Tableau of Lies

SW Gallien

Virginia Beach, Virginia

Library of Congress Control Number: 2025925389

ISBNs

978-1-970816-39-6 **(E-Book)**

978-1-970816-40-2 **(Paperback)**

978-1-970816-41-9 **(Hardcover)**

From the Author

"Write what disturbs you, what you fear, what you have not been willing to speak about. Be willing to be split open."

- Natalie Goldberg

I've always reached for pen and paper the way some people reach for a prescription bottle. Writing has been my way of making sense of chaos, of holding shadows up to the light. Stories saved me—they've always been my compass when the world felt too heavy.

As a kid, one line from *Knight Rider* embedded itself in me: *"One man can make a difference, and you are going to be that man."* I've carried that ever since—not as a call to heroics, but as proof that one voice, one story, one small act of courage can shift things. That belief shapes everything I write.

If you're here, chances are you've carried something—shame, regret, or just the weight of being human. Maybe you've been told your story disqualifies you. I want you to hear the opposite: you're not disqualified. The past doesn't get the final word.

This is only the beginning.

No one knows the depths of darkness we dance with in our minds. - SW Gallien

"I write to give myself strength. I write to be the characters that I am not. I write to explore all things I'm afraid of."

– Joss Whedon

To Mom

My fiercest believer. You saw the storyteller in me before I had words for it. You watched me build worlds in notebooks as a child, and held faith when those pages grew darker. Even when you didn't understand where the shadows came from, you never stopped seeing the light in me. When I didn't know if I could finish this, you never doubted that I would. This book is proof that you were right.

To My Husband, My Love

Joe, you see the truest version of me, even when I come undone. You've stood steady through the wild ideas, the unraveling doubts, and the moments when belief in myself slipped through my fingers. You never flinched. You reminded me of my worth, even when I couldn't see it, and gave me the courage to let this story breathe. Your strength made room for my voice.

To Thena

Proof that sometimes the right collaborator appears out of nowhere, drinks no coffee, and still somehow knows exactly what to say. You helped me organize the storm I carried for years with impeccable timing, endless patience, and insight that was uncannily precise.

To the darkness that touched my life—

You did not ask permission. You slipped in, quiet and patient, reshaping my edges. I met you young, not knowing your name, only the weight you carried.

You taught me what to fear.

You taught me what to fight.

Because of you, I learned to recognize the light—not by its brilliance, but by the way it made me feel whole.

Knowing you did not break me.

It made me.

Table of Contents

CHAPTER ONE

Deception

"False face must hide what the false heart doth know."

SAMANTHA

"STOP! Please... nothing happened. I don't even know him!" I screamed, as if raising my voice could break whatever dark possession had taken hold of my husband, Alex.

"You're lying, you little bitch." He yanked me close. "I'll beat it out of you if I have to." His hand clamped around my face, his whisper hot with whiskey. "I'm doing this because I love you. He's trying to mess with your head. I have to teach you who's the master in this house."

"Alex, please..." I pleaded. "You're hurting me." His grip twisted my forearm—I just wanted him to stop. I had done nothing more than smile at the young man who waited on our table.

"I saw you, and you're lying to me. You are mine! You are married to ME!" He shoved me into the wall.

I never saw his hand move. The backhand landed bright and hot. The room spun; my head throbbed. He kept ranting about the waiter, accusing me of lying. Then his hand was on my neck.

1

I tried to fight him off, but he was stronger. The pressure closed in until everything went cloudy... then black.

I woke up on the living room floor. The house was silent. I held still a moment, testing what hurt before I tried to stand. Getting up wasn't difficult; looking in the mirror was. Fingertip bruises marked my neck. My lip was split. A crimson handprint blazed across my cheek. Not a nightmare. I was awake.

Alex had yelled before. He'd said things that chilled me. But he had never put his hands on me... not like this.

Ice. I need ice. In the kitchen, I pressed an ice pack against my cheek and winced as the cold found the sting.

The phone's shrill ring startled me. I didn't want to answer. I had no voice for anyone. The ringing stopped—then started again.

"Damn it." I snatched up the phone. "Hello." My voice was hoarse.

"Samantha Woods... I mean, Samantha Devereux, where are you?" Rachel's raspy voice was unmistakable.

"Rach, I'm—wait, where exactly am I supposed to be?"

"We were going shopping." A pause. "You forgot, didn't you?"

"I'm sorry. I have the worst headache—pressing ice to my head

2

as we speak."

"You don't have to lie to me. I know you hate shopping by now. You promised me," she teased, half-playful, half-whining.

"Rachel, I'm not up to it today. We can go next weekend—catch the Labor Day sales." So far, no lies.

"I'll recruit Marcus to keep me company. Call me when you feel better." She hung up quickly.

Marcus Underwood was reason enough to cover up what had just happened and brave the world outside. I adored Marcus. We'd met back in middle school—casual acquaintances and frequent competitors in forensics and orchestra. Names, banter, a little flirting—fun, harmless. Nothing came of it until I started seeing Alex and Rachel met Marcus in college. Suddenly, flirting felt like crossing a line.

I found myself wanting to spend more time with Marcus than with my fiancé. I should have paid attention to that. I introduced them, and the rest was history. They got engaged shortly before I married Alex. At least someone got their happily ever after.

The sting in my cheek had faded a little. "Just the thought of Marcus makes things better," I murmured, then snorted at myself. "Great. Now I'm talking to myself out loud." There was nothing funny about any of this.

What had happened to Alex? We'd been having a nice dinner, talking, and then... he tried to choke me. I replayed the evening. What had I done to make him think I was "into" the waiter? I'm friendly by nature. I smile at everyone—strangers, people who open doors, waiters, even the grumpy old man who steals the Sunday paper. Maybe that needs to stop—wouldn't want Alex thinking I'm flirting with the mailman or the garbage guys.

Anger dulled the pain. I hadn't done anything wrong. And he hit me. Never again.

ALEXANDER

"I just had to put her in her place. No woman of mine is going to flirt with strangers," I roared as the third whiskey hit the table. I can always draw attention, and tonight was no different—two co-eds competing for a smile. I'd probably enjoy both before the night was over—that was the plan until I locked eyes with Jerome. My father.

Jerome Devereux, late fifties, more striking than most men half his age. Steel-blue eyes, a presence that steals a room without a word. In seconds, he siphoned off the attention I'd been bathing in. He slid into the seat across from me, casually waving away my admirers. Neither of us spoke.

4

"Can I get you something from the bar, sir?" the waitress asked—cute, but not dressed for it.

"A scotch."

"How would you like it?"

"In a glass." Jerome never bothered with pleasantries.

"Mr. Devereux, you certainly know how to put a young girl at ease," I said, glaring. "He wants it neat. Make it a double. Best you got."

"I was told you were in a mood." Without blinking, he took my whiskey, tipped it, and poured it onto the floor. "Perhaps that will help clear your head."

"Why are you here?" My fists clenched.

"You haven't introduced your wife to the family. Does she even know we exist?" He raised a hand. "Don't be stupid. I know she doesn't. Otherwise, she'd be packing her bags and calling an attorney about your trust."

"That's where you're wrong. Samantha will never leave me. I'm all she has—Mommy and Daddy are dead, no siblings. She's mine, and too scared to leave."

"No, son. Right now, she's naïve. Early twenties, if that. If she has no family, you need us all the more. How else are you going to keep it together?" His gaze dared me to argue.

I slammed my fist on the table. "You don't know her. She's a sweet kid, a good girl. She obeys without even realizing it."

"That will change. She got up off the floor where you left her. Took a phone call. Made a snack. Watched TV. Your behavior will change her—quickly."

"So you've got one of your goons following me again?"

"I've got both of you followed. She's boring—for now. You, on the other hand, have quite the list of extracurriculars. Care to see the photos?"

"What's the end game, Dad? What do you want?" There's always an angle.

"Bring your new wife to meet the family tomorrow. Let's say four o'clock. Drusilla and Craig will be dining with us. Perhaps you can tell your little wife what you really do when she thinks you're at work."

He stood, tossed a twenty on the table. "That's for the scotch she never brought. See you tomorrow. Don't be late."

I wanted to break his face. Instead, I left the bar with both co-eds.

Around four in the morning, I slipped out of an off-campus

apartment, leaving two naked co-eds in sheets I'd never see again. Random women were easy—no strings, no demands. Wives were work. I was exhausted, and tomorrow would be hell. Whatever Jerome had planned would wreck a good thing— having whoever I wanted while my wife thought I was at work, plus a pretty little thing at home to handle the house and dinner.

Jerome would ruin it, and Samantha would learn more in a day than she had in two years.

At home, the living room screen looped the menu. She slept on the couch. I sat and watched her. Monogamy meant nothing to me, but I hadn't meant to hurt her. Her lip was swollen. Faint finger marks on her neck. Minimal evidence. She still believed I had a special contract at Fort Bragg. I said it was top secret; she never asked. I trained her to live in my lie. No access to my accounts. No idea what I'm worth. I'd keep it that way—until she was pregnant or her inheritance ran dry. Either would lock her in.

Now Jerome would crush it—just to piss me off.

SAMANTHA

The glare through the bay window woke me. The smell of coffee drifted in from the kitchen. I sat up slowly, scanning the room. He was at the stove. When he turned and met my eyes, he smiled like nothing had happened.

7

"You're certainly in better spirits today." My voice was cold.

He crossed to the couch and reached for my hand. I pulled back.

"I deserve that, Sammie." He only used "Sammie" when I was angry. "I screwed up. I'm so sorry."

"Sorry?" As if that word could erase a handprint.

"Yes, sorry. And I'm going to have a lot more to apologize for after we talk. Please... hear me out. Please don't do anything crazy?" His hands closed over mine.

"So... don't slap you or choke you for no reason? Is that what counts as crazy?" I yanked my hands away. It wasn't just anger. It was hurt.

"Sam, don't be a bitch about it. I screwed up, and I've got some things to tell you that are going to make you mad at me for completely different reasons. But I need you today. I need you the way I was there when you lost your parents."

He tossed my parents into it like a bargaining chip. He was there when I lost them. For a long time, I thought that meant something. People make mistakes... right?

"Don't talk about my parents. Not while you're begging forgiveness for being a monster."

"Monster?" He sat back, baffled, almost wounded.

8

"What do you call a man who hits his wife? Who screams in her face?" My throat burned. I didn't want to cry, but the tears came anyway. "You want to talk about my parents?" I wiped my face, breathing slow. "If my father ever did to my mother what you did to me... she'd kill him." I held his gaze, waiting to see which version of him I'd get.

He began to cry. He dropped to his knees, body shaking, apologies spilling over each other.

Maybe he'd snapped. Maybe it was a mistake. Maybe he really was sorry. Part of me wanted to pull him close and promise a better tomorrow. Another part wanted to kick him while he was down.

"I'm going to shower. When I come out, we'll talk." I wasn't good at being cruel. "Pull yourself together and get off the floor." As I passed, my hand brushed his shoulder—an instinct I hated.

JEROME

"Sir, it appears they may reconcile. She's still in the residence, and your son is preparing breakfast. At present, it looks like a normal Saturday morning between them."

"Thank you. Have your relief contact me at the first sign of discord."

"Yes, sir."

I turned from the window of my office. Outside, Drusilla watched her son during his riding lesson. The sight pleased me. Drusilla had been molded to marry into the Devereux family. Loyalty, legacy, appearances. I trusted her more than my own children: ruthless, often cruel, fiercely protective of her boy.

Horatio.

I despised the name at first—too antique—until Drusilla reminded me that in *Hamlet,* the survivor is Horatio. Loyalty and survival. Drusilla and I had plans for the child. Now, Horatio is a four-year-old on a pony.

Watching Drusilla with her son drew my thoughts to my other daughter-in-law—the newest addition to the family. Samantha.

Insignificant.

She was not Devereux stock. A prized stallion required a mare of equal pedigree. I have little interest in horses, but I value bloodlines. My son's choice did nothing for the family's prospects.

Arrangements had been in place for Alex to marry suitably: a woman who understood her place, took direction, guarded family interests. Samantha possessed no leverage, no useful secrets. In that sense, dull.

Except for one detail.

She was close to Marcus Underwood. That alone made her worth cultivating.

SAMANTHA

Steam faded from the mirror, leaving the damage clear. Split lip. The proof on my cheek already fading—maybe something I could hide.

In the kitchen, Alex had outdone himself: waffles with Nutella and bananas, coffee, fruit, and bacon. It was almost impressive. I poured orange juice and sat at the counter.

"Want syrup with your waffles?" he asked, sweet as sugar.

"No, thank you. I'm not hungry." I lied. I was starving, but I wouldn't give him that. "Besides, you know I only eat crispy bacon." It was a weak attempt, but I wanted to mean.

I caught the flicker of irritation, though his smile held. "You could have told me before your shower you weren't hungry, so the food wouldn't be wasted."

"You could have told me you're a jealous man with a temper. Are we even, darling?" The sarcasm surprised even me.

"Of course, my love." His shoulders said he wanted to grab me, but something held him. "I have some things I need to tell you."

I waited. No encouragement. No questions. Just waiting.

"We're having dinner with my family tonight."

I choked, juice spraying the counter. "You don't have any family."

"Don't be ridiculous, Sammie. Everyone has a family. I just haven't been in touch for a while."

"You told me they were gone. You refused to talk about them. You lied."

"Yes, Sammie, I lied—get over it. My family is complicated. To me, they were gone... but that's changed. And that's not the only thing I've lied about."

"I can't say I'm surprised." My hands tightened on the glass.

"I don't work on base. I don't work at all. I'm a man of leisure. I lied so you wouldn't come after my money."

"What do you mean you don't work? What money?"

"This house, the furniture, the car—paid for with my mother's inheritance. I live off my trust. If I'm a good boy and return to the fold, I'll have much more to spend as I please."

I pressed my palms to my face, holding myself together.

"Sammie, say something." He hated silence. I could hear him fidget.

"Alex, I need a minute." My words were muffled behind my hands.

"I need to know you understand. That we can move past this little bump in the road."

My head came up. "Which bump, Alex? The lies about your family and your job? Or the fact that you put your hands on me because of a waiter? Which am I meant to 'move past'? Or all of it?" I pushed back from the counter and started toward the door.

"Sammie, baby... please—"

"You've got a lot of nerve asking me to move past anything." I didn't look back.

He didn't follow. That surprised me—and didn't.

From the living room, I heard the blinds snap shut. "Have fun watching me now, Father," he muttered.

We avoided each other until mid-afternoon. He appeared in my office doorway. "We need to leave by three-thirty."

I didn't answer.

When I emerged at 3:15, he waited in the living room. I wore a white blouse, dark-wash jeans, and my favorite boots.

"You look beautiful."

I didn't acknowledge it. He could see I'd been crying.

"I think you might be more comfortable in something a little more upscale for my family."

"I'll wear what I please." I checked my purse.

"Are you ready to go?"

"One thing first." I still didn't look at him. "Tell me the truth. Can you do that?"

"Of course. After everything, I owe you that."

"I think I already know the answer, but... what do you do when you pretend to be at work?"

Silence.

I glared at him. "Where are you? What do you do?"

He licked his lips. "I bang every girl I can."

It shook me. I said nothing. I'd expected another lie.

"I drink. I see women, sometimes more than one at a time. And I spend my money having fun. Now that you know the truth—and my father's involved—everything is about to change."

I tucked my hair behind my ear. "We have somewhere to be, and I hate being late. Shall we?" My voice stayed even.

He followed me to the door, locking it behind us. I could feel it—his control slipping. He could too.

JEROME

"Sir, they're leaving now. Alexander closed the blinds earlier; we've lost the visual. We'll need audio for the level you requested. He's on to us."

"We'll address additional resources later, David. Keep the team small. You know what my son is capable of, and I won't bankroll your entire staff to keep his name out of the papers."

"Yes, sir. Shall I follow them?"

"No. I know exactly where they're going."

I replaced the receiver with deliberate precision, a faint smile tugging at my lips. With traffic, they'd arrive at four. That left a brief window to confer with Drusilla and Craig.

As if summoned, Drusilla entered the study, Craig—my eldest—following. Drusilla crossed the room to kiss my cheek, the act calculated and unhurried. Craig stiffened. He knew, perhaps better than anyone, that between Drusilla and their son, he'd become expendable.

"How are you this afternoon, Jerome?" Drusilla's voice carried the polish of private schooling and a debutante's training. She was stunning—handpicked for Craig, her finishing paid for by the estate. Her accomplishments meant little to Craig.

"You look radiant, my dear. Excited to meet the newest addition?"

15

"I'm curious. She seems... ordinary. What did Alexander see in her?"

"Perhaps it was the novelty of choosing without Father's hand in the arrangement," Craig remarked dryly, taking his private chance to remind them both of his dissatisfaction.

"Son, you have a beautiful wife and an adoring son. What more could you want?" My tone was lightly chiding; I knew Drusilla had never been Craig's preference.

"I have my son, and for that I'm grateful—assuming you and Drusilla don't ruin him." Craig's gaze was hard. His greatest fear: Horatio molded into one of them.

"Since you love him so dearly, perhaps check on him now," I said smoothly. "Let Drusilla and me discuss business."

The dismissal was expected. Craig nodded and withdrew. He hated us almost as much as he hated his brother.

When the doors closed, Drusilla turned. "What should we do about him?"

"Craig? Nothing—for now. He generally keeps to his rules. Any issues I need to be aware of?"

"Someone will catch him eventually. His... habits won't stay hidden. And how do we keep him and Alexander's wife from becoming allies?" She sank into a leather chair.

"The same story we've used with the staff. Keep him on a leash. It's the only matter where Alexander will be useful. For all his indiscretions, your brother-in-law has never sunk to Craig's depths." I rested my chin on my clasped hand, expression unreadable. "I grow tired of my sons' weaknesses."

"They're hardly boys, Jerome. They're grown men—and eventually they'll answer for their... sins." Her voice was silk over steel.

"That day may come, but not today." I leaned back, tone calm, words precise. "Tonight, distract our guest while I speak with Alexander. Make her uncomfortable. Overwhelm her. We'll all dress formally—heighten the tension. I don't know how much Alexander has told her."

"I understand."

"No, not yet." His gaze sharpened. "You will when I explain the rest. My plan depends on Samantha believing there's no hope for Alexander's redemption."

Drusilla's reply was cool. "There is no hope."

"I also need her afraid—for her life—of both my sons. Do what you do best, my dear. Intimidate her. Break her. By any means necessary. I didn't want her in this, but she's in the game now."

"Yes, sir." She rose gracefully. Whatever I had in mind, she would soon know her part. Until then, Samantha would be her newest project—someone to mold, train, torment.

Drusilla smiled as she closed the doors. This would be fun.

CHAPTER TWO

The House of Devereux

"I know not how it was—but, with the first glimpse of the building, a sense of insufferable gloom pervaded my spirit."

SAMANTHA

The drive took nearly an hour in late-summer traffic through Spring Lake. Alex hadn't said where his father lived—only "north of Fayetteville, past Spring Lake up 87." I'd been this way with my parents on trips to Raleigh or Greensboro, but never to anywhere like this.

Eventually, he turned onto an isolated road outside Cumberland River. Pines pressed close, cicadas thrumming in the heat. After miles of green, the trees gave way to a field so vivid it looked painted. At first, I thought it was a golf course—impossibly green, immaculate. No flags. No ponds. Just curated land. In the distance, a structure rose—too vast for a home, too solemn for a clubhouse.

Alex slowed at the ornate iron gates, punched in a code. The metal groaned open, cameras watching as we passed. My stomach tightened—not only from the sheer scale, but because this world had been sealed away from me until now. Dating, planning a wedding, even vows—and he'd never spoken of them.

The manor revealed itself in pieces: pale brick in afternoon light, black shutters cutting against softness, then the breadth of it, sprawling, commanding. Up close, the symmetry felt too precise, the beauty airbrushed past human. Awe, yes—threaded with something colder.

Alex cut the engine at the front steps. A man waited at the door. For a second, I hoped—maybe this was Jerome.

"Try not to look so impressed," Alex murmured. "They feed on envy and fear. Wait here."

He greeted the man—Sampson, the butler—then took my hand. "He's not a tour guide. Let's meet my... Daddy." The word dripped mockery.

"This is the house?" My voice sounded smaller than I wanted.

"Yes. Maybe now you understand why I never brought anyone here before marriage. Who could say no to all this?"

I stared at the mansion, its perfection pressing down like a portrait too polished to be real. Alex rang the bell. "Game face, sweetheart. Lion's den."

* * * * * * *

The door opened. A tall blonde stepped onto the porch, every movement polished.

"You're late, Alex. You know how he hates that."

"Dru," Alex said flatly. "Did you sharpen your fangs before we arrived?"

"Ever the charmer." Her smile was smooth, practiced. "Is this the wife you didn't want us to meet?" She stepped toward me, hand extended. "I'm Drusilla Devereux. Married to his older brother, Craig."

"It's a pleasure. I'm Samantha—but my friends call me Sam."

Her smile flickered, cool. "Samantha, please come in."

The house swallowed us. The foyer stretched wide and bright, sunlight pouring from high windows onto polished stone. Chandeliers glittered above, staircases swept upward, portraits lined the walls. Dazzling, but not familiar.

Every sound echoed too far. My boots scuffed, ordinary against the pristine marble, reminding me I didn't belong. The air smelled of polish and age, layered with too many flowers. Their sweetness dragged me back to the funeral home—lilies and roses so heavy I could hardly breathe. I pushed the memory down, but dread clung.

Alex smirked at my discomfort. Of course he did. He lied about his family, his work, and now paraded me like proof.

ALEXANDER

She tried not to stare, but I saw it—the widening eyes at the gates, the manor, the marble. Awe, confusion, maybe fear. It pulled at something in me I didn't expect.

This was never the plan. I didn't want her here. Bringing her risked everything I'd built apart. I told myself I'd kept her away for her sake. Truth was simpler: I liked her naïve, untested.

Her boots caught my eye. Scuffed, the same ones she wore in Fayetteville. Out of place here. She shifted in them, already feeling it. Better that she know early what this place demanded.

The door opened. Drusilla appeared, polished as always. Polished, sharp, and hard like a diamond on all edges. Samantha was softer, with darting eyes, jeans and boots like someone who'd wandered onto the wrong stage. I preferred her that way.

I reached for her hand. She didn't pull away. She never did.

SAMANTHA

Drusilla slid her arm through mine, steering me like I already belonged to her. The threshold gave way to an entrance hall, vast and gleaming. She led me straight into a library of dark shelves and leather spines, wax and polish sharp in the air. A vase of flowers sweetened it—too sweet. A chair faced away from us.

22

"Meet Jerome Devereux, Alexander's father."

I stepped forward, voice catching. "It's a pleasure to meet you, sir. And Drusilla, please—call me Sam."

Drusilla's smile sharpened. "What makes you think we're friends?" She swept out, closing the doors behind her. The sound echoed like a lock.

Jerome rose, taller than Alex, salt-and-pepper hair, striking blue eyes. Handsome, yes—but in a way that examined. Judged. As if I'd already failed.

He circled me slowly, measured. "At least she has manners, Alexander. You should have helped her dress for dinner."

Alex was still behind me. My stomach dropped.

Jerome took my hand, lips brushing it gently. "Lovely. She is lovely. Your brother failed to say how much so."

Alex's voice was flat. "Interesting. He wasn't invited to my wedding. None of you were. Yet he attended."

Jerome's eyes never left mine. "Why keep us away from such an occasion?"

"So the occasion could stay happy," Alex said.

Their eyes locked. The air thickened.

Jerome gestured to a chair. "Samantha, sit. Alexander, find your brother. I'd like a moment with my daughter-in-law."

JEROME

She tried to hold herself with dignity, but I saw hesitation in the way her eyes flicked to the door.

"Would you care for a drink?"

"Water, thank you."

"Because you're driving... or pregnant?"

Her blink betrayed her. I leaned back, let the question hang. The staff brought drinks, then we were alone again.

"One matter first. Did my son have you sign a prenuptial agreement?"

"No."

"How much did you know about our money before you married?"

"Enough to think he had a house and a car, because of his mother's life insurance. I believed he worked on base. I thought we'd build a life on salaries."

Honest. Dangerous. I believed her.

"Alexander will work here now. You'll spend time here as well. We have expectations."

I pressed her—school, plans, age. Provincial. Unremarkable. She'd need polish. "If you'd spent an hour with us before the wedding, you wouldn't have gone through with it."

Her hand brushed her arm. She didn't realize I noticed. "Keep him happy and you'll have little to worry about," I said softly. "Telling him no never ends well. Especially for women."

Fear kept her quiet. Silence was answer enough.

DRUSILLA

Jerome dismissed Samantha. She stepped into the entryway as Alexander arrived with Craig.

"Samantha, this is my eldest son, Craig Devereux," Jerome said.

Craig caught her hand, kissed her knuckles with smooth charm. "Brave of you to marry into this circus, sister-in-law."

She pulled back too quickly. A tell. Jerome saw it. So did Alexander, jaw tight.

"Drusilla, take Samantha on a tour," Jerome instructed.

"Yes, Jerome." I turned. "With me, Samantha."

Her boots echoed off rhythm as I led her through the back halls. "You ride?" My tone said I already knew.

"No. Never had the chance. You know, being poor and all." The sarcasm was unpolished, raw.

"At last, some backbone. You'll need it in this family."

25

She frowned. "So you are testing me."

"Somewhat. Don't mistake me—we're not friends. I'm too much like Jerome for that. He picked me for Craig. He had someone picked for Alexander, too, but Alex ran first."

Her eyes widened. "Arranged marriages? This family is—"

"Rich." I cut her off. "The kind that keeps its name clean no matter the stain. Jerome paved the way for me to be a matriarch in this family. I studied abroad. Learned language young."

We walked toward the meadows. Horses grazed under a bleeding sunset. She stopped. "It's beautiful."

"A mausoleum," I corrected. "That's where people who refuse to fall in line end up."

Her head snapped toward me. "Why are you telling me this?"

"Alex's mother is buried there. Family secrets, too. Some you'll never know. Others you'll wish you could forget. You seem like a nice girl, Samantha. Nice doesn't last here. Average doesn't cut it. This is survival of the fittest."

I let silence stretch as we returned. At the steps, I slowed, meeting her eyes.

"There was never a dinner. You were brought here to be seen, weighed, measured. Tonight was about you—how you carried yourself, how quickly you flinched, what you'd say when pressed. Consider it your first test."

I let the words hang, then added, "You and Alexander should leave soon. Craig's blood will be running hot."

SAMANTHA

Alex waited on the veranda, leaning against a column, eyes sharp. "Were you nice to my wife, Dru, or did you suck the soul out of her already?"

"Go home, Alexander." She brushed past. "And keep her away from your brother. You know what I mean."

His arm slipped around my shoulders. For once, I was relieved to feel it. "I don't understand," I whispered.

"Not here. Someone's listening."

I remembered Jerome's cool warnings, the cameras, Drusilla's eyes. Silence seemed safer.

Sampson stood at the front with keys in hand. Alex took them, guided me to the car. The gates opened, releasing us. The ride home was loud with pounding music, bass rattling the speakers. I didn't ask him to turn it down. Maybe he needed the noise. Maybe I did too.

At home he crouched by the car, hands working quick near the wheel well. He held up a disc, metal flashing. "They were tracking us," he said, almost pleased. "So predictable." Any other day, I would've laughed. After the cameras and Jerome's questions, I didn't.

ALEXANDER

When I came inside, I tapped a finger to my ear and tilted my head toward the backyard. Too many ears in these walls.

"It's a beautiful night," I said. "Let's sit outside."

She grabbed a bottle of water from the counter. "Beer?" she asked over her shoulder.

"Yeah."

We sat in the porch swing, the night air cool, carrying the faint sweetness of honeysuckle. She handed me the bottle, her eyes wary, like she was already bracing for whatever I might say.

"What did your father want?" she asked.

I took a long chug before answering. "A better school for you. Babies. Better English. More time with the family. And Drusilla—she wants you to stay away from Craig."

Her brows knit. "Why would I be around Craig in the first place?"

"Don't take it personally. Craig's a danger. I know I hurt you,

Sammie, but Craig..." I hesitated, shame edging my voice. "He'd do much worse if he had the chance. He's a predator. Dru knows it, and he likes you."

She shuddered. "Has he ever—?"

"Yes." The word came out heavier than I wanted. "My father's covered for him more than once. Even in the manor itself."

For a flicker, I saw her soften—almost believing me, forgetting. Almost. That flicker was all I wanted, all I needed. And then it was gone, replaced by that look I knew too well: questioning, measuring, deciding if I was worth the risk.

"What do we do now?" she asked.

"We play along. For now. Stay close to Jerome or Dru. And if Craig ever comes here when I'm not home—don't let him in. Pretend you're not here."

She nodded, but I could see the wheels turning in her head. Always turning. Always doubting. Always asking why behind those amber eyes.

The pressure rose in me, something raw and consuming. I told myself it was because of her—because she mattered too much. Because loving her made me want control, made me want to hold on tighter. If I didn't, I might lose her. That thought made the edge inside me sharpen until it cut.

It snapped before I could stop it. I stood too fast. "Come with me."

Her head tilted, cautious. "What is it?"

"Don't question me." The words cracked sharp, sharper than I meant. But once they were out, I didn't want to take them back. They felt necessary, the only way to keep her still, to keep her mine.

I reached for her hand, gripping too tight. I felt the tension in her body, the way she tried to pull away. "Alex, that hurts."

Her eyes locked on mine, wide, afraid. And in that moment, the fear should have broken me. But it didn't.

Instead, I told myself it was proof—proof that I loved her enough to lose control.

And I didn't let go.

SAMANTHA

I yanked my hand free. "Stop. You're scaring me."

But the look in his eyes froze me in place. They weren't Alex's eyes anymore—not the boy who steadied me after my parents died, not the husband who kissed me under fireworks at Disney. His gaze was darker, stripped of the man I knew, something raw and dangerous breaking through his skin.

Before I could move, his hand tangled in my hair, yanking me down the hall.

"Alex—please!"

"I want you. Now." His voice was jagged, a stranger's.

"Not like this," I begged, stumbling against him. "Please, not like this—"

My words only seemed to feed him. The world snapped white with pain as his palm cracked across my cheek. I hit the mattress hard, the metallic taste of blood flooding my mouth.

"Shut up," he hissed, shoving a hand over my lips. His weight pressed me down. "I want what's mine."

Terror clawed at my chest. I thrashed for air, biting his palm, but his hand only shifted, closing around my throat. Another blow blurred the edges of everything, darkness closing in until there was nothing left to fight.

ALEXANDER

She went still beneath me, her body slack, and for a moment I thought I'd gone too far. Panic shot through me sharp and cold—but then I caught the shallow rasp of her breathing, and relief steadied my chest.

I left her on the bed, whimpering. I walked to the kitchen,

opening the freezer with hands that shook more than I wanted to admit. A plastic pack of ice slid into my grip. Cold, solid. Something to fix what I'd broken.

Back in the bedroom, I sat beside her. Her hair clung damp to her cheek. I brushed it back gently, pressing the ice pack against the swelling that was already rising where my hand had struck. "Baby, I'm sorry," I whispered. "I don't know what came over me."

Her eyes fluttered, unfocused. She rasped, "Why?"

"It wasn't that bad," I said, keeping my tone soft, careful. "Come on, you like it a little rough."

She whispered, "No." A tear slipped free, sliding across her temple.

For an instant, guilt burned. That tear should have stopped me cold. But I couldn't let it. Instead, I told myself it meant something else, that she cared, that she felt me in a way no one else ever had. Her hurt was proof of how deep this ran between us.

I smiled, letting it stretch slow across my face like reassurance. "Sometimes we have to change things up," I murmured, as if I'd given her a gift instead of pain.

She gathered what was left of her clothes, stumbling toward the bathroom. I heard the lock turn, the water roar to life. She was hiding, but I told myself she just needed space. She'd come around—she always did.

I sat on the edge of the bed, rubbing my hand where her teeth had broken skin. The sting was sharp, grounding. This hadn't been cruelty; it was passion, raw and consuming. Proof of how much she mattered to me. If she didn't matter, I wouldn't have lost control.

When the shower finally cut off, I slipped out. Better to give her the night, let her cool off. Tomorrow, she'd understand. Tomorrow she'd remember she is mine.

CHAPTER THREE

The Gilded Mask

"The mask, given time, comes to own the face beneath."

SAMANTHA

The Thursday before Labor Day weekend, the air was a wet blanket over campus—humidity so thick the desks stuck to our arms. Genevieve fanned herself with a syllabus while Rachel tried to coax me into plans.

"Pool party," Rachel sang. "We'll melt otherwise."

Genevieve rolled her eyes. "I have to work. Let's plan for tomorrow."

Rachel gave an exaggerated pout, then shrugged, undeterred. "Fine. Tomorrow then. So, Sam... what's the family like?"

"Different. I have to be taught how to act in society. Debutante lessons for the poor relation." I let the last words drip in my best antebellum drawl.

That made them laugh—until Marcus spoke. "I could help you with that." Something in the way he said it made my skin prickle.

No chance to respond before Genevieve noticed. "What happened to your face?"

I shifted my hair so it fell just right. "Walked into a cabinet."

She snorted. "Fine. If cabinets are throwing hands, I'm out." Her eyes lingered too long, suspicion sharpening into something closer to concern.

Rachel frowned, softer. "Lunch at least, Sam. You need it."

"Maybe," I said, though we both knew I wouldn't.

By the time the professor dimmed the lights and launched into cell structure, my mind was gone. Words blurred on the slides, formulas I normally absorbed without effort. All I could think about was Genevieve's jab, Rachel's curiosity, Marcus's steady gaze.

And Alexander's world. My new world.

I stared down at my notebook, the page still blank twenty minutes in, fingers clenched around my pen until they cramped. My chest felt tight, like the air in the classroom had thickened.

When the lecture ended, chairs scraped, backpacks zipped, and everyone shuffled toward the biology lab across the hall. I stood too, but my feet refused to follow. The thought of fluorescent lights and disinfectant made my stomach twist.

Instead, I slipped out the side door into the late summer sun.

The rose garden was too hot for hiding, but I went anyway. The last blooms hung on against the humidity—some still full, others already browning.

I sat on the low brick wall, arms wrapped around myself, trying to breathe.

At least these flowers still had roots. They weren't perfect— some fading, some half-dead—but they belonged here. The air smelled green and damp, touched with soil.

The manor's flowers were different. Cut. Arranged. Pretty for a day, maybe two, then already wilting. Their perfume, too heavy indoors, clinging until it reminded me of funeral homes. Pretty for show. Not meant to comfort.

That felt closer to me than I wanted to admit—taken from where I belonged, trimmed down to fit someone else's picture. Polished on the outside, breaking underneath.

I pressed my palms into the rough brick, holding on. The roses had roots. I wasn't sure I did anymore.

MARCUS

I hesitated at the side door, then followed her out. Across the quad, I spotted her in the rose garden, perched on the low wall like she was carrying something too heavy to set down.

By the time I reached her, she didn't turn. She just kept staring

36

at the late-summer blooms, still hanging on though the season was shifting.

"I thought you hated roses," I said quietly. "Why come here?"

Her eyes didn't leave the flowers. "Don't you have a class to be in?"

"Same one as you." I lowered myself onto the wall beside her, close but not crowding. "This seat taken?"

She didn't answer. But she didn't tell me to leave either.

"I hate red roses," she said finally. "Cut ones especially. They're everywhere—apologies, condolences, declarations of love. Always roses. I like rose gardens better. At least those are alive. They stay where they belong."

I understood. I'd grown up in the Devereuxs' shadow long enough to know how much of that house was for display—arrangements and appearances, everything meant for show.

So I asked, careful, "What flowers do you like?"

Her answer came soft, almost surprised at herself. "Orchids. They're not dead or dying. Just beautiful in their little pots."

The words hit harder than she meant them to. Somewhere along the way, she'd stopped feeling rooted.

Her eyes welled before she could stop them. Tears slipped fast, and she covered her face, mortified.

I pulled a handkerchief from my pocket and offered it.

She gave a wet laugh. "Who even carries a handkerchief?"

"Someone who knows it'll help you fit in with your pretentious new family," I said.

The joke landed wrong and right at the same time. She let me pull her into a brief hug, her shoulders shaking against me, before she straightened.

"Come on," I said softly. "Let's get back before Rachel sends a search party."

SAMANTHA

Back among friends, we slipped into the lab a minute late. The professor's eyes cut up from the attendance sheet, sharp enough to sting, before he went back to his notes. Rachel mouthed *what took you so long?* across the bench, but didn't press. She never did in public.

Genevieve, of course, raised one eyebrow. "Nice of you to join us," she murmured, her pen already moving in neat, deliberate strokes.

I hunched over the microscope, adjusting the focus, pretending cell walls and stained nuclei demanded all of me. Easier than meeting Rachel's gaze.

Slides passed back and forth, pencils scratched. Rachel leaned in just enough to whisper, "You're okay?" Her tone made it half question, half plea.

"Fine," I muttered, too quickly.

Genevieve cleared her throat, sharp. "Some of us are trying to learn, remember?" She flicked her eyes between us, then back to her notebook.

By the time the professor dismissed us, Genevieve's bag was already zipped and lined up in perfect order. Rachel bolted too, muttering something about her dad needing the car.

That left Marcus leaning on the desk like he had all the time in the world.

"We should work on those refinements," he said.

I narrowed my eyes. "What does that even mean?"

"Wardrobe. Nails. Heels are about to become a new reality for you." His grin tilted, sly but not unkind. "I've got ideas—and a connection to help us out."

I groaned, dragging my hands down my face. The thought of being remade, packaged, dressed for a stage that didn't feel like mine exhausted me before we even started. "I don't really have a choice, do I?"

"Not really." He slung his bag over his shoulder, grin tugging wider. "But I promise it'll hurt less if I'm the one coaching you through it."

I rolled my eyes. It all sounded like some form of torture. And why did this beautiful boy want to help with my makeover montage? A fleeting thought about his sexuality crossed my mind, but there was no question—Marcus was a ladies' man.

He slung his bag over his shoulder. "I'll drive."

ALLISON

From the street, the salon was dark, the CLOSED sign still in the window. I'd left it that way on purpose. Marcus had called in a favor, and for Marcus, I always found a way.

The bell over the door jingled as he stepped in with a girl at his side. Samantha. She looked nervous, like she wasn't sure if she belonged. I'd seen that look plenty of times—girls trying to measure up to someone else's world.

"Sam," Marcus said, "this is Allison—my cousin."

Cousin. My brows lifted, but I let it slide. If that was the story he told her, it wasn't mine to contradict.

"So this is the lucky girl," I said warmly, offering a smile.

"Marcus says you need the works."

She flushed. "Am I really that hopeless?"

"You're not hopeless," I said, tilting her chin gently toward the light. "Just a few rough edges. That's easy to fix."

Marcus jumped in with his grin. "You're perfect. But you want to fit in with your new family. Are you ready?"

She hesitated, then gave a half-smile. "I guess I'm as ready as I'll ever be."

"Allison's one of the best," he added, kissing my cheek.

I gave him a look—half amusement, half reminder that polish wasn't everything. But I understood what he was trying to do. If presentation made her feel stronger, maybe that was worth something.

"Marcus, go grab us some lunch," I told him, looping my arm through Sam's and steering her toward the back. "Give us forty-five minutes. I'll start with the painful stuff."

He winked at her as he left. She looked like she was walking to an execution, but she followed me anyway.

I'd built a life outside of the Devereux shadow. She was walking into it. I couldn't change that, but I could make sure she walked in at least looking the part.

SAMANTHA

The "painful stuff" turned out to be waxing. Of course.

I gritted my teeth as Allison worked, grateful for her steady stream of chatter to fill the silence. Twins at home, late-night feedings, juggling school and this salon—she was easy to like, warm without forcing it.

It helped a little. Until the next strip came off.

Why do we put ourselves through this? The thought wasn't new, but it burned hotter than usual. Waxing, nails, makeup, hair, heels—all the things we're told we "should" be doing. My skin stung, and I groaned under my breath at the absurdity of it.

Allison only smiled, like she'd heard it all before. Then, almost idly, she asked, "So... what's the makeover for?"

The question caught me off guard. Her tone was casual, but her hands stilled just long enough for me to notice.

I hesitated, then gave her the safest truth I could. "My husband's family... they move in circles I don't. Events, dinners, galas. Apparently, I need polish."

For a heartbeat, something flickered in her expression—recognition, maybe memory—but she smoothed it away. "That makes sense," she said lightly, pressing the strip down again.

By the time Marcus came back with food, my nails were coral-bright, drying under a fan. He insisted on feeding me fries so I wouldn't smudge them. I rolled my eyes, but let him. Half-amused. Half-exhausted. Mostly grateful.

Afterward, Allison set to work on my hair—layers, highlights that caught the light just enough. Her hands were quick but careful, transforming me piece by piece while she talked about tiny, ordinary things: her kids, her clients, friends outside these walls. Normal things. The kind of talk I used to have with Rachel or Gen, back before my life bent into shapes I hardly recognized.

Almost four hours later, I stared at the mirror. Smooth skin, glossy hair, bright nails. A different woman looked back. Different enough, maybe, to pass in Alex's world.

"Allison, thank you," I said, reaching for my wallet.

She waved me off. "Marcus took care of everything. Just promise you'll come back."

MARCUS

"She's sweet, not a Devereux, though." Allison said once Sam was out of earshot, watching through the glass as Sam tilted her head, studying the reflection like she didn't quite believe it was her own face staring back.

"I know," I said. Too much. Too fast.

Allison's brow arched. "But I thought you were dating Rachel."

"I am," I answered, sharper than I meant. "Samantha's her best friend."

"And married to a Devereux," she added. "Alexander Devereux."

"Say it plain, Allison."

She folded her arms. "You've got no business standing this close to her. Not if you care about her. Not if you care about yourself. You're in love with her."

I looked away. The words hit harder because they were true. "That's impossible. Whatever it is—I'll hold it."

Allison's tone softened, but her warning still cut. "Devereux men don't play fair. You've already got one against you—the husband. Don't stack the odds."

I forced a smile. "You know me."

"That's what I'm worried about," she murmured. Her gaze flicked back toward Sam's reflection under the salon lights. "Marcus... don't tell her who I am. Not now. Maybe not ever."

I frowned. "She deserves the truth."

"She deserves a chance," Allison shot back. "Knowing I'm his sister won't help her. It'll only tie her closer. I cut those ties for a reason. Don't drag me back."

Her voice wavered—barely, but enough for me to hear the fear underneath.

Before I could answer, movement outside caught my eye. A woman leaned against her car across the lot, phone tilted our way. Pretending to scroll. The angle was wrong. She wasn't taking pictures of herself.

I shifted, blocking the view. Eyes. Always eyes. Even here.

SAMANTHA

By the time I picked up my car and drove home, the strangeness of it all had settled in. My hair felt lighter without the weight of its old length, brushing just past my collarbone now instead of trailing down my back. Chestnut strands caught the light with a warm auburn sheen, styled into an easy elegance that looked nothing like my usual messy-bun coed self. My skin still stung where it had been waxed raw, and my nails—bright, glossy coral—flashed every time I gripped the wheel.

I looked like someone else. Someone polished. Someone built to fit into a world I hardly knew existed. And yet when I caught my reflection in the rearview mirror, the amber eyes looking back at me were still mine—unchanged, a reminder that no matter what they altered, some part of me remained.

The house was quiet when I pulled in—too quiet. I unlocked

the door and stepped inside. The low hum of the television drifted from the living room, though I knew I'd turned it off that morning.

"Alex?" My voice carried thin through the silence. "Honey, are you home? I have a surprise for you."

"I have a surprise for you too."

The voice wasn't Alex's.

Craig.

My stomach knotted tight. "How did you get in here?"

"I was invited." He stepped forward slowly, eyes raking over me with a languid ease that made my skin crawl. "You look... different. Polished. Lovely."

My throat tightened. "Thank you," I said softly, though the words felt wrong in my mouth. It wasn't gratitude; it was a reflex, a shield against the unease prickling down my spine.

"Don't be modest." His smile curved faintly, a performance more than warmth. "It suits you. Just remember... in this family, playing the part matters more than you think."

The words landed wrong—too smooth, too rehearsed. I couldn't tell if it was threat, warning, or both.

"Craig."

Alex's voice cut sharp from the hallway. He moved between us, all cold authority, his presence filling the space. "Samantha, go into the kitchen. My brother was just leaving."

"Not before I deliver this from dear old dad." Craig slid an envelope from his jacket, waving it lazily, as if the message inside were nothing more than a party invitation.

I didn't move until Alex's eyes locked on mine. His voice dropped, low and firm. "Go."

CHAPTER FOUR

Hard Lessons

"Force, and fraud, are the two cardinal virtues."

CRAIG

I watched her slip past, head down, clutching those bags like proof of something. New hair, coral nails, a brighter smile painted on a pale face. A makeover—Marcus's doing, no doubt. She looked polished now, less hometown girl. Dru would shred it—too brassy, too eager, never enough. But Jerome? He'd be pleased. He liked the rough edges filed down, liked to believe he could turn anyone into a Devereux.

Those bags almost made me laugh. Off-the-rack, mall-store clothes would never stand up to Drusilla's scrutiny or Jerome's impossible standards. She didn't know that yet. To her, this probably felt like a transformation.

She stopped short when she saw me.

"What are you doing here?"

Only a brief interaction before Alex's voice echoed, "Go," Dismissing her from our conversation.

Her shoulders stiffened. She turned away, vanished into the kitchen, and the moment shrank down to just the two of us. Alex's eyes fixed on me. "What message?"

I reached inside my jacket, pulled out the envelope, and handed it over. Thick, heavy. My father's handwriting across the front.

Alex turned it over in his hands. "What's inside?"

I kept my tone even. "I know better than to pry." A lie.

He stared at me like he wanted to cut the words from my throat. For the first time in years, I wondered if even Jerome underestimated how much damage a man like him could do once he finally blew apart.

ALEXANDER

Photos. That was my brother's delivery.

Samantha and Marcus in the rose garden at campus. At a salon. Shopping. Laughing over lunch. Another set with Rachel there, like her presence made it all harmless.

Harmless isn't letting another man feed you at a salon. Harmless isn't letting him pick your clothes.

Marcus was slick. Well-mannered, groomed—the kind my father trusted in our circle. I'd seen the way he looked at Samantha before the wedding. Polite smiles covering something hungrier.

One shot in the stack caught my attention more than the rest— inside the salon. Marcus's so-called "cousin" smiling at

Samantha. I knew those eyes. Devereux eyes. Light gray-blue, the kind you didn't forget. I didn't care what story Marcus spun—Allison was not a coincidence. She'd been gone a long time, but not so far she couldn't be useful. And Marcus? Of course, he'd keep her close. The two of them always huddled on the sidelines, misfits together.

When I walked into the kitchen that night, I didn't raise my voice. I set the envelope on the counter and told her to explain. She said Marcus was helping her "fit in" with my family. Like that was his place. She studied the picture of him feeding her fries, tapped it with her fresh manicure, and said, "Babe, I'm sorry. You're right—it looks bad. I didn't think how it would look to someone else. I just didn't want to ruin the nails while they were wet, that's all." Her voice softened, careful. "If it bothers you, we can go by and I'll introduce you to Allison. Clear everything up."

I touched her hand lightly, let my voice ease. "I believe you. I know you didn't mean anything by it."

But inside, the thought pressed sharp: naïve doesn't make it okay. Not in this family. Not with me.

"How about we drop the whole thing and you show me what you spent our money on."

She didn't miss a beat. Went into the bedroom, laid out

dresses, shoes, and accessories in neat rows. I nodded at each one. Better than before. She promised she'd practice walking in the heels. She kept talking, trying to keep the peace, and I let her. The moment had passed. For now.

"Anything else you want to tell me?" I asked.

"Nothing much else has happened."

Lies. I saw the looks in the pictures.

No need to fight her over Marcus tonight. Better to let her think it was behind us. Because men like Marcus always get bold. And when they do, they make mistakes.

I'd been patient. Too patient. After Craig's stunt and those photos, I could feel her slipping, twisting from my grasp. That wasn't going to happen.

On Saturday morning, I woke her with breakfast in bed—French toast, her favorite. She looked surprised. "Wear something comfortable," I told her. "We'll go up to Raven Rock. Spend the day together."

She looked relieved. Maybe even a little eager. She thought the matter with the photos was settled, that I'd chosen calm, chosen to let it go. To me, it meant something else entirely. Proof she loved me. Proof she wanted us. Proof she could still be guided, shaped, corrected. My love will keep her safe, even from her own mistakes.

I packed sandwiches, strawberries, champagne—set the scene. If she could relax, if she could remember how good we were together, maybe she'd quit wasting her time on other people.

The hike started fine. She laughed at something I said, looked almost like the girl I married. Mid-afternoon now, the air cooler than when we started. Pines shedding needles, the first yellow-gold leaves turning on the ridge. A storm was rolling in, distant thunder pressing closer with each step.

On our way back, she stumbled on a root, and I caught her by the arm. For a second, she looked up at me the way she used to—trust in her eyes, relief at my steadiness. My touch meant safety to her.

I could have held her there. I could have let that trust stand.

But the sky had already turned, and so had I. The image of Marcus feeding her flickered sharp in my mind, the way she smiled at him, the way she let him close.

You don't let people steal from you, my father's words came back.

I pulled her off the trail, backed her against a tree. For a heartbeat, she thought it was passion—her lips parted, waiting for a kiss, eyes bright with the hope that we were still that couple in the woods. She didn't see what was really coming.

"Do you know how my father taught me not to steal?"

She blinked. "What?"

"You're stealing from me," I said.

"The shopping? That was my money."

Her eyes sparked—confusion, maybe even defiance. "Alex, this isn't stealing."

"Not money. Time. Giving it to another man. To other people." Marcus's face flashed again, her lips parted in that laugh. I took a breath. "So I'll ask again—do you know how my father taught me not to steal?"

She whispered, "No."

I kissed her cheek. "I'm sorry. This is because I love you. You have to learn."

I covered her mouth before she could argue. The rock was right there. One swing against her arm and she dropped all fight, just a muffled scream.

"Breathe, Sam," I said. The anger burned off the second I'd done it. Now it was just about fixing what was broken. "Let's get you to a doctor."

We passed a park ranger on the way out. I didn't miss a beat—told him she'd tripped after we'd been drinking champagne. Let him focus on the alcohol, not anything else.

By the time we hit the main road, I knew how to make her love me again.

The one she relied on.

The one she couldn't imagine leaving.

Lesson learned.

DR. ELI SINCLAIR

I've worked in emergency medicine nearly thirty years. You learn not to take cases home with you—until one refuses to let you go.

For me, that was Elizabeth Devereux.

Sixteen years ago, her husband brought her in. Bruises that didn't fit the fall. Fractures that told a different story. But she never spoke the words, and I never asked hard enough. When she was found at the bottom of the stairs years later, the coroner called it an accident. I let the silence stand. It's the weight I carry into every exam room.

These days, I work most weekends so my staff can be home with their families. My weekdays, I give to free clinics and domestic violence programs. Penance, though it never balances the scale.

So when the Devereux name came across my chart that Saturday afternoon, my gut tightened.

Samantha Devereux.

Elizabeth's daughter? The family lived in the area. It was possible.

On paper, it was minor. A hairline fracture. Clean. No setting required. But the bruising was wrong. The story was wrong. Hiking at Raven Rock, a slip on the trail, her husband said. I've heard cleaner lies.

And the husband — he hovered too close. Concern is one thing. Possession is another.

"Mr. Devereux, would you fill out paperwork with the nurse while we finish? Then you can both be on your way."

"She only hurt her arm." He didn't move.

I'd seen that before—men who don't let their wives breathe without permission.

"It's protocol," I said, and drew the curtain between us.

"Mrs. Devereux—"

"Sam," she corrected.

"Sam. Are the painkillers helping?"

"I'm fine. Can I go home now? No offense, but I don't like hospitals."

"I've signed your discharge. But I need to tell you something."

Her eyes narrowed. Fear, suspicion—I couldn't tell.

"Is it worse than a fracture?"

"No. You're perfectly healthy. I just think your husband is more dangerous to you than hiking will ever be."

Her lips parted, ready to deny it. I didn't let her.

"Shh. Take this." I slid my card into her hand, low, practiced, discreet. "I work with people who help women leave dangerous situations. If you need help, call. Day or night. Be safe."

Her fingers closed around the card, but she wouldn't meet my eyes. She wanted to. I could feel it. But fear is a tether she couldn't cut.

I stepped out before he returned. He gave me a polite nod—the kind that says more than words. The kind that says I see you.

This time, I hadn't stayed silent. It wasn't enough. It never would be. But it was something.

By then, the sun had already set, the ER lights carrying the weight of another long Saturday night.

And if I were a betting man, I'd put money on Samantha not being Elizabeth's daughter. No, I think her husband is the same boy who once stood over his mother's broken body at the foot of the stairs.

ALEXANDER

When we got home from the hospital, Sam disappeared into the bedroom without a word. I knew she wouldn't come out unless I made her. I'd gone too far—again.

It had started fine. Breakfast in bed. A day in the woods. Then I broke her arm. Because she was trying to please my family... and it was another man helping her do it.

I couldn't stay in the house with that silence pressing in. I grabbed my keys and left. I'd get her something while I was out. A peace offering. Not flowers—she hated them, for reasons I'd never understand. She was complicated like that. Twenty years old and still more girl than woman, but she had this way of pulling men in without even trying. Craig wanted her. Hell, maybe even my father wanted her.

Sam wasn't the most beautiful woman in the room, but she was the one you remembered. She could blend in with everyone else, but there was a light in her—sweet with an undertone of venom—that made people look twice. That was what drew me to her.

And what I was going to take from her. Strip it away the same way my father had done to my mother.

Jealousy burned hotter than anything else in me. I'd seen the way other men looked at her—innocent conversations in her mind, but I knew better.

When I came home earlier and found Craig in my house, I imagined the worst. I remembered the maid at the estate when we were boys—Craig, fourteen, me, twelve—caught in something that left her shaken and crying. Better to put the blame on Craig—he had the face for it. Everyone believed it anyway.

But love does that to a man. My kind of love, anyway. It's not flowers and breakfast. It's protection at any cost. Even if she doesn't understand it.

I drove around for hours before stopping at a jewelry store just before closing. Bought her a charm bracelet, added a little boot charm. A reminder of us—of what bound us together, good and bad.

The next morning, I left her sleeping when I went out. My mind was in chaos, I needed space to think. I'd handled the problem yesterday. She'd remember the lesson. Remember, I'm the one she answers to—not my family, not the nosy ER doctor. Me.

By the time I came back, her car was still in the driveway. The blinds in the living room were tilted just enough for me to see her moving around inside, carrying a bag into the bedroom. Packing.

I expected anger. I didn't expect her to try and leave—not again. She was too scared to follow through.

I walked inside. She must've seen me pull in because she was hiding in the bathroom. Like a door would stop me. I could've dragged her out right then. But no. Let her think she had space. Let her cool off.

The doorbell rang just as I grabbed a beer.

Drusilla stood there with one of our doctors.

"What's this?" I asked, keeping my voice level.

"Checking on your wife," she said smoothly, stepping inside without waiting for permission and marching to the master bedroom. The doctor followed.

I didn't like Sam being alone with either of them, but Drusilla never showed up without Jerome having a hand in it.

From the bedroom, I heard Drusilla's voice, "Let our doctor look at you."

Sam's voice came back sharp. "I went to the hospital. Why are you here?"

I didn't catch the doctor's reply, but the tone was calm, practiced. He'd send his report later.

I stayed in the hall, listening for the shift in her voice that meant the fight was draining out of her. It didn't take long.

Drusilla came out, expression unreadable. "Keep calm, for once. She's not going anywhere. Not tonight."

I met her eyes. "Her decision or yours?"

"No matter. It was the right one." She walked out without another word.

The doctor paused at the door. "I'll send the notes to your father."

Of course, he would. Everything went back to Jerome.

When the house was quiet again, I could hear water running in the bathroom. The rest of the house had gone dark, night pressing at the windows. She was probably staring at herself in the mirror, wondering if she was broken. She didn't need to wonder—I'd decide that for her.

Either way, she wasn't leaving. Not now. Not until I said so.

SAMANTHA

The months blurred into something that barely felt like living. By late November, I was scribbling out invitations for the New Year's party, my hand cramping over names that belonged to strangers, not friends.

Sunday through Thursday, I stayed at the Devereux Estate, "learning" under Drusilla's eye. Friday and Saturday, I went home to keep up appearances.

I had different roles depending on where I stood: student on campus, debutante-in-training for Marcus, wife for Alex, a mix

60

of student and servant for Jerome and Drusilla. None of them felt like me.

One morning before heading to the estate, I caught my reflection in the mirror: heels, a sleek pantsuit Jerome had insisted on, my hair polished smooth and glossy. The woman looking back at me belonged in their world, not mine. She was someone I barely recognized.

The very next day, when no one was scheduled to come by, I stayed in a hoodie and leggings, hair twisted into a messy bun, while I addressed the last of the invitations. A small rebellion, petty maybe, but mine. Those quiet refusals reminded me I still existed somewhere under the roles they kept handing me.

I lied to my friends. Lied to myself. My parents would've been ashamed if they knew I was still with Alex. I was ashamed. But my arm healed quickly after Raven Rock, and Alex had been... perfect. Too perfect. Like it never happened. That unsettled me almost more than the violence had.

Jerome decided I'd take the spring semester off, then finish my bachelor's at a "respectable institution" in the fall. Translation: the one he picked. He wanted me with Drusilla more. "So, you'll be comfortable running the house if needed."

Drusilla was tolerable when Craig wasn't around, almost warm with her son, Horatio. She made it her mission to keep him from turning into Craig. I wondered if that was possible.

I learned more from the staff than from any Devereux. Jerome's public money came from real estate. The rest came in whispers—cartels, mafia ties, the kind of gossip that only grew in places where servants knew to lower their voices. Juicier stories slipped through cracks when Dru was away: Craig was accused of assaulting a maid at fourteen and knowing more about his mother, Elizabeth's, death than he ever said. Some blamed Jerome. Some blamed Alex. The reports never added up. One day, Craig was the monster in their stories, the next, he was the kindest of the Devereux, while Drusilla was painted as the true villain. None of it made sense, except for one constant: everyone believed the house was bugged.

That I believed.

Alex and I, we both kept tabs on the family. I just didn't tell him everything I heard. Pleasing the family, keeping Alex happy. Miserable, but effective.

One afternoon, as I finalized the guest list, Jerome walked into the kitchen.

"You have an office," he said.

"I can keep an eye on operations better from here," I answered without looking up.

"Graduation is next weekend."

"Yes, sir."

"You haven't planned a dinner party."

"I have plans with my friends. Didn't think the Estate needed the burden of a community college celebration."

"Very well. Drusilla's reports are impressive. You're learning quickly."

"Do I get a gold star?" The words slipped before I could stop them.

"That was uncalled for," he said, looking at me like I was a letter delivered to the wrong address.

"Where will you continue your education?"

"I figured you and Dru had that mapped out already."

"The tone, Samantha."

I straightened my back, swallowing every question that wanted to rise. Why do you get to decide? Why can't I finish what I started? Why do I feel more like a project than a person?

"Is there anything else?" I asked.

"Has Alexander told you our plans?"

"No."

"When he announces, act surprised. Your husband is going overseas to monitor certain interests. You will stay here."

Why me here? Why not with my husband?

"If I'm not going with Alex, I'll stay at my home."

"This is your home." His voice was final. "When will you have your first child?"

"When we're ready."

It wasn't his question to ask. And I was in no hurry to bring a child into any of this.

"Let's aim for before he leaves. Then we will discuss your request to maintain your home."

His words settled over me like chains.

I left before I said something I couldn't take back.

JEROME

I watched her go, the door closing softly behind her. Even in retreat, there was that faint stiffness in her shoulders—a tell she hadn't yet learned to mask. She was adapting quickly, yes, but still wore her defiance in the form of leggings and a hoodie. Comfortable. Careless. Ordinary. Not Devereux.

Alexander let her drift about this way, and perhaps that was the root of his weakness—satisfied with a wife who looked like any girl off the street when she could be so much more. Perhaps it was a lack of confidence in himself.

Samantha was still in the stage of being dressed up, paraded in borrowed silk, polished for rooms she didn't yet know how to command. But I recognized potential when I saw it. She had good bones, as they said in the trade. Foundation worth investing in. With refinement, staging, and the right pressure, she would not simply pass—she would look, act, and walk as though she had always been part of the plan.

She thought herself clever, feeding Alexander scraps she believed would wound me, imagining herself his little spy. Let her. A pawn that fancied itself more could still serve, until it overreached. I would take the measure of her loyalties when the time comes.

Alexander would bristle at being sent to Tokyo. He already seethed at Marcus's nearness, suspected too much when his wife's gaze lingered where it should not. Jealousy was Alexander's bluntest edge, but I know how to use a crude tool. Rage weakened men, cracked them open.

And Samantha... she might yet prove the perfect test. Beneath the cotton and bravado, there was spirit. Wit. Even courage. Qualities I both admired and distrusted. I would give her just enough rope, just enough room to reveal herself.

Rachel remained on the board, though unsteady. Still valuable, but unstable pieces had a way of toppling—and sometimes, collapse was more useful than endurance.

The real card, though, was the one none of them suspected: Alexander's chances of fathering a child were slim. He'd contracted mumps as a boy, and though no doctor had ever spoken with certainty, I understood. Not impossible, but improbable. Knowledge to be held close until it can be played for maximum effect.

Timing was everything.

Alexander dispatched overseas. Samantha left at the manor. Marcus hovering close. Drusilla—Drusilla never played better than when Samantha was on the field.

Early evening shadows stretched across the room as I poured another measure of scotch, savoring the fire in my throat. The game was moving. The pieces were aligning.

And Samantha—whether she knew it or not—was being renovated, step by step, into exactly what I need her to be.

CHAPTER FIVE
Whispers & Lies

"When devils will the blackest sins put on, they do suggest at first with heavenly shows."

ALEXANDER

Graduation parties bored me. Too many congratulations, too many fake smiles, too many idiots pretending the future was theirs to claim.

Samantha's friends crowded our living room, squealing over Rachel's new jewelry as if she'd just won an Oscar.

Marcus was in the middle of them, laughing with Rachel, Genevieve, and Samantha like he belonged there. Rachel teased him first. "I still can't believe you ended up in Bio 151 with us. What was that—community college remedial?"

Genevieve piled on, grinning. "Samantha had to keep you from blowing up the lab."

He threw his hands up in mock surrender, chuckling. "I needed the credit to graduate on time. My school was full, and you three were lucky enough to get stuck with me."

They laughed together, easy and warm. Too warm.

When Samantha reached for another tray of glasses, Marcus

stepped in before I could move, taking it from her hands with a grin. "Careful, Sam, you'll drop it."

She rolled her eyes, but she smiled. Too easily.

It made my jaw clench. She was my wife, not his to help, not his to tease.

Later, he slid onto the couch beside me, trying that familiar, boyish tone—like we were still kids playing basketball in the driveway. "She's not flashy at all. That has to be a little odd for the manor crowd, but it suits her. Gotta be one of the reasons you fell for her. Or do you prefer her debutante alter ego?"

I didn't blink. "I prefer her naked." Deadpan. Sharp enough to cut. "You prefer high maintenance."

His jaw ticked, but he said nothing. Good.

I stood, lifting my beer bottle, and the room's chatter dulled. Eyes turned.

"I'm going overseas on a contract."

The silence that followed landed like a slap. Even Samantha froze.

I smirked, enjoying the sting. "Aren't you all happy I'll be gone for a year?"

Her smile wavered, brittle. She stepped close, her voice low enough for only me. "Alexander, not now. This isn't the right time."

She meant to soothe, but all I heard was correction. In my house. From my wife.

Gasps, awkward laughter, eyes darting between us. They didn't know how to take it. That pleased me.

In the kitchen, I popped another beer. The hiss sounded too loud in the quiet house. Samantha followed, arms crossed, her face tight.

"Don't call me down in front of your friends."

"Babe, we were celebrating and you just killed it," she spoke soft, but there was bite.

"Think of all the whoring you can do," I shot back, low enough for only her.

Her eyes widened. Bad sign. She never understood how close the line was.

SAMANTHA

I saw it in his face—the way his eyes darkened, how his shoulders rolled forward like he was squaring up for a fight. He was drunk. Angry. Dangerous.

I didn't argue. I smoothed my voice. "Hey guys, let's call it a night," I told the others, walking into the living room with the brightest smile I could fake.

Rachel and Marcus didn't question it. Genevieve clung to me a little longer, whisper sharp against my ear, "If you ever need out, call me."

I laughed it off until her car pulled away.

Inside, the kitchen was empty. The bedroom, too.

"Alex?" My voice cut through the quiet. His car was still here. I moved from room to room until I found him in the guest room. My office.

"What are you doing?" I tried for playful.

"What are you and my father hiding from me?"

"I'm not hiding anything." I turned for the hallway, but he yanked me back. My shoulders slammed into the wall.

"Alex, look at me—please." I brushed my fingers against his cheek, pleading.

For a heartbeat, he stilled. His eyes searched mine. Maybe. Just maybe.

Then his jaw clenched.

"Do you love me?" His voice came low, sharp. Silence was dangerous.

"I married you."

"I asked if you love me." His whisper burned.

"I did."

The punch knocked the air out of me.

"Do you love me?" he shouted.

"No safe answer," my mind raced. But I forced the words. "Not anymore."

Another blow. Then another. A kick. Every second was calculated: don't scream too loud, don't fight too hard. Just survive.

He dragged me into the bedroom. Bruised, stripped. His voice was cold, almost conversational. "It's been weeks since I had my wife under me where she belongs."

When he was done, he tossed a towel at me. "It'll be much easier if you love me and treat me the way I deserve. I'll be back in a few hours. Clean up, or there will be hell to pay."

The front door slammed.

ALEXANDER

The night air hit me, cold and sobering. My knuckles ached. My stomach churned.

I shouldn't have done it. Not like that. Not tonight.

But she pushed me. Corrected me in front of her friends, in my house. Let Marcus stand too close, laugh too easily, take trays from her hands like she needed him. Like she wasn't mine.

I told myself it wasn't my fault. She made me do it—made me prove I still owned her. That's what a husband was owed. That's what Jerome never understood.

Still... I couldn't leave it as it was. Not if anyone asked questions.

Pulling out my phone, I scrolled past every name until I landed on Marcus. Of all people. It burned to choose him, but he was the only one whose number I had.

He answered on the second ring.

"She fell," I said flatly. "In the garage. Organizing hiking gear. Refused to see a doctor. I've been called out on work—I can't be there. Can you check on her?"

Silence stretched. I hated that hesitation.

"I don't have Rachel's number," I added, sharper than I meant. "You were the only one I could reach." A pause. Then, lower, deliberate, "And you know how it is with the Devereux. Some things stay quiet."

Not just a lie, but a warning.

The lie tasted sour, but I told it anyway. A fall. A clumsy accident. Nothing to see.

Marcus agreed. Good. He'd do as told—or else.

I hung up, bile rising. Guilt twisted in me, hot and raw, but I shoved it down. She'd learn. She had to.

MARCUS

The porch light burned overhead when I rang the bell. Twice.

Samantha cracked the door, pale and rigid. "Forget something?"

"Alexander called me," I said. "Said you'd fallen in the garage. Refused a doctor. Thought I'd check."

Her eyes widened. Surprise flickered before she smoothed it away. "He... he called you?" The words slipped out too raw.

"Surprised me too, Sam."

That told me enough. Whatever happened tonight, she hadn't expected me. And she sure as hell hadn't expected him to send me.

She stepped back, tucking herself into the shadows.

"He said you fell? In the garage? Putting away hiking gear?"

Her eyes darted. "I... slipped." The words came too fast, too thin. The story didn't match. Too late, she realized it, her face tightening before she forced a shaky nod. "Yes—the gear. I slipped trying to move it."

Her breathing hitched, shallow, like every inhale cost her. One arm stayed tight across her stomach, as if she could hold herself together by force.

That decided it. "You're going to the hospital."

"My coat is in the garage," she murmured.

I nodded, went to fetch it. The garage was empty. No hiking gear. No sign of a fall.

When I came back, she didn't meet my eyes. She was pale, shaking, holding herself together by threads. I wasn't about to pull them loose.

We drove in silence. Every mile, I replayed Alexander's voice. Flat. Cold. *Some things stay quiet.*

Not just a lie. A warning.

DR. ELI SINCLAIR

Second time in three months. Different day, same woman. Samantha Devereux.

Her name on the intake chart stopped me cold. Bruised ribs. Shoulder injury. Story: fell while storing hiking gear.

I pushed through the curtain. Samantha sat on the gurney, left arm cradled. Her hair was pulled back, but not neatly—hurried, like she'd tried to make herself presentable and missed. Her eyes were too wide for a "simple fall."

74

"Mrs. Devereux," I said evenly, "I hear you took a tumble?"

She nodded; gaze fixed on the floor. "Yeah. I was putting away hiking gear in the garage. Lost my balance."

I eased into my chair, flipping through her chart. "Same side as last time?"

Her head snapped up, surprise flashing before she smoothed it away.

The exam confirmed what my gut already knew. Tenderness along the ribs—clustered, not diffused. That was a fist, a kick, not a shelf. The shoulder: subluxation. No abrasions, no attempt to catch herself.

"Did you land on your arm?" I asked carefully.

She shook her head. "No, I hit the shelving." Too quick. Too practiced.

Elizabeth's ghost loomed. Different woman, same lies.

"You know," I said, clinical, "these injuries are more common in contact sports. Football. Wrestling. Rugby. Car wrecks. A simple fall doesn't usually leave this pattern."

Her shoulders tensed. "I told you what happened."

Silence stretched. She stared at the curtain, at the floor, anywhere but me.

I finished the exam, keeping my hands gentle. "We'll treat the shoulder subluxation and bruised ribs. Sling for comfort, a week or so. The ribs will hurt with twisting, laughing, breathing—expect that. Bruises will fade in two, maybe three weeks, but the tenderness may last longer. I'd like to keep you overnight as a precaution."

A lie. If she stayed, she'd be safe.

She nodded, relief flickering when the conversation shifted to clinical.

I signed off the chart, my pen hovering. Two visits in a few months. Injuries that didn't match. The same family name.

I lowered my voice. "Samantha. I'm going to ask you one more time. Are you safe at home?"

Her lips parted, trembled, then closed. "I'm fine."

The words were rote. Scripted. Just like Elizabeth.

I wrote it down anyway: suspected non-accidental trauma. And I told myself I'd remember her face.

When I opened the curtain, he was waiting. Maybe a brother, maybe something else. Clearly, he was anxious, worried about her. I leaned toward him.

"Get her out of there," I murmured. "He will kill her if you don't convince her to get out."

CHAPTER SIX
Half in Shadow

"Every truth has two sides; it is as well to look at both, before we commit ourselves to either."

SAMANTHA

Back in the room, Marcus sat close beside the bed, his hand resting lightly on my forearm. Not possessive. Not insistent. Just there. Solid.

I could still hear Dr. Sinclair's words ringing in my ears: *He will kill her if you don't convince her to get out.* The weight of them pressed harder than the bruises.

Was I disrespectful? Did I correct Alex in front of everyone? Did I make him look small? I replayed it in my head, searching for the moment it turned. He wasn't in control when he drank—not fully. That much I knew. But was it me? Was it because I told him *not now?*

And why Marcus? Of all people, why call Marcus? He hated Marcus near me. That was the point. Punishment, or proof I belonged to him, no matter who saw the mess.

The ache in my stomach dragged me back to the floor of our bedroom, his words cold and casual. *It's been months since I had my wife under me, where she belongs.* My chest tightened, bile rising. Was it rape if it was your husband? The question twisted like a blade. My skin burned with shame, and still I wasn't sure what to call it.

Sinclair's voice tangled with Marcus's whisper. *Get her out.* They thought I hadn't heard. But I had.

I searched Marcus's face. His jaw was set, eyes dark—he believed Sinclair. That terrified me more than if he'd dismissed it.

Finally, Marcus spoke. Quiet. Raw. "I didn't think Alexander was capable of this."

"It was a fall," I said quickly, the lie bitter on my tongue.

He shook his head. "Sam, I saw his temper even when we were kids. He didn't grow out of it—he grew into it." His hand pressed a little firmer. "I'll get you out."

And then, like a dam breaking, Marcus kept talking. His childhood in the Devereux shadow. The way he had loved me for years. How Rachel had been a stand-in for what he really wanted—with me.

I shut my eyes. Why now, Marcus?

"I can't do this, Marcus. Neither can you. Not to Rachel. And Alex would—"

He kissed me. Maybe to silence me. Maybe because he couldn't help it.

I kissed him back.

Shame flooded me instantly, hot and suffocating. Not just betrayal of Rachel—but because some desperate part of me wanted him, maybe I always had.

MARCUS

Her lips were softer than I'd imagined, tentative, like she knew this could only ever be borrowed time. I should have stopped. But when Samantha didn't pull away, I let myself kiss her. Let myself imagine, just for a heartbeat, that we were possible.

I pulled back first, afraid if I didn't, I never would. The words slipped out. "I love you, Samantha."

Her eyes widened. Guilt flashed. Her breath caught too sharp, ribs flaring with pain. And here I was, piling more on her.

"Marcus, no. Rachel's my best friend."

"I know. And Alex—"

"It's not the husband part that makes me feel guilty," she whispered. "Rachel would never do this to me. And I—" She cut herself off, but what she didn't say hung heavy.

I didn't push. Instead, I held her gaze. And what I saw unsettled me most: the shadow of Sinclair's warning in her eyes. *He will kill her.* She hadn't denied it. She'd absorbed it.

She signed herself out of the hospital against Sinclair's orders. I stayed with her through every step, then drove her home.

It was wrong, unnatural, to see her this way. Shoulders hunched, eyes downcast, every step measured as though the air itself choked her.

A spark of anger flared hot in me, anger that Alex would do this. But anger wouldn't help her. She needed gentleness.

She winced trying to lift her arms, so when she finally sat, I took the brush from her dresser and ran it gently through her hair, slow and deliberate.

That was all I could give her: steadiness where he gave chaos, care where he gave pain. My hands said what my mouth couldn't—that I would never be like him.

The contrast was unbearable. The violence she'd endured, and then this—quiet intimacy, trust in something so small, so ordinary.

JEROME

The next afternoon, I went to the house. Alexander was at the estate—I'd arranged it. That left me the opening I wanted: Samantha alone.

The furnishings were comfortable, meant to be used, not admired. No gilded mirrors or carved mantels. Just clean lines, soft fabrics, spaces lived in instead of staged. A home chosen for function, not statement.

Samantha matched it. Curled on the sofa in jogging pants and a hoodie—bruised, arm in a sling. Not careless. Simply ordinary. Deliberately so.

"My son did this to you?" I asked.

Her lips twitched. "I fell in the garage."

I let out a dry laugh. "No, you didn't. Don't lie to me—you're terrible at it."

"I fell," she repeated, voice thin.

I smirked. "And my wife broke her heel, toppled down the stairs, and snapped her neck."

Her throat worked. A nerve struck.

"I can help you," I said.

"Arsenic or cyanide?" she shot back.

I leaned forward, voice calm. "Be honest. I will let you choose."

She startled. "You know what he'll do if he finds out I've talked to you."

I waved it off. "I told you before—my sons have their flaws. I need strong daughters and grandchildren to carry on my name. I can protect you, just like Drusilla."

Her chin lifted. "I don't want to be anything like Drusilla."

"One Drusilla is enough. We need balance—someone warm, approachable. The staff works better when you're around. Elizabeth was like that."

Her eyes hardened. "It did her a lot of good."

Heat cut through me, but I mastered it. Only once had I failed with Elizabeth. Never again.

"You don't know how or why Elizabeth ended up at the bottom of those steps," I said evenly. "Remember that."

"What do you want from me, Jerome?" Her frustration brewed.

"Truth."

She gave it. The broken arm. This beating. The rape. Her voice cracked. "Truth enough for one day?"

I kept composed. Inside, I seethed—not at her, but at Alexander. Reckless. Wasteful.

So I smiled.

"Are you smiling?" she demanded. "Proud of what your son did to me?"

"No. I smile because you're angry. Anger is useful. Self-pity isn't. I'll handle Alexander. Spend time with your friends. Especially Marcus."

Suspicion flashed. She thought it a trap. She wasn't wrong.

Pieces moved. Alexander contained. Craig managed. Drusilla loyal. Marcus useful. And Samantha, if she harnessed her anger, might be forged into something formidable. A queen instead of a pawn.

I rose, kissed her forehead like a priest blessing a parishioner. "Alexander is out of control. Let me get him caged."

I left her then, with more questions than answers—exactly as intended. But her words echoed: Alexander wasn't merely reckless. He was a monster.

MARCUS

Sunday morning, Rachel had already taken over Sam's kitchen. She bustled, chirping, determined to play nurse. She pushed Sam toward the shower, waited outside the door, even dried and fixed her hair.

By the time she settled Sam on the couch with a blanket, Rachel looked proud. "Genevieve will be by later. Until then, you pick the first movie."

Sam's eyes found mine. Sharp. Quiet.

"Star Wars," she said.

Rachel groaned. "No ma'am. Comedy, not sci-fi." She jingled her keys. "I'm going for Starbucks and cake pops! Marcus, keep her here, she's known to run." Then she was gone.

Her trust stung. She left Sam in my care without hesitation. And I had already betrayed her.

The silence was heavy. Sam rose, tugging the blanket tight. "Alex's office has all the DVDs," she said without looking back.

Instinct pulled me after her. My hand brushed hers. "Are we going to talk about the other night?"

She stiffened, flinched. "Maybe we shouldn't."

"I can't tell you I love you, kiss you, and pretend it didn't happen."

"Maybe, we can."

She pulled a box set from the shelf, suddenly close. Her perfume cut through the dust. Her eyes caught mine and gravity pulled me under. I kissed her, urgent, desperate.

She stayed rigid. Pain flickered across her face.

The phone rang. Merciful.

She answered, face shuttered. Rachel—called into work. Leaving me alone with Sam again.

Her voice was tight when she hung up. "She's my best friend, Marcus."

"I know. And Alex—"

"Those people are insane." Her eyes blazed. "Jerome came

yesterday. He knew Alex could be violent. He told me to spend more time with you. Even said Craig would arrange it."

Jerome moving pieces.

I reached for her again, pulled her close. She didn't fight, but I felt the way her body tensed, ribs guarding the pain. I kissed her softer.

Her palm pressed flat to my chest, stopping me.

"Not while you're with Rachel. Not again."

"It's just a kiss."

"You know it's more. And I can't deal with that now." She turned away, "You need to leave."

There was nothing left to say. I pulled myself away, leaving her standing there.

SAMANTHA

I curled back onto the couch, blanket clutched tight. One of Rachel's DVDs looped on the menu. A love triangle, betrayal, happy ending.

It lasted ten minutes.

Alex's fists. His boot in my ribs. Sinclair's warning. Marcus's kiss.

Every memory layered until my chest squeezed tight. My ribs screamed, the sling bit into my shoulder.

I was trapped in my body. Worse, trapped in my mind—replaying, replaying.

Rachel trusted me, and I had betrayed her the second I let myself feel it. Yet the ache of Marcus's lips dulled the rest.

No way back. No way forward.

And Jerome—Jerome of all people—had promised protection.

The Devereux machine was closing in. Every angle, every breath, hurt.

I hit stop on the remote, silencing the laughter. The room fell back into silence, heavy and watching.

GENEVIEVE

The drive over felt longer than it should have. My thoughts circled the same loop: I was never a fan of Alex's. Too perfect. Too polished.

Sam and I had drifted since the engagement. I chalked it up to newlyweds. Then came the bruises. The flimsy stories about injuries. The arm, the ribs. None of it added up.

And now—another ER visit.

I knocked once before letting myself in. Sam was curled on the couch, blanket wrapped around her. Smaller than I'd ever seen her.

"Hey, trouble," I said softly.

Her face lifted, tired but grateful. "Gen."

"Garage shelves, huh?"

She flinched. "That's what I said."

I tilted my head. "Sam, you drink so little. You've never been reckless. You don't have to tell me," I added gently. "Just... don't lie. Not to me."

Her eyes glossed. Silence sat heavy.

I grabbed the remote. "Star Wars? It's streaming now."

Her laugh was fragile. "You know Rachel won't let me."

"Rachel's not here. And if anyone needs *A New Hope* right now, it's you."

She leaned back, wincing. I didn't press. For now, it was enough to sit side by side, the blue glow painting the room.

SAMANTHA

Graduation had come and gone at the start of December, but instead of feeling like I'd stepped into something new, I felt myself shrinking.

Jerome kept me shadowing Drusilla—cocktail parties, dinner service. Days blurred together in floral arrangements and forks that always seemed wrong.

In the bathroom mirror that night, I studied the reflection I barely recognized. My ribs ached, the shoulder twinged. Bruises faded, but I still searched for them.

On the hanger beside me waited the gown Drusilla mandated: purple silk, low neckline, hem brushing my knees. It demanded to be seen.

Physically, I was mending. Outwardly, I looked the part. Inside, I was hollow.

Last year was all cocoa and twinkle lights with my parents. This year, the estate glittered like a set piece. Formal gowns replaced pajamas. Polite laughter replaced belly laughs.

Now it was New Year's Eve. Another Devereux gala. Another parade of strangers judging my smile. Jerome had been explicit: greet every guest at the door. A test.

Better this year than last. Last year, on New Year's Eve, I buried my parents. This year, I bury myself in silk and call it survival.

MARCUS

I'd booked the reservation weeks ago, back when I still thought being engaged to Rachel was the right move.

Sitting across from her now, over candlelight, I felt the weight of what I was about to do.

Her eyes still carried the brightness from the night I proposed— dimmed, but there. She cut into her entrée and smiled.

"So... we need to talk dates. Long engagement? Short one?"

I set down my fork. "Rach, let's not get into this tonight."

"We have to talk sometime. People are asking me."

"It's our wedding, not theirs."

Her shoulders stiffened. "What is it with you lately? I need to start planning."

I thought of Samantha. The kiss. Sinclair's warning. The promise I'd made to myself.

"I think we need to slow down."

Her fork clattered. "Slow down? You asked me to marry you."

"I rushed it. Too many things changing."

Her voice went cold. "So now you want to call it off? This is humiliating."

"Always thinking of yourself," I snapped. Cheap shot.

She tugged at the ring. "Then you can have this back."

I caught her hand. "Keep it. Sell it. Use it for school. I'm just... not ready."

Her breath hitched, but when she spoke, it was steady. "If we're not engaged, we're not together. I can't go back to dating you."

The finality should have hurt more. Instead, guilt pooled—for ending it, and for why. Because I loved someone else.

She dabbed her eyes, composure snapping into place. "Samantha's going to be surrounded by those people tonight. She needs us there. We're still going to the party."

I nodded. "Yeah. We'll go."

CHAPTER SEVEN

The Board is Set

"Life is a kind of Chess, in which we often have points to gain, and competitors or adversaries to contend with."

ALEXANDER

By the time the chandeliers were lit and the champagne flowed, I was already bored. From across the ballroom, I nursed my drink and studied my wife.

Samantha was radiant in purple silk—Drusilla's doing, no doubt. Posture sharpened, smile practiced, but her eyes? They gave her away. That wasn't Samantha smiling at my father's guests. That was my training shining through her. She was mine, down to the bones that broke when I needed to remind her.

She didn't look at me until she felt me staring. Her spine stiffened, her gaze slid across the room, and when our eyes locked, I let my smile stretch slow, deliberate, and walked toward her.

"You look ravishing, Mrs. Devereux," I murmured, brushing the necklace at her throat with my fingers. "Whatever will I do without you on the other side of the world?"

Her lips curved, but her words carried teeth. "Probably the

same thing you do when I'm sent to Father's house. Your... appetites."

I adjusted the pendant so it lay flat, dragging my knuckle across her collarbone. Her pulse jumped beneath my touch. "You needed that arrangement as much as I did," I whispered against her ear. "Don't forget, I can still get to you. Want to test me on that?"

I kissed her cheek, smiling at the way she forced her body not to recoil. She hated me. But she wasn't leaving. Not unless I let her.

The door opened behind her. She turned, expecting another stranger. Instead—Rachel and Marcus.

Rachel went straight to Samantha, clinging too tightly, eyes rimmed red, face blotched from crying. Pathetic. My wife softened instantly, wrapping her arms around her as though Rachel's heartbreak outweighed everything else.

And then—there it was.

Samantha's eyes slid to Marcus. And Marcus... made a gesture. Quick, small, but I caught it. His hand twisted, like slipping a ring off his finger.

My drink froze halfway to my lips. Samantha understood him instantly. Her shoulders knotted, her stomach clenched.

The engagement was over.

Rachel clung to Samantha, mascara smudging, while Marcus kept his expression careful, too careful. But his eyes betrayed him. He looked at her with something he didn't bother to hide—not from her. Desire. Possession.

And worse? She looked back.

My pulse roared in my ears. They thought they were subtle. They thought I wouldn't notice. But nothing escaped me. Not in my house. Not in my world.

Marcus Underwood was playing a game. A game he would lose. And Samantha, she was about to learn what happened to people who thought they could outmaneuver me.

DRUSILLA

As soon as I glided into the entrance hall, I felt like a woman who owned every eye in it. Red silk, slit high, neckline low, honey-blonde hair catching the chandelier light. I was groomed for this role, but tonight I played it to perfection.

"I invited them," I said when Alex asked about the guest list. "Samantha needed a break from people she neither knows nor likes. Genevieve was intolerable, but these two will do."

Her gaze flicked between Marcus and Samantha—sharp, measuring. She saw the crackle of something neither of them

93

intended to show. Marcus, careful. Samantha, measured in return. The exchange told her more than words ever would.

Amusement curled her lips, but unease lived beneath it. Perhaps Samantha was learning too quickly. Perhaps she was learning to play.

I turned away, swallowed by the crowd, leaving perfume and tension in my wake.

RACHEL

By the time I followed Samantha upstairs, I was desperate to escape. The house was too much—marble floors, glittering chandeliers, people who looked at her like she didn't belong. Like I didn't, either.

Her assigned room was bigger than my entire apartment. I laughed through my nerves as I opened doors—closet, bathroom—each one more ridiculous than the last. Lavish. Absurd. Not for a girl like Sam.

We stretched out across the bed, and for a few minutes we were our old selves again—though dressed better, painted into someone else's world. We talked about the future, about disappointments, about endings.

Finally, I forced out what I needed to hear myself say. "I'm leaving for Wilmington single. He called it off." My voice barely shook. I didn't cry. Not yet.

Sam took my hand. She said the right things, the safe things.

"Who knows what the future holds—for either of us."

She gave me a weak smile, and there it was—her tell. Normally she'd rage for me, call him a coward, curse the nerve of a man stringing me along only to walk away. But now she was careful. Too careful. Not just protecting me. Protecting him.

That's when it hit me. I was the fool.

"How long, Sam?" I asked.

At first, she looked surprised. Then caught.

"Samantha Woods, how long?" My voice cracked. I was crying now, and I didn't care.

"Rachel, it's not—"

"It's not me." I swallowed, collected myself. "Tell Marcus to find his own way. Or maybe just take him home with you."

I stood, cold and steady. I was done. And then I was gone.

SAMANTHA

The door clicked shut behind Rachel, and silence rushed in to fill the space she left. My hand still rested on the bedspread where hers had been, empty now, colder than it should have been.

I hated myself. For the look in her eyes. For the tremor in her voice. For being the reason she had to say those words.

I hadn't pursued Marcus. I'd tried to keep the friend line clear. But he had a way of being where I needed his help the most, woven into the edges of my life until the lines blurred. And I'd let it happen. Now Rachel knew. And it didn't matter how careful I thought I had been. To her, I was the betrayer.

I stood, moving to the gilded mirror above the vanity. The reflection that stared back at me hardly looked like the girl Rachel had once known. My lipstick had faded; I reapplied it with hands that trembled. I dabbed tears from the corner of my eyes.

The diamonds at my throat felt heavy. More leash than lavish. I adjusted the clasp, lifted my chin.

I wanted to run, to chase her down the stairs, to beg her to understand. But what could I say? That I never meant for it to happen? That I'd tried to fight it? Excuses, all of it. Rachel deserved more than excuses. When that door closed, so did years of friendship. If the roles were reversed, I would feel the same.

I straightened my shoulders, smoothed the silk over my hips, and pinned my mask back in place. Out there, beneath the chandeliers, they expected poise. They expected Mrs. Alexander Devereux.

Inside, though—inside I was unraveling.

And still, I opened the door and stepped back toward the light.

CRAIG

She drifted down the staircase. Despite her finery, she was out of place among the laughter, perfume, and the clink of glasses. She looked uncomfortable. Sad. I wondered if it was the party— or that little friend of hers. Cute, but not my taste. Neither of them were.

Odd that Rachel slipped straight for the door. Without Marcus.

I stepped into Samantha's path.

"My brother said you looked stunning tonight. Those Drusilla's diamonds?"

"Yes. She was kind enough to loan them." Something had shaken her. Wonder if the friend caught on.

"Is your little friend abandoning you?" I asked, tone light, almost playful. "She seemed..." I let the pause stretch, watching her shift beneath it.

"She's not well. Rachel isn't feeling up to the crowd," Samantha said. "I need to find her date, let him know he'll need to find his own way home."

I nodded toward the glitter at her throat. "You know, I can

never remember when I gave those to Drusilla. Was it after I cheated, or an anniversary? Funny how memory works."

The line fell like a stone, too sharp for a party joke, but I smiled as though it amused me. People believed more in my cruelty than my truth.

She looked for an escape, and salvation arrived on a silver tray.

"Mrs. Devereux. Your husband needs you in the billiard room," Sampson said.

She nodded and slipped away quickly.

I kept the smile, though something pinched in my chest as I watched her leave.

JEROME

The billiard room smelled of smoke and liquor, familiar and comforting. I sipped my scotch, content to let Alexander strut for Marcus, who pretended not to notice. They played their parts as expected.

When Samantha entered, I spread my hands in mock benediction. "Is she not a vision? Lovely—though perhaps something a little longer next time."

Alexander gave her a perfunctory glance. "Beautiful." Desire without devotion. Lust without love. Predictable.

Samantha arched a brow. "I could not agree more, Jerome. We can discuss it tomorrow with my stylist." She tugged lightly at the hem of her dress—humor edged with defiance.

I turned to Marcus deliberately. "And what do you think, Marcus? Does she fit here?"

The boy startled, and so did she—proof Samantha had not realized he was present. Marcus cleared his throat, uneasy.

"She seems to be fitting in well. Careful, she has a mind of her own." His gaze flicked toward Samantha as he said it, like a private compliment.

Interesting. Not clever, but telling.

Clever girl, I noticed the way Samantha ignored him. "Alex, Rachel left early. It looks like Marcus will need a ride back to town." She did not look at Marcus—she looked only at her husband, smoothing the edges before they could fray.

I set down my glass. Tone mild, decision absolute. "Samantha, you can see Marcus home. Alexander has had quite a lot to drink. It would be best for him to stay here."

Alexander glared, silent. Perfect.

The board was set. All as intended.

ALEXANDER

I couldn't stop watching them. Even in the ballroom, with strangers pressing around me, my eyes found Samantha and Marcus. Always them.

He lingered too near. His body angled toward her. Always her. And she—she gave him those careful looks. Small. Subtle. But I saw.

My jaw ached from grinding. My grip threatened to shatter the glass in my hand.

Father wasn't watching her. Or Marcus. He was watching me. Measuring the tremor in my hand, the predator's focus in my stare. He knew exactly what I wanted to do. That's why he smiled.

"Alexander has had quite a lot to drink tonight," he said smoothly. "After the midnight toast, perhaps you should see that Marcus gets home safely."

Not a suggestion. An exile.

I understood. He wasn't sending me to Tokyo to honor me. He was moving me off the board.

I am not a pawn, like the rest of them.

The countdown began. Samantha's practiced smile stayed

painted on. My whisper cut against it, "You think I don't see it? The way you look at him?"

Her lips barely moved. "Not here."

"Not here," I echoed, gritting my teeth in something like a smile.

The clock struck twelve. I kissed her hard, deep, claiming her for every watching eye. She kissed back—what else could she do? But her lips were cold.

Father's hand landed heavy on my shoulder. "That's enough for tonight. Samantha, take Marcus home."

Protecting them. Not me.

Let him think distance would dull this fire. When I came back, there would be no distance left.

SAMANTHA

The cold air bit my skin sharper than I expected. For the first time all night, I could breathe—though my lungs still felt bruised. The smell of champagne clung to everyone else, but I hadn't touched a drop. I thought I'd be driving Alexander home, not Marcus.

Jerome's words still rang: *Take Marcus home.* Not a suggestion. An order.

Marcus walked beside me, coat folded over his arm, silence heavier than Alexander's rage. I kept waiting for the snap, the sigh, the disappointment I'd learned to expect. The reflex lived in me.

By the time we reached my car, I realized I was clutching my little beaded bag so tightly my knuckles hurt. The words slipped out before I could stop them. "That was humiliating."

Marcus opened my door, leaning in just enough that our hands brushed. A rush burned through me I couldn't afford.

"Not for you," he said.

I slid into the seat, forcing myself not to shiver. "For Alex, then."

He circled, slid into the passenger side. "And Jerome. He wanted everyone to see who holds the leash."

The gates stood wide. I didn't breathe right until the estate vanished in the rearview. Alex's kiss sat on my lips like a bruise, his whisper burrowed in my ear: *You think I don't see it?*

Marcus finally broke the silence. "He knows, Sam. Alexander knows something."

My grip tightened on the wheel. "Then why agree to go? Why let Jerome ship him off like a child?"

"Because Jerome is not to be disobeyed. Even by Alex. Drunk and jealous makes him look weak. But you..." His voice softened. "You looked perfect."

A bitter laugh caught in my throat. "Perfect? That's not how it feels."

"You were," Marcus said. "That's why he's afraid of you."

Perfect for what? Jerome's game. Alexander's punishment. A dress I wanted to rip off and burn.

"So," I whispered, headlights cutting into the night. "Where do we go from here?"

CHAPTER EIGHT

Knight Takes Pawn

"At the end of the game, the king and pawn go into the same box."

MARCUS

Rachel's face haunted me. Part of me hated myself for it. Rachel deserved better than to be strung along, better than to have her heart broken for someone who couldn't give her the same love back. I'd wanted to let her down gently, wait until she moved, maybe let the distance do the work.

The way her eyes had shone, hurt, betrayed, when she realized what she'd always feared. I hadn't lied to her. Not exactly. But I hadn't told the whole truth either. And the truth was sitting beside me, hands gripping the wheel so tightly her knuckles blanched.

Samantha's question lingered between us. Where do we go from here? It hung in the air, heavy, demanding, and I had nothing to give her. No plan. No promise. No answer that wouldn't risk breaking her further or putting a target squarely on her back.

I wanted to reach for her. To tell her that I loved her. That I'd walk through fire to get her out of this place, away from

Alexander, away from Jerome. That Rachel had been the cost of it—the life I was supposed to build sacrificed for the one I couldn't let go.

But I didn't.

Because silence was safer than hope. Safer than lies.

I pressed my palms flat against my knees, grounding myself in the hum of the tires on the highway. A dozen words burned at the back of my throat, each one dangerous. I thought of Rachel's voice, the way it cracked when she whispered my name, and then of Sam, here and now, carrying both of us forward even while her own hands trembled. The guilt doubled back on itself—two weights pulling me apart. I told myself that if I just kept quiet long enough, the night would swallow the choice I was too much of a coward to make.

So I stared at the road instead, at the sweep of headlights cutting through the dark, letting the question hang there unanswered until it pressed against my ribs like a stone.

And then the flashing red lights appeared ahead, strobing against the windshield, breaking the moment before it crushed us both.

SAMANTHA

Marcus sat beside me, quiet, staring out the window, his face lit in harsh slices by the passing streetlamps. I wanted to reach for his hand. But Rachel's words still rang in my head: How long?

And the whole time, all I could think about was protecting Marcus. I had betrayed Rachel in ways I never thought myself capable.

I squeezed the steering wheel like I could break it in half. His lack of an answer did not make it any better. Where do we go from here?

The silence in the car pressed on me, louder than the hum of the engine. I could feel Marcus's presence beside me like a weight, every shallow breath of his measured, controlled, while mine wanted to spiral into panic. My mind replayed the look on Rachel's face—hurt, betrayed, the way her voice shook when she asked me if it had been going on all along. I hadn't answered her honestly. Maybe I hadn't even answered myself.

I gripped the wheel tighter, my knuckles burning white, because if I let go, even for a second, I was afraid everything would collapse. He was staring out at the night like he could disappear into it, and I kept wondering if he already had. Was I only holding onto smoke? Was I just the temporary place he landed after setting fire to everything else?

A horn blared from the next lane, snapping me back, but even that sound couldn't shake off the thoughts. My pulse raced. If I spoke, I might say something I couldn't take back, something about love, or guilt, or how I would choose him again despite knowing the cost. And I wasn't ready for his silence to be my answer. Not yet.

So I drove on, pretending the road was steady under me, pretending the green lights were absolution. But inside, all I felt was the sharp edge of a question that neither of us seemed brave enough to touch.

MARCUS

Sirens broke the silence, light painting the inside of Sam's car in harsh pulses of color. At first, I thought it was just another DWI checkpoint, but then I saw the smoke—thick, black, curling into the sky.

I leaned forward, my chest tightening. "Slow down—look."

Flames licked the roofline of the apartment complex before I even registered what I was seeing. My apartment. My place. Gone.

"Shit." The word slipped out before I could stop it.

Sam pulled closer, but a firefighter waved us back.

I shoved the door open, ignoring the heat that hit me like a wall.

Gravel crunched under my shoes as I stepped toward the barricade, Sam calling my name behind me.

"Sir, you need to stay back," an officer barked, holding out an arm. The badge on his chest glinted in the firelight, face hard with routine.

"My apartment's in there," I said, the words breaking out before I could stop them. My throat felt raw already, smoke searing down into my lungs.

"I'm sorry." His tone didn't change. "Everyone's been evacuated. There's nothing you can do. I stood there, useless, watching everything I owned burn. Clothes, furniture, my books, my photos—every trace of the life I'd tried to build after Mom died.

The fire cracked and roared, and I felt hollow, like the heat had already scorched me from the inside out.

Sam's phone rang. Her voice was tense, low when she answered. Jerome. Of course. Did he already know? I only caught her side of it, but the instructions were clear enough: take me back to her house.

I wanted to protest. To tell her I didn't need saving, just a ride to a hotel. But I had nothing left except the clothes on my back, and the tux was uncomfortable enough already.

So I nodded when she told me, and I followed her back to the car.

My home was burning behind me. I had lost it all, but it was her hands trembling on the wheel. Part of me was grateful that the fire left me with only one place to go—with her.

SAMANTHA

The fire still burned in the rearview mirror, a glow in the sky that looked too much like the end of something. Marcus sat quiet beside me, his jaw tight, and the flames reflecting in his eyes long after we left them behind.

"I guess we know where we are going now." It was a sad attempt at humor.

He laughed. Weak, like I told a bad dad joke.

I gripped the wheel harder. I should've felt relief—Alex was at the estate, drunk. For once, the house we lived in would be mine alone. But bringing Marcus there? That was something else entirely. Alex had not approved that.

I could smell the smoke in his clothes, sharp and acrid. Mine too, I suppose. He didn't say a word, but his silence was louder than anything. Everything he owned, gone. And me—here I was, stealing glances at him, thinking about his hands on my face, his mouth on mine, when his life had just been reduced to ashes.

What is wrong with me?

Jerome's voice echoed in my head from the phone: *Take him home. Let me handle Alex.*

Handle him. That was the way Jerome said everything. Smooth. Controlled. Like, even disaster was something he was three moves ahead of.

I pulled into the driveway, heart hammering as if headlights might suddenly sweep in behind us, as if Alex might appear out of the shadows and catch me with Marcus walking into our house. My hands shook when I killed the engine. Alex's car was in the garage. He would not be leaving the manor on his own.

"Come on, let's try to wash this night away," I said, my voice steadier than I felt.

Inside, the silence pressed down. No music, no drunken voices, no footsteps pacing. Just the two of us.

I found Alex's clothes for him, the thought alone was enough to make me want to laugh or cry—Marcus wearing what belonged to my husband. The irony of it was stranger than fiction.

As he disappeared down the hall toward the guest bath, I leaned against the kitchen counter, pressing both palms flat to keep from unraveling. Alex had whispered at the party that he could still get to me. But right now, Marcus was here. Safe. Close. And that scared me more than Alex ever could.

I pulled the bourbon from the cabinet and poured. I didn't drink often or much, but tonight called for it. I welcomed the burn in my throat and the warmth that followed. Not sure if I was drinking it to settle my nerves or dull the emotion.

The pipes creaked down the hall—Marcus turning on the shower. I closed my eyes, steadying myself.

My thoughts in chaos. Rachel's tears. Her voice questioning—how long?

Marcus's hand on mine. Alex's whisper in my ear. I wished I could make all the noise be quiet, just for a little while. One more drink, draining the glass dry.

I peeled off the purple silk, letting it fall to the floor like a lie I no longer wanted to wear. I turned on my shower, stepping into the spray as hot as I could stand it, letting the water sting over bruises that were almost faded. I caressed old wounds.

What had I done to deserve it?

Why was I taking chances?

Why did Jerome instruct for Marcus to come here?

The steam blurred everything—the mirror, the tiled walls, my judgment.

Alex's whisper—*I can still get to you*—crawled under my skin.

I tilted my head back into the spray, as if drowning would be easier than deciding what I wanted or needed to do next. Clearly, I was not making the best decisions over the last few years.

MARCUS

The water pounded over me, but it didn't touch the fire still burning in my chest. My apartment—gone. My engagement—shattered. My life—reduced to smoke and embers.

And Samantha. Just down the hall, behind another stream of running water. I pictured her, shoulders tense, eyes heavy with secrets. She was stronger than she knew, yet so fragile.

I should've stayed in my lane. I was not hiding my affections well. But I was done watching her suffer in silence. Done being guarded. I could get her out.

I stepped into the master bath. I opened the curtain.

SAMANTHA

My heart seized. It was him. Marcus. Stepping inside, water dripping down his chest, his eyes locked on me like I was the only thing left standing in his world.

Fear flared first—sharp, electric. Then relief. Then something far more dangerous... want.

"Marcus—"

He moved closer. His hand touched my arm, gentle, testing. Steam curled around us, closing the distance that words had always left gaping. My body betrayed me. I should have recoiled, but I leaned closer. His hand was steady, reverent, nothing like Alex's cruel grip. The steam thickened, and so did the silence. I should have told him to leave. I should have pushed him away. But I didn't. I wanted him.

He brushed a strand of wet hair from my cheek. I closed my eyes, leaning into it. God help me, I was lost. His lips found mine—careful at first, tasting steam and salt and the faint copper tang of fear. I kissed him back, desperate and tentative all at the same time.

My back against the cool tile, his mouth moved to my throat, then my jaw. I realized what it felt like to be touched without cruelty. Gentle. Devouring, but not destructive. The water went cold before I remembered to breathe. He shut it off, wrapped me in a towel like I was precious to him. So gentle, so foreign. For the first time in months, I didn't feel like property. I felt seen. I felt safe.

MARCUS

I carried her to the bedroom. She gasped—not fear, surprise—and pressed her face against my chest. She was trembling, though whether from the cold or from us, I couldn't tell.

I laid her on the bed, slid in beside her, and pulled her close. She stiffened at first, the way someone does when they've learned touch means pain. So I held still. No pressure. No demand. Just warmth.

Little by little, her body softened against mine. She let out a shaky breath, then another, and I felt the moment she gave in—not to me, but to the comfort of being held.

My whole body screamed for more, but restraint was the only proof I had that I wasn't like him. So I stayed steady, anchoring her in the storm. Her breaths lengthened, slow and uneven at first, then deeper. By the time her fingers curled into my hair, she was asleep, clinging to me as though she'd finally allowed herself to rest.

SAMANTHA

Sleep claimed me in his arms, not from fear, pain, or exhaustion, but with the strange peace of being held without expectation.

When I woke, the night had passed. His arm was still draped across my waist, heavy and protective, his breath warm against the back of my neck. For one fragile moment, I let myself sink into it. I wanted the moment to last forever. I wanted it never to have happened. Both truths lived in me like rival hearts. *Who the hell am I? I'm not this person.*

The light was merciless, spilling across us, showing everything I wanted hidden. For one breath, I let myself believe it. His words. His promise. A life beyond this cage. Then the weight came crashing back: Rachel. Alex. Jerome. The Devereux barbed wire twisted around my name. I slipped from the bed, clutching the sheet—

"Leaving me already?" His voice cut across the room. He looked like both salvation and ruin.

"I love you, Sam. I want to get you out." He forced the words past the ache in his throat. "Will you let me?"

His question cut deep, sharp as a blade. I wanted to say yes. To believe him. But love had been a weapon in Alex's mouth, a cage disguised as devotion. No one had asked my permission in months. No one had waited for my answer.

"I don't know," I whispered. It was the only truth I had left, and it was filled with fear.

MARCUS

It wasn't enough. It would never be enough.

I sat up and gently pulled the sheet to draw her close. I cupped her face in my hands. "I love you, Sam. Don't pretend this is nothing."

Her eyes filled—fear, longing, guilt, all tangled together.

"Marcus..." Her voice cracked. "Rachel's my best friend. Alex is still my husband. How can I—"

"I know, Sam?" I drew her into my lap, cradling her. "I know."

SAMANTHA

My voice broke. "Every kiss feels like betrayal. Every touch feels like a death sentence. But when you held me last night..." I stopped, laid my head on his shoulder, breath shaking. Alex was the only man I'd ever been with. And this—none of this felt like him. Could that be what love really was? I didn't trust it. I didn't trust myself.

He kissed me softly. "It's okay. If you're not ready, it can wait." For now, he could wait. As long as it took, he'd wait. He pulled me back into the bed beside him. We lay in silence until my phone rang.

For one fleeting hour, I had almost convinced myself the world outside didn't exist. Then Alex's voice snapped it back. "Father wants some bonding today. Be back out here by four for dinner." Not a request. A reminder. "Bring me home with you tonight." Click.

I dropped the phone like it had bitten me. Marcus didn't need to hear both sides of the call to know who it was.

"He's pulling you back," he murmured. My silence was answer enough. I traced my fingers along the line of his jaw, committing it to memory in case it had to be the last time. "It was foolish to think this could last."

He caught my hand, pressed his lips to my palm. "It doesn't have to end here."

"Yes, it does." My throat burned. I knew this could not go on. Alex would kill us both. Some women said that to be dramatic, but I know him. *He. Will. Kill. Us.* And he already suspects something.

Marcus wanted to argue—wanted to tell me he'd burn the whole estate to the ground before he let Alex drag me back—but the Devereux orbit devoured everything it touched.

Jerome's voice still rang in my head: *We need strong daughters. I can protect you.* But no one could protect me from Alex. Not Jerome, not Marcus, not anyone. I pressed my face into Marcus's shoulder, pretending just for a few breaths longer that maybe this was possible.

Hope is cruel.

CHAPTER NINE

Queen's Watch

"Man is tormented not by things, but by the views he takes of them."

DRUSILLA

I lifted the binoculars again. In the kitchen, Samantha and Marcus stood too close, heads bent toward one another, shoulders brushing, laughter hushed. Not a kiss, not quite. But the glow on her face told me enough—happy, softened. They looked like a pair toasting their first New Year's Day together. A dangerous fiction, but one I could use.

I lowered the glasses, started the engine, and rolled the Escalade into the driveway of Samantha's little Fayetteville house. Alexander's house, technically—but for now, hers.

Time to see how little Samantha handles pressure.

At the door, I pressed the bell and waited. Too long. Long enough for her to smooth her blouse, to tuck away whatever softness Marcus had drawn out of her.

When she finally opened, her hair was still damp, her buttons slightly askew, confirmation, at least to my eyes.

"Drusilla, what a surprise." No smile offered.

"I was out and thought poor Marcus could use some clothes," I said smoothly, stepping inside without waiting, arms full of folded fabric and a bakery bag. "And cinnamon scones for you, of course. After last night..." I let my voice trail off delicately, savoring the flicker of terror in her eyes.

She snatched the bag. "Thank you. I'll make coffee."

"The house is charming," I remarked, drifting toward the kitchen. "Have you called a decorator yet?"

"No. I think Jerome plans to keep me hostage at the estate while my husband is in Tokyo—not much point." Her voice was dry, her hands busy with the coffee pot. "But I'll be sure to guard the silk cushions for you."

I smiled. "I've sat on worse. You do hate me, don't you?"

"I don't hate you. Not exactly."

Before I could reply, Marcus entered. His hair was damp, his polite smile stretched thin.

"Hello, Drusilla. Nice to see you again."

"Marcus," I purred. "Samantha was just assuring me I'm not terrible. How kind." I let my gaze settle on him. "Any word on the apartment?"

He shook his head. "It's New Year's Day—offices are closed.

But when I do hear '*I expect it'll be what we already know.*' Probably a total loss." His voice was weary, cautious.

"Then stay here," I said easily. "Alexander will be gone for a year. Samantha will primarily be at the manor. The house should not sit empty. She will only be here a few days a week."

Samantha's shoulders stiffened. "Not sure Alex will approve."

"I'll speak with Jerome." I sipped the coffee she had poured, unbothered. "Marcus?"

He hesitated. "It makes sense... for now."

His caution pleased me. Better wary than defiant. Defiance had to be broken.

"Good. I'll arrange it." I stood, gathering my purse. "Thank you both for the coffee. Dinner at four, casual. Don't be late. Marcus, Jerome hates for dinner guests to be late."

"I appreciate the invite, but—"

"We will see you and Samantha at four."

At the door, I turned back, smiling bright and sharp as glass. "You'll be in good hands with Samantha, Marcus. She is learning quickly."

Back in my Escalade, I laughed softly. An act of arson and the smallest nudge. That was all it ever took.

MARCUS

I stood at the window, watching Drusilla back her Escalade down the driveway. Something about the way she smiled at us before she left stuck in my gut. "I don't like the fact that she showed up here like that."

Samantha was stacking dishes in the sink, movements too calm to be natural. "I think you're being paranoid. Maybe she was just... worried about you."

"Worried about me? No, likely." I echoed, jaw tightening.

I stepped behind her, slipped my arms around her waist, needing her body as an anchor. "I've got to figure some things out," I murmured into her hair.

She tilted her head—not pulling away, but not melting either. Guarded. "Running already?"

"Planning," I admitted, kissing her shoulder. "If I take you with me, I need a real plan first."

Her body tensed. "Alex will—"

"Never find us. We can leave when he goes to Tokyo." I tightened my hold. "Once I get you away, I'll never let him near you again."

But even as I said it, I felt her retreat, not in her body, but somewhere deeper.

SAMANTHA

I turned to face him, words heavy. "Promises are easier made than kept, Marcus. You think you want this... us... but you don't know the price."

"I know I love you," he said too quickly.

My lips twisted. "The last man who loved me broke my heart— among other things." My hand brushed unconsciously at my ribs. The words weren't playful. They were scars.

MARCUS

Her eyes slid past me to the glass door. She stepped outside, leaving me with coffee and silence.

Drusilla had dangled the idea earlier, me staying here while Alex was overseas. It was everything I wanted and everything that would damn us. If Alex came back, we'd have to be gone before his feet touched the threshold.

Through the glass, I watched Samantha fold her arms tight across her chest, braced against a storm only she could see.

I slid the door open and joined her. "Sam."

"You're thinking of him," I said. Not a question.

She let out a humorless laugh. "I don't get to stop thinking of him. Whatever path I follow, he's the hurdle."

"Focus on me instead."

Her shoulders tightened. "That's not how it works, Marcus. He's in my head. You don't erase that with promises."

I brushed her hand until she let me lace my fingers through hers. "Then I'll stop promising. I'll prove it. One day at a time. I'll keep showing up. That's all I can give you."

Her eyes shimmered with something like hope. Not trust—not yet. But hope.

DRUISILLA

From the road, I lowered the binoculars, lips curving as the girl finally let Marcus take her hand. Perfect. Predictable.

Jerome thought himself the master, but I had always known the truth: the smallest strings, pulled at the right moment, could set everything tumbling. One fire. One lost apartment. One well-timed visit. And now Samantha was already moving toward the boy—already playing house, as if this really were their first New Year's morning together.

I dialed Jerome.

"Yes, my dear." His clipped tone told me he wasn't alone.

"You'll be pleased. They've only just emerged from the bedroom. They look... hungry."

"Are we certain?"

"I'm certain enough."

The line went dead. I lifted the glasses again, catching Samantha's hand, and swallowed in Marcus's. The girl actually looked happy.

Fool. She thought love was her lifeline. She didn't see the snare.

CHAPTER TEN

The Price of Love

"The misery of man proceeds not from his wants, but from his desires."

SAMANTHA

I drifted into the yard, mind heavy. The grass was still damp, January air clinging cold against my skin. Last night, it was guilt that kept me awake—Rachel, Marcus, the way my heart pulled toward him when it shouldn't.

Marcus said he loved me. I believed he did. Being near him was easy. But love? Love took courage, and I had none left.

The truth I couldn't admit: I felt guiltier about Rachel than Alex. Alex had strangled our love the moment his hand closed around my wrist. Rachel trusted me. And I was betraying her.

Still, Marcus made me feel lighter. Almost myself again. That terrified me.

"I'd love to know what that internal monologue is about," he said softly, startling me.

"One bridge at a time." I forced a smile. "Sometimes my thoughts scare me." I hesitated, then blurted, "Did you love Rachel?"

His brows knit. "You know I care about her. But I've always loved you."

"How do you know it's love, and not just... something else?"

He stepped closer. "Have you ever seen me look at anyone the way I look at you? Have I ever been careless with you, your feelings?"

Something inside me shifted. I stepped into him, close enough to feel his warmth. "Marcus, I want to be with you. But I can't say I love you. Not yet. And I don't know how we will ever be together."

"I love you," he said, steady.

"I know."

The corner of his mouth quirked. "Okay, Han."

I giggled despite myself. He pulled me into his arms, and I let him. But Rachel's voice still whispered in the back of my mind: *How long, Sam?*

MARCUS

When she stepped into me, I knew. She couldn't say the words yet, but "not yet" was enough.

I kissed the top of her head. She smelled like coffee and cinnamon, the pastries Drusilla brought, twisted into this moment. Maybe they thought they'd set us up. Maybe they had.

Rachel's face flickered in my mind. Her red-rimmed eyes, trembling hands. I hadn't lied to her, not exactly. But I'd known. From the beginning, I'd known.

Samantha's voice pulled me back. "If I stay... if I try... promise me you won't turn into him. Promise me you won't make me regret this."

I covered her hand with mine. "Never. Not in this lifetime."

SAMANTHA

I wanted to believe him. Wanted it so badly it hurt. But saying love was easy. Promises were easy. Surviving the aftermath was not.

Still, I didn't step away.

Because even as guilt gnawed, something else was stirring—hope.

I wanted to leave. I wanted to be with him, to believe him. But I wasn't sure I was brave enough to leave, strong enough to survive what came after.

And hope was the most dangerous thing of all.

CHAPTER ELEVEN

The Offer

"Gold is the spur to do and suffer."

MARCUS

The silence at dinner that evening clung to me as we left the table. I sat across from the woman I love and her husband. Conversation had been minimal. Jerome reiterates plans to send Alex to Tokyo. Sam tried to control her responses, but I caught the slight smile when Jerome said Alex would likely be gone a year, maybe more.

After the meal, Jerome beckoned me into his library. Smoke from the night of the fire still lingered in my thoughts—thick, choking, the kind that stayed in your lungs even after you stepped outside.

He gestured to a chair across from his desk. "Sit, Marcus."

The leather was too big, too soft, like it might swallow me whole. My palms itched as I rested them on my knees.

"Your mother was important to this family," Jerome began, as though continuing a conversation I hadn't heard. "More important than you likely realize. I made her a promise—to see that you had the tools to succeed."

His words struck harder than I expected. I swallowed. "She never mentioned—"

"She wouldn't have." His tone cut off any doubt. "But I honor my commitments. You have proven yourself loyal to Samantha, patient when she needed patience, steady when she might have faltered. I've taken note. And I intend to see that loyalty rewarded."

I shifted, not sure where this was going.

Jerome leaned back, fingers steepled. "I've endowed your education. Law school, fully funded. And until then, during the completion of your undergraduate studies, I am offering you a paid internship with the family's attorney. You'll gain exposure to corporate practice—mergers, acquisitions, the work that sustains this family."

The words buzzed in my head. Endowments. Internships. Promises made to my mother. None of it fit together. "I... I appreciate that, sir. Truly. But my interest leans toward criminal law. Maybe family law."

A faint smile crossed his lips, sharp at the edges. "Idealism has its place, Marcus. But idealism rarely pays the bills. Practicality, discipline—those are the stones of a foundation worth building."

I couldn't look away from him. He was measuring me, weighing me.

"I'll do my best."

"You will." His eyes narrowed slightly. "But understand me. When I invest in a man, I expect a return. This is no charity. You've shown me resolve. Patience. Perhaps even courage. Traits I can use. Don't let ambition cloud your judgment. Untethered ambition destroys men. I will see you remain tethered."

My chest tightened. Help or shackles—I couldn't tell.

Jerome reached into a drawer and placed a folder on the desk. "Your stipend. Sign nothing tonight. Take it. Think. But know—the moment you accept, you are bound. Consider carefully, Marcus."

The weight of it was heavier than paper had any right to be. "Thank you, sir." The words scraped out, brittle.

He waved me off, already dismissing me. "Go. Eat. Sleep. Study. The rest will come."

I stood, folder clutched too tightly, and crossed the library. The latch clicked behind me, and I stepped into the hall. My chest still felt tight, Jerome's words pressing heavier than the silence of his library.

And then I saw her.

Samantha was standing halfway down the corridor, framed by the muted light of a wall sconce, arms folded against herself as though the air in this house never warmed her. She lifted her head when she noticed me, and for a second her eyes softened—relief, recognition, maybe even worry.

Everything inside me twisted.

Jerome had just handed me a golden ticket: law school, paid for. An internship, a future. A ladder out of every uncertainty I'd ever known. But tied to him. Tied to this family.

And there was Samantha. The woman who wanted nothing more than to be free of them.

If I accepted, I could give her a way out. Money. Power. Influence. I could keep my promise—never let Alex near her again, never let Jerome's games break her down. But would she want that, knowing it was built on Jerome's coin? Built on his leash?

Her voice broke the silence, quiet but steady. "Are you alright?"

I managed a nod, but the truth knotted in my throat. Because the only thing I was sure of, standing there in that corridor, was that the future Jerome had just placed in my hands might not be the same one Samantha wanted.

And I didn't know which choice would lose her faster—taking it, or walking away.

"Are you alright?" she asked again, softer this time.

I forced a breath. "Fine. Just... a long talk."

Her brow furrowed. She didn't believe me, not really. Samantha always saw too much.

"What did he want?"

The folder in my hand felt heavier. Jerome's voice echoed in my head: *When I invest in a man, I expect a return.*

I swallowed. "Said he was... impressed with me. Wants me to spend more time around the family attorney. Something about... opportunities."

She tilted her head, studying me like she was trying to see what I wasn't saying. "That sounds... good?"

I laughed, short and humorless. "Yeah. A dream, I guess."

But it didn't feel like a dream. It felt like a trap.

Her hand brushed my arm, just for a second. "Be careful, Marcus. They don't give without taking."

The folder slipped slightly in my grip, and I tightened my hold. *I know,* I thought. But I only nodded, because if I said anything else, I wasn't sure I could stop myself from telling her everything.

And I didn't want to see the look in her eyes if she asked me not to take it.

SAMANTHA

The library door opened, and Marcus stepped out, clutching a folder like it might burn through his hands. His face was pale, eyes darting as though he wasn't sure where to put them. I barely had time to meet his gaze before Jerome followed.

"Ah," Jerome said, his voice smooth as ever, "the future always arrives sooner than expected." His eyes flicked over Marcus, then settled on me, as if weighing where to place us on his invisible board.

He laid a hand lightly on my shoulder. To anyone else, it might have seemed paternal. To me, it was a dismissal.

"You should spend the weekend at your own home, Samantha," he continued, tone decisive, already arranging my steps for me. "Time is short before Alexander departs for Tokyo. Make use of it."

A shift in the air made me turn. Alex stood just inside the hall's threshold, his brow furrowed. For the briefest moment, there was softness in his eyes—not joy, not even warmth, but something that looked like longing. The words *spend the weekend with him* seemed to hang between us, and though he didn't smile, I saw the tension ease around his jaw.

Marcus shifted beside me, uncertain, but Jerome pressed forward. "You, however," he said to Marcus, "will remain.

There are matters I wish to acquaint you with. The family's affairs, the duties that sustain us. You'll find it... educational."

Marcus opened his mouth, a protest forming, but Jerome silenced him with a faint lift of his hand. "Consider it an investment. Your law school ambitions will require grounding. The kind of grounding only experience can provide."

Marcus nodded, not quite in agreement.

"Then it's settled." And with that, Jerome swept past us, leaving the air heavy in his wake.

ALEXANDER

I watched my father disappear down the corridor, his words sharper than blades. Samantha stood frozen, Marcus hovering too close.

My house. My wife. And yet, somehow, my father's game.

I clenched my fist against the smooth oak paneling, forcing myself not to let it show. Whatever Marcus meant to her, whatever expression passed between them when they thought I wasn't looking—I didn't like it. I didn't understand it.

But I saw it. And I always noticed.

The house was always my father's domain, every stone and shadow bent to his will. And now Samantha...

She stood there, caught between confusion and exhaustion, like a songbird in a storm. Marcus hovered near her, too close. Too damn natural. My father saw it. I saw it. And she—God help her—pretended not to.

My grip on the glass tightened until I thought it might break. She was mine. My wife. My anchor. She had forgotten that, but I'd remind her. Before Tokyo, I would win her back.

Not with rage. Not with bruises. With love. Real love. The kind that protects. The kind that binds.

I thought of my mother. The way her heel snapped. The sound of her body striking marble. People said it was an accident. I said it was an accident. But I knew better. Chaos always begins with one weak moment. One lapse. And I swore I would never let it happen again.

But I had let it happen. I was Sammie's chaos. Sammie. Back when she smiled at me like I was her world. Back when I could make her laugh until she cried, and she believed in us before the family swallowed everything.

I had been the monster. The bruiser. The storm. I had taken that smile and replaced it with pain. And still... still I wanted to save her. But it was me she needed to be saved from.

Maybe she would be better off with him. No. She was mine.

Love and control weren't opposites. They were the same coin, two sides pressed so tightly they couldn't be pried apart. Control was love. It kept her safe. Without it, there was only chaos.

Jerome understood that. He never raised a hand to my mother the way I had to Sammie. His control came from love, and it kept him untouchable. I hated him for it. I envied him for it.

If I could bind Samantha to me, she would see.

I had sacrificed too. I had given up the nights blurred by whiskey and whatever woman I could find. The reckless hunger that once ruled me was not what it was. My father had beaten me into a shape I never wanted. If I had to endure that, I could overcome this.

Because in the end, she would see. Control wasn't cruelty. Control was devotion. Control was proof that I would never let her fall.

I would make her happy again. I would make her safe.

And she would be mine. Always mine.

But as she glanced toward Marcus, just for a heartbeat too long, unease stirred sharp in my chest. I forced it down.

Love demanded control. And control demanded silence.

CHAPTER TWELVE

The Fragile Truce

"The chains of habit are too weak to be felt until they are too strong to be broken."

The highway unspooled under the headlights, quiet and black. He set his hand on mine. I didn't pull away—I knew better—but I didn't close around his either. It just sat there: his warmth pressing into me, my fingers stiff.

He broke the silence. "Sammie..." Low, hesitant in a way I barely recognized. "I owe you an apology."

My stomach tightened. I watched the dashboard and waited.

"I lied. I was afraid. I didn't want you to see me the way my father sees me—weak, a failure, something to control. The women, the drinking, the temper... they were ways to forget. Ways to prove I wasn't just his puppet." A bitter laugh. "All I did was become something worse."

The words stung, truth bent into something useful to him.

"I hurt you," he said finally, thumb brushing the back of my hand.

"It's unforgivable. I know that. But, Sammie..." The name from another time cracked something in me.

"When my mother died, I started clawing through the dark. She was the only one who saw me without the weight of this family. When she fell, I lost the only proof I wasn't born broken."

Silence pressed harder.

"I can't undo it. But I'm asking you to forgive me. Not because I deserve it." His grip tightened—gentle, unyielding. "Because I don't know how to keep going if you don't."

I watched his reflection in the glass. To anyone else, he might have looked like a man baring his soul. I knew better. With Alex, confession and control were braided so tightly you couldn't tell where one ended and the other began.

And God help me, part of me wanted to believe him anyway.

Once, he had been my rock. The night my parents died, he held me through the sterile light and told me I wasn't alone. That was a year ago. We'd been married less than that, and already he'd become the darkest shadow in my life.

Forgive him? The girl my parents raised would have said yes. Marriage meant endurance, prayer, promises held tight even when they frayed. But the woman sitting here, bruised and worn thin by his hands, didn't know what forgiveness looked like anymore.

Jerome's voice slid back over my skin: Samantha remains here... and she must not be alone. A planned heir before Tokyo. A transaction.

And here was Alex, begging. Love and control, always the same coin—just turned in his palm.

I closed my eyes and wondered which was worse, believing him, or not.

His thumb kept moving, tentative, and steady. I didn't pull away. I didn't offer anything back.

"Your dad once talked to me," he said quietly, "about the kind of marriage he believed in. Biblical. Lifelong. Enduring all things." A pause. "Your mom said it too—marriage is forgiving every day."

Of course, he remembered. My mother, with a dish towel over her shoulder, peaceful and certain. *Marriage is forgiving every day.*

My throat burned. "It's one of those easier-said-than-done things," I managed, voice thin. I pressed my temple to the cool glass to keep from crying.

"Maybe it doesn't have to be so hard, Sammie," he murmured.

The softness cut deeper than anger ever did. For a moment, I saw the boy from the hospital waiting room.

Then the barbed wire tightened: A child before Alexander leaves.

Headlights swept our driveway. The house rose—familiar and

suffocating. He killed the engine. My hand sat in his, heavy as stone.

ALEXANDER

The engine ticked. She slipped from my hand like it weighed too much. At the door, her keys fumbled; I took them, opened it, and she went straight to tidying—mail squared, coat hung— her version of breathing.

I hovered at the bourbon cabinet. Habit. Reflex. I didn't open it.

I thought of the way she flinched at the sound of a cap. Somewhere along the way, I'd taught her to braid liquor to rage.

"Maybe we start here, it's still New Year's Day," I said. "No more drinking. Not for me."

A letter slid from her fingers. It wasn't a grand promise; it was real.

SAMANTHA

No drinking. I searched his face for the trick that usually followed when he sounded gentle. There wasn't one. Not yet.

Laughter wanted to come—bitter. As if pouring liquor down the drain could rinse away the pain. But something cracked in me, just a hairline, enough to let air in. I remembered the boy who said, you're not alone, Sammie.

"That's... something," I said.

He nodded like I'd handed him a reprieve. Then he set the bottles in the sink and turned them upside down.

I stayed back until disbelief tugged me forward. I touched his arm—light, not guiding. He glanced at me with something quiet, almost gratitude. When the last bottle ran out, the kitchen felt hollowed and strange.

We bagged the empties together. Pallbearers.

At the door, I rose on instinct to brush a kiss to his lips, a nightly habit. He turned and gave me his cheek.

"I had too much at my father's," he said, almost apologetic. "You don't want that taste." He stepped away. "I'll shower. Wash it off."

He'd never turned from a kiss. The refusal felt more intimate than wanting.

By the time I came to the bedroom, steam still on my skin, the bed was dim and quiet. Alexander not present.

ALEXANDER

I sat on the edge of the guest bed, hair damp, and shirt hanging loose at my shoulders. The familiar master bedroom waited across the hall. I heard her come out of the shower. She would be laying in out bed. I need to be with her, but tonight I couldn't. Not after the look in her eyes when I turned away.

Not after the feel of her lips—habitual, cautious, almost hopeful I could change. I would, I'd prove it to her.

She came to the doorway, confusion shadowing her features. "What are you doing in here?"

I looked up at her, steady. "You need time, Sammie. And I need to prove I meant what I said. So tonight, I'll give you both."

Her breath caught, and for once I didn't press her to answer. I let the words settle. Serious. Final.

She crossed the room slowly, perched on the edge of the bed beside me. The space between us was charged, not with heat but with something harder—uncertainty, fragile possibility.

"Are we really going to try to start over?" Her voice was small, almost childlike. "Can we?"

I turned my head to her, searching her face. "If you'll let me."

The silence stretched. She worried her lip between her teeth, then finally whispered, "Stay in our room tonight. Just... stay."

I exhaled slowly, the weight in my chest loosening just enough to nod. No sex. No demands. Just the bed we once shared, in the quiet. A fragile truce, maybe even a beginning.

And for the first time in a long while, the monster stayed quiet.

SAMANTHA

The bedroom was dim, with only the faint glow of the streetlight seeping through the blinds.

Alex climbed in bed, his broad shoulders outlined beneath the quilt. He faced away from me, his breathing even but not deep enough for sleep. I had spent so long bracing for the monster that I had almost forgotten the man—the one whose broad frame once made me feel safe, the one I fell in love with before fear swallowed me whole. He was still beautiful. And that, somehow, was the cruelest part.

I slipped beneath the covers; the sheets cool against my skin. And then the memory came, unbidden: another body lying beside me. Marcus. His arm was heavy around me, his warmth anchoring me in the dark. No pressure. No demands. Just comfort. Just breathing in tandem. I swallowed hard and turned toward the ceiling, willing the thought away.

But this was the same bed. The same house. And now Alex's silence pressed against me instead. He didn't reach for me. He didn't even turn his head.

ALEXANDER

I kept my back to her, eyes open in the dark, listening to every shift of the sheets. I could feel her there—her tension. Close enough to touch, close enough to breathe in, but I didn't move. Not this time.

It wasn't easy. God, it went against everything in me not to roll over, not to pull her against me until she had no space left to doubt where she belonged. That had always been my way: take the moment, force it into shape, and remind her I was stronger. But look where that got us.

I lay still. Let her think I was asleep. Let her decide whether she wanted me. Maybe silence could do what force never did.

The guilt sat heavy in my chest, a weight I hadn't known how to name until tonight. I thought of my mother—how quickly her life ended in a single instant of chaos. I swore I'd never repeat it, never let weakness spiral into destruction. And yet, here I was. I'd become Sammie's spiral. Her darkest moment.

But I could change that. I would change that. If I could make her believe it, maybe I could believe it too.

I tightened my jaw and stared into the dark. I'd give her this silence, this space. But before I left for Tokyo, I would win her back. I'd give her a reason to hope again, even if it meant carving away pieces of myself I'd never wanted to lose.

She was mine. And this time, I'd prove it without breaking her.

I woke to warmth at my back. Her warmth.

Samantha had curled against me in the night, her arm draped across my chest, her face tucked into the hollow of my shoulder. It was instinct, I knew that. She did it in her sleep, always had, unless she was too hurt, too afraid. Still, I let myself believe it meant more. That maybe, just maybe, some part of her still wanted me.

I turned carefully, not wanting to break the fragile spell. Her hair spilled across the pillow, her breathing soft and even. She looked younger like this, untouched by the shadows that always lingered in her eyes when she was awake. My Sammie.

I lifted a hand, brushing the strands back from her face. My thumb traced the line of her cheekbone, feather-light. She stirred, her lashes fluttering before her eyes opened to mine.

For a moment, neither of us spoke.

Then her voice came, hushed, still rough with sleep. "Alex..."

The way she said my name, it was enough to make me forget everything else.

"You still curl up to me," I whispered, my hand lingering against her skin. "Even when you don't mean to. Maybe that's the part of you that knows we can still work."

Her lips parted, but no words came. I could see the battle in her eyes—the doubt, the guilt, and the fear. But she didn't pull away.

And that was enough. Enough to keep me holding on. Enough to make me think I hadn't already lost her.

SAMANTHA

He wasn't wrong. As a child, I reached for my parents in the dark; later, I reached for Alex, until fear taught my body to stay rigid. So why now?

I wanted to say it wasn't a choice, but the words stuck. Maybe love wasn't completely gone. The thought scared me. My muscles loosened anyway. His arm came around, he was careful. For a few breaths, we were just two people in a bed with daylight pressing at the blinds.

I didn't say I forgave him. I didn't say anything. I let him believe. I let myself believe.

ALEXANDER

For the first time in longer than I could admit, I felt something that wasn't rage or jealousy.

I lowered my voice to a whisper meant only for her.

"I can be a better man, Sammie. For you. For us."

Her lashes fluttered. A fragile smile. "We'll see."

It weighed more than any vow—and she still didn't pull away. She fell back asleep, curled beside me still.

SAMANTHA

The first thing I noticed was the quiet. No weight beside me in bed, no steady breath at my shoulder. Just the morning light and the faint smell of coffee drifting in from the kitchen.

For a moment, panic tightened in my chest. But then I heard the clink of a mug against the counter, the low hum of the coffee maker. Alex.

I slipped out of bed, padding down the hall barefoot. He was at the counter, hair damp from a run, a sheen of sweat still clinging to his skin. When he saw me, he lifted a mug and pressed it into my hands before I could ask.

"Morning," he said, leaning in to brush a kiss against my cheek. Quick, almost casual—but it startled me. Not in the way his temper did. This startled me in the way good things sometimes do, things you've forgotten you could have.

My hand rose to my cheek before I could stop it, and I caught myself smiling. "You're bright-eyed and bushy-tailed." The words tumbled out, absurd and clumsy. I actually laughed under my breath. "I've never even said that before. My mom did. Not me."

The moment hung between us, warm and awkward, like sunlight finding a corner it hadn't touched in years.

Alex leaned back against the counter, his own mug in hand, eyes tracing me in a way that didn't feel sharp this time. Softer. "Your mom had good lines," he said quietly. "She knew how to make things stick."

The mention of her tugged something inside me—sudden, tender. Before I could respond, he shifted, voice steady. "That's part of why I've got plans for us today. Something I think she would've liked. Something I think you'll like."

I tilted my head, wary but curious. "Plans?"

He gave me that half-smile, the one that used to undo me when we were younger. "Dinner, symphony, a night at the Hayworth. They're doing John Williams—your favorite. I thought we'd get away for a little while. Just you and me."

ALEXANDER

We beat the traffic to Raleigh. While she changed, I paced. When she stepped out—black pants that moved like a skirt, plum wrap tied at her waist, I caught my breath and pushed the heat down. Not tonight. Not like that.

Dinner came first, my safe play before the main event. A corner booth, candlelight, the kind of menu she'd always liked. I let her order, just listened. Laughed when she teased me for mangling the French on the wine list. Rolled my eyes at her mock scolding when I admitted I picked the place because it was five minutes from the concert hall.

Then the symphony. I'd planned it for her, but when the brass crashed through the opening bars of Star Wars, even I felt a jolt in my chest. She lit up like the stage was hers, eyes wide, humming along under her breath. Her right hand was moving gently as if she were conducting. I barely watched the orchestra. I just watched her.

And somewhere between Jurassic Park and Indiana Jones, the thought came, clear and simple: This is what it could be. This is what it should have been all along.

SAMANTHA

My feet ached; my heart didn't. In the restroom, my phone buzzed.

Marcus: Are you okay? Why won't you message me back?

My throat closed. He had been my lifeline. We were naked together two days ago. But Alex was trying. *Marriage is forgiving every day*, Mom's words rung in my ears

I sent a thumbs-up. I'm fine. Then I blocked his number. The silence stung—and felt clean.

Outside, Alex waited under the marquee. We walked like any other couple, comparing favorite cues. Back at the hotel, steam fogged the mirror. When I reached for my cosmetic bag, he stepped from the shower with a towel at his hips. No embarrassment, just memory.

I took a towel and pressed it between his shoulders. He shivered. I kissed the curve where the neck meets the shoulder.

He turned, eyes searching. "Are you sure? I—"

"I'm sure," I whispered. "Kiss me."

He did—lifting me like I was nothing, carrying me to the bed. No words after that. Just husband and wife trying to find each other again.

It could work.

ALEXANDER

Morning, and she was beside me, draped over me like she belonged. Chosen. She chose me.

She woke and smiled faint. "Good morning, husband."

"Good morning, wife."

SAMANTHA

The words felt borrowed and heavy. The room smelled like soap and him. For a heartbeat, it was easy. Then the reminder: one night doesn't erase a year.

I didn't pull away. Not yet. For the first time in too long, his weight didn't feel like a prison. It felt almost safe again.

Almost. He would leave for Tokyo soon. And who would he be when he came back?

CHAPTER THIRTEEN
Shifting Pieces

"In the very cradle of our being, fate plants the seeds of our end."

DRUSILLA

The library smelled of polished oak and Jerome's cigars, the same scent that had clung to the house since Elizabeth's day. Late afternoon light pressed thin through the drapes, the hour when shadows lengthen but lamps are not yet lit. I held a brandy I had no interest in drinking, only studying the firelight caught in its surface. In the glass, reflections warped—truth bending, masks shifting. More useful than the taste.

Alexander was leaving in two days. That much was settled. What unsettled me was the quiet shift in his wife.

I had watched Samantha like a hawk, expecting fractures— Marcus's nearness, the fire, and the staged sympathy I had orchestrated to draw them closer. All the pieces were there. Yet instead of breaking, she had crawled back to Alexander, back to his bed.

Foolish. Pathetic.

She had even blocked Marcus's number. What kind of weak woman tried to salvage a marriage with a man who had bruised her, broken her? Whatever misfortune came to Samantha now, she would have no one to blame but herself. And if she ruined the careful plans Jerome and I had laid—well, then she deserved what was coming.

Jerome sat across from me, flame cupped to his cigar, his expression unreadable in the haze. Finally, he exhaled, ember glowing. "He surprises me."

I arched a brow. "Alexander?"

"He's shown restraint these past weeks. A degree of control I did not expect. I understand he gave up the drinking." His tone was smooth, measured, as though this were some quarterly report and not his son's marriage. "He has steadied her. Had her falling in love again, or close enough to it. And with Horatio's equestrian event at the end of January, she has performed well enough in appearances."

The words soured on my tongue. "Love. If she calls that love, she deserves every bruise he gives her."

Jerome's gaze slid to me, cool and precise. "You're letting distaste cloud your judgment. All I require is that she produce a child. If Alexander manages it without knowing more than he should, I care little which son she warms to."

I masked my irritation with another swirl of brandy, watching the liquid's surface fracture the lamplight. He always spoke of his sons as if they were interchangeable parts in a machine—replaceable, adjustable, and disposable.

But Marcus. Marcus was supposed to be the lever. My lever. And now Samantha's sudden resolve had cut him loose.

"Then it falls to me to correct course," I said. "Alexander may believe he's reclaimed her, but Marcus will remain in that house. Proximity will do what scheming could not."

Jerome did not argue. He simply smoked, filing my words into whatever ledger ticked behind his eyes.

But for a heartbeat, through the smoke, I thought I saw something else, softer, a warmth. Some flicker of hesitation about the girl now caught between his sons.

Then it was gone. Snuffed out like the ember falling to the tray.

No matter. I would tighten the noose for Samantha myself.

MARCUS

The east wing smelled of polish and hay, the manor's two worlds colliding as I stacked programs for Horatio's equestrian event at the end of January. Jerome's pride on display, his name gleaming across the top.

Beside me, Samantha's hands busied themselves with ribbons, twisting the fabric too tight, knuckles pale. Her mind was miles away.

I couldn't hold it back anymore. "You blocked me."

Her head snapped up, eyes wide. Then, just as quickly, the panic smoothed into something practiced. "It must've been an accident."

"An accident?"

She scrolled her phone, tapped, and held it toward me. "See? Fixed. You're unblocked." A playful smile, as if it were nothing.

It wasn't anything. She was lying.

"Why?" My voice stayed calm, but my chest tightened.

Her hands folded around the ribbon again, more careful this time. "Because Alex and I are... trying."

The word hit like a blow. Trying.

I wanted to rage, to shake sense into her, to tell her you can't build a life from ashes and call it forgiveness. But not here. Not with staff in the hall. Not with Drusilla's eyes everywhere.

So I nodded once. Clipped. "I see."

Silence stretched, thin as glass.

We finished our work without another word—programs stacked, ribbons tied. An afternoon of pretending we weren't burning.

And all the while, Jerome's folder weighed on me. Samantha retreated from my embrace, while they bound me tighter to the house.

SAMANTHA

Bright ribbons in red, blue, and gold fluttered against the January gray, pinned to the chests of children far younger than I expected. Their ponies trotted briskly, coats gleaming, manes braided with bows. It was all foreign to me—the rules, the applause at the right moments, even the way the mothers spoke in hushed, reverent tones as though this arena were a chapel.

I clung tighter to Alex's arm. He smelled faintly of coffee and aftershave, his warmth grounding me in the cold. The last few weeks had been better. He hadn't touched a drink. I'd hear the bass of music pulsing from the garage, the metallic clang of weights, sometimes even his voice singing—rough, off-key, but alive. It was better than the silence of bottles clinking in the trash. Better than before.

When a gust cut through, I pressed close. He chuckled, bought two steaming cups of cocoa, and pressed one into my hands. For a moment, it was easy to pretend we were any other couple, just out on a cold Saturday, watching children ride ponies.

That illusion broke when I spotted Marcus. He leaned against the white rail, coat collar turned up against the wind, expression unreadable as he watched the course.

"Marcus," Alex said, voice cool.

"Alexander." Marcus's nod was polite, detached. Then, softer: "Samantha."

We exchanged the bare minimum of courtesies, my smile brittle around the rim of my cup. Someone—Marcus, maybe—remarked on the cold, and I laughed too brightly.

Then Alex shifted, hand warm and heavy at my back. His words were low, meant only for Marcus. "Take care of the house while I'm away. But leave what's mine alone."

The edge was unmistakable, and my heart jumped. Still, I told myself it was only his protectiveness, his way of drawing a line before leaving. Almost flattering, in its way.

A cheer rose from the crowd just then. We turned as Horatio guided his pony neatly over a low fence, ribbons bouncing against his jacket. He looked so small, so serious, his concentration far older than his years.

"That's my grandson," a voice said behind us.

Jerome. He strode forward, coat immaculate, cigar unlit but turning slowly between his fingers. He nodded to Alex, then to Marcus. His eyes, sharp and assessing, lingered on the three of us as though weighing each against the other.

Marcus straightened. "I'll let you enjoy the event," he said, and with a brief nod to me, excused himself into the crowd.

Jerome stayed, watching Horatio's round with a faint smile that didn't quite reach his eyes. "He's performing well," he said. "Focused. Knows what's expected of him."

Alex's arm tightened around mine. "He's a Devereux," he replied. "He'll deliver."

Jerome hummed, neither agreement nor denial, just that cool ledger-keeping sound of his. My cocoa had gone lukewarm, but I held it tight, listening as father and son spoke about Horatio as though he were a horse on the auction block rather than a boy in the ring.

And all the while, I stayed pressed against Alex, convincing myself this was safety. This was love.

ALEXANDER

The morning of departure.

Samantha was curled against me, her hair spilling across the pillow, breath warm against my chest. For a moment, I stayed still, memorizing the weight of her, the quiet peace of our bed. Then I slipped free and dressed in silence, careful not to wake her.

The past few weeks had been like when we first married—laughter in small moments, shared meals, her hand in mine. A honeymoon phase reborn.

I thought of the equestrian event two days ago, how the wind had cut across the field and she'd leaned into me for warmth. I'd pulled her close, bought her cocoa, felt her smile against my shoulder. For once, she had looked content—mine again, as she should be. That memory steadied me now.

And yet, Marcus. Standing there at the rail, eyes too steady, words too calm. I hadn't missed the look that passed between them, no matter how quickly she smoothed her smile. My warning had been clear enough, but the thought still nagged.

She stirred, blinking awake.

"You should've woken me," she murmured, her voice husky with sleep.

I set a cup of coffee on the nightstand and sat beside her. Gently, I brushed a strand of hair from her face, fingers lingering for a breath. She looked so peaceful then—soft, unguarded, the way she had on our honeymoon mornings not so long ago.

"You needed the sleep," I said.

She smiled, chiding, and wrapped both hands around the mug.

"I'll miss you, Sammie," I told her, letting the truth of it sit in my chest. "But I'll be back for the Garden Party in April."

"April." She repeated it softly, as if marking time.

We started our morning the way we always did, her laughter still lingering when I loaded my bags into the car. By midday, I was gone, the road opening toward the airport and the work waiting for me in Tokyo.

CHAPTER FOURTEEN
The Poisoned Picture

"Suspicion is a heavy armor, and with its weight it impedes more than it protects."

DRUSILLA

I called for Samantha two weeks before the spring gala, The Garden Party. When she stepped inside my office, I welcomed her with the softness she expected.

"I hear you and Alexander are doing well. It delights me, Samantha. Truly." My smile curved sweetly, but it didn't touch my eyes. Then I let the pause sharpen, the silence growing long enough for her nerves to prickle.

"As your sister in this family, I should tell you something."

Samantha's breath caught. Perfect.

"Alexander is drinking again," I said gently, almost mournfully. "And apparently, enjoying the company of other women."

Her head shook so fast it almost looked childish. "No. No, I'd know. He's trying. We've talked. I'd know."

Pathetic. I slid the folder across the table, nails tapping the glossy cover.

Inside: photographs. Alexander was at a bar, leaning close to a petite brunette, and her hand on his arm, his head bent toward her. I let the silence stretch before I said the word: "An escort, maybe."

Samantha's face faltered, denial and doubt tangling together until one ate the other.

I held back a sigh. What kind of woman crawled back into bed with a man who bruised her, begged for his affection like a stray dog hoping for scraps? She had been handed freedom—Marcus all but laid it at her feet—and she'd thrown it aside to cling to the illusion of a marriage.

Weak. Foolish. Sentimental.

Not like me. I had chosen survival, calculation. I had cut myself away from hope years ago and, in doing so, secured my son's future. Love was a weapon, not a lifeline. Samantha still hadn't learned that lesson.

But her weakness could be useful.

It didn't matter whether the photographs were true. It never mattered. Suspicion alone was enough. Suspicion carved cracks where loyalty once lived, and cracks were how I bent people into place.

She stammered something—a thank you, an excuse, a prayer—I

hardly listened. She gathered the photographs with trembling fingers and fled, shoulders hunched as though she carried the weight of betrayal itself.

I sat back, smoothing my skirt, satisfied. Alexander's sudden attempts at redemption had threatened to unravel everything Jerome and I had built. But suspicion—suspicion would always bring her back in line.

JEROME

Drusilla poured the brandy with her usual precision, the crystal glowing in the firelight. She was smug tonight, her lips curved as she slid a photograph across my desk.

Alexander is at a bar. A woman leaning in, too pretty, too obvious.

I glanced at it once before setting it aside. *"Manufactured."*

Her eyes narrowed. "And effective. Reports from the estate said Alexander has been... impressive. Control. Restraint. Even charm. It was becoming inconvenient."

I let the silence linger, enjoying the faint tick of irritation in her jaw. She wanted praise. She would get efficiency. "So you staged this."

"The girl, who knows?" she admitted smoothly. "The photographer arranged. Samantha saw what she needed to see."

I leaned back, steepling my fingers. The fire cracked, and for a moment Elizabeth's face rose unbidden—the night she told me Alexander had her smile. Her mouth firm, her eyes certain, the way she looked when she knew a truth I hadn't spoken. It flickered, then vanished. Sentiment was a dangerous indulgence.

"Alexander's progress does not change his nature," I said at last. "He may try to soften his edges, but in the end, he is still mine. Still predictable."

Drusilla's smile sharpened. "And Samantha is pliable again. She'll cling to Marcus for comfort. It will move faster this way."

I studied her. To Drusilla, Samantha was weakness, foolishness. But I had watched the girl closely. Beneath the softness, there was steel. She survived Alexander. She bent but did not break. That made her valuable.

"Do not mistake fragility for weakness," I said quietly. "She is malleable, yes, but she endures. That is why she will matter."

Drusilla tilted her head, curious. "You almost sound impressed."

I let the faintest smile ghost across my lips, then killed it. "Impressed or not, she serves her purpose. The boy will be gone soon. The girl will remain. And Marcus—" I tapped the forgotten photograph with a single finger. "Marcus will be useful if he learns where his loyalties lie."

The brandy burned warm down my throat. Drusilla thought the photograph was a victory. To me, it was a tool. A reminder. The pieces were moving exactly as I intended.

CRAIG

I listened to my father and his wife play god in someone else's life. They both sat with their drinks of choice—Jerome with his cigar and scotch, Drusilla with her brandy—quietly counting their assumed victories.

The silence stretched until I broke it. "What happens when the house of cards falls? Have either of you thought about that?"

Jerome didn't even flinch. He never did. "She is safe here," he said, as though safety were something he could dictate into existence.

"But she's not always here, Father." I let the pause hang, then added, "And my brother has a way of blowing hard enough to topple the neatest stacks."

Drusilla set her glass down with a soft click, her eyes narrowing just enough to betray annoyance. "Then the question isn't if it falls, but how we minimize the fallout."

Jerome exhaled smoke, patient, deliberate. "You both assume collapse. I plan for endurance. She bends. She survives. That is enough."

I leaned back in my chair, smirking. "Until she decides surviving isn't worth it."

That earned me a glance—first from Drusilla, sharp and suspicious, then from Jerome, cool and unreadable. For a moment, I wondered if I'd overplayed the line. But then the moment passed, swallowed by the haze of smoke and the clink of ice in a glass.

They thought they had her measured. They thought they had me, too.

But games like this never ended clean.

MARCUS

The corridor outside my room was quiet, the kind of silence that settles heavy after dinner at the manor. I reached for the handle, ready to shut the world out, when I heard it—soft, muffled, but sharp enough to cut through the stillness.

Samantha's sobs.

The door across from mine hung slightly ajar. I knocked once, gently, then stepped inside.

She was perched on the edge of the bed, clutching a manila envelope like it was the only thing holding her together. Her shoulders shook, eyes red, face streaked. When she looked up, I saw her fracture wide open.

The envelope slipped from her lap. A photo slid free across the carpet—Alex, drink in hand, some woman leaning toward him like they'd been caught mid-flirt. It gleamed too perfectly, every angle just right. Too perfect.

Still, it gutted her.

I bent, fingers brushing the glossy edge, and the words tumbled out before I could stop them. "He was never going to change. But you tried. God, you tried."

Her hands pressed harder against her face, but it didn't stop the tears.

I sat beside her, useless, fumbling. "You don't have to carry this anymore, Sam. Not for him. Not for them." My throat caught, the truth clawing its way out. "I can take…"

Her head snapped toward me, eyes sharp through the blur. "Can what?"

The rest curdled on my tongue. I forced it into something safer. "I can take you home. If you don't want to be here."

I waited. Waited for her to tell me to leave. To ask me to stay. Nothing. She just sobbed.

Her phone buzzed against the bedspread. Alex.

She didn't move for it. Didn't even flinch.

"Maybe you should talk to him," I said, softer than I meant. The words tasted like ash.

I stared at the photo in my hand. Too clean. Too neat. Staged. I knew it. But if I told her it was staged, she'd run back to him. If I let her believe, she might finally run. I said nothing—and hating myself for both choices was the only truth I had left.

Her phone buzzed again. Alex's name lit the screen. She didn't move.

I stood, slow, like any sudden movement might shatter her completely. "I'll be down the hall if you need me," I said. My voice felt too thin for the weight in the room.

She nodded, not looking at me, her arms wrapped tight around herself.

The hardest part wasn't leaving—it was pulling the door shut without making her feel like I'd abandoned her.

So I left it cracked, light spilling into the hall.

And then I walked away.

CHAPTER FIFTEEN

Fractured Lens

"We are always deceiving ourselves in our hopes."

SAMANTHA

The room swallowed me whole once Marcus slipped out. The silence pressed against my ears, heavy and absolute.

My phone buzzed again. A text this time. Probably already asleep. Sweet dreams, Sammie.

The words blurred as new tears stung my eyes. I tossed the phone aside and changed quickly, pulling on an old cotton shirt and soft pants, something that might have belonged to another life.

The king-sized bed dwarfed me. I curled on my side, knees tucked to my chest, clutching the pillow like it might stop me from breaking. I had believed him. I had believed Alex when he said he was changing—when he poured out the bourbon, when he took me to the symphony, when he said he wanted to try. For a few fleeting months, I had believed.

And now the photo wouldn't leave my mind—the glass in his hand, the woman at his side.

My stomach twisted. Marcus was right across the hall. Marcus, who had shown up again and again. Marcus, whom I'd pushed away, and who somehow still came back when Alex betrayed me. Maybe he really was the one who could save me.

The phone buzzed a third time. This time it wasn't a text.

Alex. Calling.

My throat burned as I swiped to answer. "Hello."

"You sound tired," his voice was warm, hopeful. "Long day?"

"Why did we even try," I snapped, my words clipped and shaking, "if you were just going to betray me so quickly?"

Silence. Then: "What?"

"Don't play dumb, Alex. A bar. A woman. Already?" My voice cracked on the last word.

On the other end, he exhaled hard. "Sammie, I had one drink. One. And I came home. Alone. Who's been feeding you this?"

The line trembled between us. His voice sharpened, tinged with something like fear. "It's them, isn't it? My family. They're twisting things."

My hand shook while holding the phone. His tone had a bite, but beneath it I heard something else—confusion. Frustration. Maybe even truth.

But I couldn't believe him. Not with the photo burned into my brain. Not with suspicion already weighing like armor across my chest.

And he couldn't convince me. Not from halfway across the world.

The silence stretched, fraying at the edges. My breath hitched, but no words came.

On the other end, I heard him inhale, then let it out sharp. Neither of us spoke.

Finally, I lowered the phone from my ear, staring at the glowing screen until it went dark.

I didn't hang up. I just... let the silence die.

I didn't know what to believe anymore.

ALEXANDER

The line went dead, leaving me staring at my reflection in the darkened Tokyo hotel window.

What the hell was that?

Why did I even try—change, soften, crawl on my knees—if she was never going to believe me? She knew what my family was. She knew how they played their games. And yet a single photo, a single whisper, was enough to send her spiraling against me.

My jaw locked, muscles burning as I paced the room.

Marcus.

Of course, it was Marcus. He'd been hovering since the start, the savior waiting in the wings. Maybe he had someone feeding her, tipping her off, planting seeds. Pull the right string and Samantha—my Sammie—would fold right into his arms.

Over my dead body.

If he thought distance gave him the advantage, he was wrong. I'd be home soon enough for the family's spring gala in April. And when I was, I'd undo whatever damage he—or anyone else—had managed to wedge between us.

Maybe I could even convince her to come back to Tokyo with me.

A fresh start. Away from their claws. Away from him.

Just me and Sammie.

Where she belonged.

SAMANTHA

The house in Fayetteville was silent, almost too neat after weeks of Marcus living here alone. At the manor, preparations for the Garden Party were already underway—the spring gala, always held on the last Thursday of April, as fixed in the Devereux calendar as New Year's Eve. No one ever questioned why Thursday; tradition was reason enough.

After days of planning and lists, I almost welcomed the quiet here. It had been over a week since Dru had pressed that photo into my hand—the same day I'd last spoken to Alex. Nearly three months had passed since he left for Tokyo at the end of January.

I'd come back this weekend, ahead of the gala, to put our house in order for his return: fresh linens on the bed, groceries in the fridge, the mail stacked neatly on the table. Tuesday, he'd be home, and Jerome had already declared we would attend the Garden Party together, as though it were a coronation.

For once, I thought I might finally have a stretch of peace. No Drusilla lurking, no Jerome setting traps with his questions, no Marcus and those looks that left me raw and unsteady. Just me, silence, and the work of putting Alex's house—our house—in order.

Then Marcus arrived.

Of course he did. His key turned in the lock like it had always belonged there. Technically, it did—Jerome had made sure Marcus was supposed to be staying here. The sight of him standing in the doorway made my chest tighten.

"You're here," I said flatly, my voice sharper than I meant.

His expression flickered, half-guilt, half-defense. "Jerome wanted me to check in. You know how he is about the house."

I knew. I also knew Jerome rarely did anything without reason.

The air between us grew heavier with each passing hour. We tiptoed around one another, sharing space but not words. Every glance seemed to stretch into something else—accusation, longing, regret. By nightfall, I could feel him watching me even when he wasn't.

By Saturday, the tension was unbearable. I found myself looking at him too long, remembering too much. The night of the fire. The night in my bed when he simply held me. The safety of it. The wanting that had never gone away.

He didn't push. He didn't need to. I was the one who crossed the line.

It wasn't passion, not at first. It was defiance. Two could play this game, I told myself. Alex had his women, his lies, his secrets. Why shouldn't I have this? Why shouldn't I take something for myself, even if it was only for a night?

But when Marcus touched me, when I let him in, the rationalizations blurred into something harder to deny. Desire. Relief. The terrible, intoxicating rush of being wanted without condition.

And in the back of my mind, a clock ticked.

Three days.

Three days before Alex came home.

I lay there afterward, the sheets twisted around me, Marcus's breathing steady at my side, and I told myself it was strategy, not surrender. I told myself it didn't matter.

But even as I whispered those lies into the quiet, I knew better.

I had crossed the line, and there was no going back.

MARCUS

Lying beside her, I knew this wasn't about me. Not tonight.

Her body was warm against mine, but the way she clung to me told a different story. She wanted to get even with Alex, and I was the weapon in her hand.

And God help me, I didn't care.

Even if I was just her pawn tonight, the line was crossed. She had let me in, and part of me believed that once the door opened, it couldn't be shut again. Maybe, just maybe, crossing that line—even in fury—meant I could still get her away from all of this.

But that thought tangled with another—the weight of everything Jerome had dangled in front of me.

It had been four months since the fire, four months since Jerome pulled me deeper into his orbit. The internship, the stipend, the trust fund he promised—all waiting on my signature. I hadn't signed. Not yet. But I was still getting paid, still working under the family attorney, learning. More often, though, I was with Jerome himself. Watching. Listening. Absorbing.

If I ran with Samantha, all of that would vanish. Jerome would never forgive me for taking her away, and Alex... Alex would hunt me to the grave.

My mind flickered back to her, to the curve of her cheek resting against the pillow. Tonight, I was a pawn in her game. But tomorrow—tomorrow, I swore—I'd be more.

The possessiveness startled me when I felt it. I couldn't justify it. Couldn't even name it. But it was there, coiled tight in my chest. She belonged with me. Not as a possession, not as something to own—but because I was the only one who truly saw her, in fact the only one who could love her without condition.

And yet... she still wore his ring.

I closed my eyes, knowing I was fooling myself. This night didn't simplify anything. It only made the Devereux web more tangled, more dangerous.

But then came the second night.

No anger, no revenge. Just the quiet pull of something we'd buried too long. Her hands weren't trembling this time. They sought me out, certain, wanting.

That night wasn't about Alex. It was about us.

I kissed her like I had always wanted to, touched her like we had all the time in the world. And for a few stolen hours, it felt like we did.

Neither of us knew what it would cost.

Neither of us knew she would carry a piece of that weekend with her long after I left for the manor.

A piece that would change everything.

SAMANTHA

Marcus slept beside me, the rise and fall of his chest steady, unhurried. I watched him for a moment, caught between tenderness and dread.

Because I didn't regret this—not Saturday night, not the night after. But I also didn't know what it meant.

Before Alex left for Tokyo, he'd been... good. The kind of good that made me ache to remember how it felt when we first met. He'd stopped drinking. Started running. Took me to the symphony, of all things. He had been gentle in ways I had almost forgotten he could be. For a brief window of time, I believed him. I believed in us.

And then he was gone.

And Marcus was here.

With Marcus, it wasn't about promises or apologies. It wasn't about control. It was about the way his hands steadied me, the way his lips pressed to mine like he was afraid I'd disappear. He gave me something Alex never quite could anymore— choice.

But even now, lying in this fragile morning peace, guilt pressed at me. I was a married woman. I had let myself be drawn into something I swore I wouldn't.

Two nights. Two choices I couldn't take back.

I pressed my face into the pillow and closed my eyes, trying to hold the contradiction together: the memory of Alex, trying so hard to change, and Marcus, here and real and warm beside me.

What did it mean? What did I want it to mean?

Marcus stirred, turning toward me. His eyes half-opened, soft with sleep, and he smiled—a small, unguarded thing. My heart caught.

I didn't regret it. But I didn't know how to live with it either.

And late tomorrow, Alex would be home.

Monday morning, when Marcus was gone, I lay awake again in the quiet house. A low hum rose in the distance, faint at first, then swelling—an airplane cutting across the early morning sky. I stared at the ceiling, skin prickling, and every nerve aware.

Alex was coming.

The sound faded, but the dread stayed.

CHAPTER SIXTEEN
Resort Game

"The most dangerous man is the one who can keep his temper in check."

ALEXANDER

I moved my flight up, determined to arrive on Tuesday. The red-eye left me ragged, but I didn't care. Ten days—that was all Father had allowed me. Ten days to stand beside Samantha, to prove myself at the spring gala, to remind her who we were before Tokyo pulled me back across the ocean.

I expected her to be waiting. I expected home. Instead, I arrived at an empty house. Father had taken her to the manor, of course. His summons always outweighed my desires. I slept alone, prowled the silence of our Fayetteville rooms alone, and did not lay eyes on Sammie until Thursday night, when the gala lights finally revealed her.

Three days wasted. Three days stolen from me.

And after this visit, who knew when I'd see her again?

—

The gala glittered, flawless on the surface—lanterns strung through the gardens, champagne like water, the right names spilling into the right ears. But beneath it all, between Samantha and me, there was brittleness. I felt it in the stiffness of her hand on my arm, in the way her eyes slipped past mine too quickly, as if she feared what she might see if she held my gaze.

It came out only once, sharp as broken glass.

"I heard things, Alex," she whispered as we drifted between tables, her lips frozen in the perfect smile Drusilla had trained her to wear. "The drinking. The women."

My chest tightened, but my smile stayed for the crowd. Only when I drew her into the corridor did I let the mask falter.

"I won't lie to you," I said, low. "I had a drink. One. I won't insult you by denying that. But there were no women. Not this time."

Her eyes searched mine, full of doubt, but she wasn't ready to fight. Not here. Not tonight.

"We'll talk after the gala," she said softly, her voice all steel under the blush-colored gown.

So I let it drop, though the weight of it followed me the rest of the evening.

But then fate served me a bitterer draught.

Marcus.

He crossed our path as we moved toward the long table of donors. "Good evening," he said evenly, though his eyes darted—toward me, toward her.

Samantha gave the barest nod, then pivoted gracefully away to greet a woman in emerald silk at the next table. Indifference, practiced and polished. Drusilla's training was written across her every move.

Which left me with him.

"Hope my house has been comfortable for you," I said, letting the smile cut at the edges.

Marcus faltered, just for a second. "It wasn't my idea, Alex. But it has been convenient, especially since I leave in a couple of months anyway. I really... appreciate it."

His words landed flat, pantomime instead of sincerity.

I saw the guilt flicker across his face. Saw how Sammie barely acknowledged him, as if he were nothing. Saw enough to know there was more beneath it.

And I catalogued every detail, every glance, every tremor, until it hardened into fuel.

—

Hours later, I stood in my father's office, fists tight at my sides.

"I'll be spending the rest of the weekend with my wife," I said, sharper than I intended. "It was your brilliant idea to let Marcus stay at my house while I do your bidding in Tokyo. He's circling her, and you damn well know it. That's what it looks like. You want him nearby, fine. Keep him here. Not in my house."

Jerome leaned back in his leather chair, unimpressed. "Alexander, he is a guest in your home."

"Then let him have the house, and Sammie can come back to Tokyo with me."

"That will not do, son." His tone was cool, condescending, the way you speak to a servant who oversteps.

"Father, I leave in less than a week. If she isn't coming back with me, then give me this much. Let me have these last few days to set things right."

His eyes narrowed, studying me like a man studies a horse for flaws before he buys it. Finally: "If you leave a mark on Samantha, you will answer to me."

The words sliced. I forced a laugh, brittle. "You'd dare threaten me?"

"You are going away for as long as I require," he said, his voice flat as stone. "To protect your wife, I keep you at a distance. It would be ideal for you to be home, fathering my heirs. But every time you feel slighted, you attack that poor girl."

"You want me to give you heirs? If I never see my wife, we'll have to arrange a test tube like you did for Drusilla and Craig."

"Careful, Alexander." His voice hardened. "You may go for the weekend. Make peace. Make her comfortable. Give her a child to bind her to you." He turned his back on me, dismissing me with his shoulders. "Do you understand?"

"Yes," I bit out.

"Then keep your hands gentle. Bruises on a wife can be explained. Bruises on a mother cannot."

I hated the way his words pinned me, but I hated more how much truth they carried.

"I can handle myself. I want the quiet with her. No watchers. No interruptions. Just the space to remind her who we are."

Jerome lifted his glass, his nod final. "Drusilla will make arrangements. A resort. Massages, dinners, the works. Romance her. Don't repeat your sins. You'll need her happy and pliant before you leave."

I caught Drusilla's smirk as she swept out to make the calls. Father's voice followed her, sharp as the crack of a whip: "And Alexander—bury that damn bracelet. It's grotesque."

The sting burned, but I bit my tongue. He didn't understand. He never would.

Because Sammie would, she always had.

And this weekend, I would make her remember.

SAMANTHA

By the time we reached Pinehurst the next afternoon, the words I'd bitten back at the gala were gnawing holes inside me. The drive wound past manicured lawns and pine-lined fairways, a place built for appearances—quiet luxury meant to soothe. But the silence in the car was louder than the golf carts buzzing across the greens.

Even the couples massage smoothed nothing but skin. His hands rested heavy in mine during the ritual, but nothing untied the knot in my chest.

Before dinner, he handed me a velvet box. Not Devereux grandeur—something smaller, discreet. I opened it with fingers that shook more than I wanted him to see. The last jewelry he gave me bore a hiking boot to remind me of a violent lesson. What would this be?

A necklace. Delicate, diamond-pinned. Not Drusilla's borrowed opulence. Not a leash in jewel form. Something that looked chosen. For me.

"It's beautiful," I whispered, brushing the pendant.

And then he said it. The words I never thought I'd hear from him, at least not like this:

"I'm sorry. For everything."

It jolted me, sharp as a slap. Alex had apologized before—after fists, after nights lost to bourbon, always dressed in excuses. But never like this. Bare. Stripped. Almost believable.

Dinner at my favorite Italian spot was warm, even pleasant. The smell of garlic and tomatoes, the sound of clinking glasses, the wine loosening my tongue, pasta filling the hollow in me. For an hour, I almost forgot the bruises, the photographs, the ache of Marcus's lips. Almost.

But when we returned to the suite, the silence swelled again, pressing against the walls like smoke. I turned to him, arms crossed, voice sharp.

"Why should I believe you? About the women."

The words left my mouth before I could stop them, sharper than I meant, and guilt burned immediately after. I had no right to ask — not after the weekend I'd spent tangled with Marcus, whispering lies to myself about survival and choice.

He didn't bristle, not the way I expected. Instead, he exhaled slowly, like he'd been waiting for this moment.

"Because I'm telling you the truth," Alex said. "I've been every kind of bastard to you, Sammie, but not this. Not while I was away. I had a drink, yes. I slipped. But I didn't betray you with anyone else. Not this time. I swear it."

The way he said it—measured, steady—was almost worse than rage. What frightened me more: that he was lying, or that he wasn't?

The necklace glittered in the lamplight, sharp points of reflection stabbing my eyes. I touched it again, as though the stones could tell me what to believe.

* * * * * * *

The next morning, I woke to lilies on my nightstand and the smell of coffee drifting through the suite. He tried. God, he tried. We laughed over golf, over my "dough balls" instead of gnocchi during a cooking class, and over his burnt toast that he insisted was "extra flavor." For once, we weren't enemies.

But peace never lasted. Not in this life.

That evening, as I zipped my dress and fixed my hair, something pressed in on me harder than silk or pearls. A late period. A suspicion.

I shut the bathroom door, heart hammering, and pulled the small box from the bottom of my travel bag. The fluorescent light hummed overhead, merciless and buzzing. The wrapper crinkled loud in my hands as though the whole hotel could hear it. Three minutes stretched into eternity.

I gripped the counter, staring at the stick as if willpower could force the truth out of it.

No plus sign. No blue.

Not pregnant.

I knew it was too soon. But my body knew. And fear knew it too.

The knock rattled the door. "Babe? You ready for dinner?"

I shoved the test deep into the trash, forced my voice steady before opening the door. "Maybe we should skip dinner... and have dessert instead."

I kissed him like it meant something. Tried to imagine Marcus's mouth, Marcus's hands, to make it believable.

Alex pulled back, his eyes searching. "You don't have to—"

"I want to," I lied, steady this time. "You're leaving, and we don't know when you'll be back. We should say goodbye properly."

He gave in, gentle for once, tender. And I let him believe.

* * * * * * *

Later, while he ordered room service, I locked myself in the bathroom again. Pressed my back against the door. Let the tears come hot, silent, unrelenting.

The tiles were cold against my spine, the hum of the fan filling the void where my sobs caught.

I had sealed myself to this family with one reckless weekend.

If a child came of it, the world would believe it was his.

And then—then there would be no way out.

ALEXANDER

The fairway stretched out below the balcony, dew still clinging to the grass, the air sharp with pine and the faint chlorine from the pool. Early golfers dotted the course, quiet figures moving across the manicured green.

I sat with coffee cooling in my hands while Samantha still slept inside the suite.

Something was off.

She'd been warm with me last night. Initiated, even. And God, I'd wanted it...needed it. But it didn't add up. If she believed I'd cheated, if she even suspected, why pull me close instead of pushing me away?

Because she's hiding something.

I forced my breathing steady, the way I'd learned in Tokyo— inhale four, hold four, exhale four. But the unease coiled tighter the longer I sat.

The sliding door creaked behind me. Samantha stepped out, hair tousled, the new necklace catching morning light. She wrapped her arms around herself, more armor than warmth.

"Morning," I said, too even.

"Morning." Her smile didn't reach her eyes.

I didn't bother with small talk. "You believed them, didn't you? About my drinking. About other women."

She flinched. "Alex—"

"Then why?" My voice sharpened. "Why come to me last night? Why now?"

Her throat worked, eyes glassing. "I just... I didn't want to fight anymore."

"Bullshit." I set the mug down hard. "What are you hiding?"

Tears broke. She tried to turn away, but I caught her chin, not rough, not yet. "Tell me."

The words fell jagged. "I was angry. I thought you cheated, so I—" Her breath stuttered. "Marcus and I... once. It didn't matter. It doesn't matter."

Her eyes locked on mine then, wide and wet. Fear. Real fear.

For a moment, the rage nearly broke me. But I forced my hands down, fists curling at my side instead of around her. If I touched her now, I'd shatter what little was left.

I swallowed the fire, forced out words flat as stone: "I'm going for a run."

She nodded, choking back a sob, and I left before I shattered.

* * * * * * *

The resort's jogging path wound between fairways and pines, past the mirrored stillness of a small lake. My shoes hit the pavement hard, each stride hammering the thought deeper.

Marcus.

He'd been there, circling, waiting. My absence had opened the door, and she, my Sammie, had let him in.

Faster. My lungs burned, but I pushed harder, rage fueling me.

I pictured Marcus's face, calm, self-righteous. The gall to touch what was mine. The audacity to look me in the eye at the gala and thank me for the house. My house. I bet he appreciated it. Every minute under my roof, circling closer to my wife.

And Sammie, barely a nod for him, as Drusilla had trained her. Indifference painted over guilt. She faltered when she looked at me, but she confessed. That mattered. She told me herself. She felt guilty. She was afraid to lose me.

Confession meant she still loved me. Guilt was proof we still had a chance.

Over my dead body would Marcus think otherwise.

Branches blurred past, my pulse drowning out everything else.

Four days. That was all I had left before Tokyo pulled me back under.

Four days to remind her who I was.

Four days to decide whether Marcus walked away from this breathing.

And God help me, I didn't know which way I'd decide.

SAMANTHA

I stayed on the balcony after he left, wrapped in the hotel robe, the morning air cool against my skin. His coffee mug sat abandoned on the table, half-empty, the ceramic ring damp beneath it.

My hands still shook, not from what he'd said—but from what he hadn't done.

I had confessed. The words had slipped out jagged, raw. I'd admitted the unthinkable—that I'd betrayed him. Even as they tumbled past my lips, I braced for the blow. My body knew the rhythm: the snap, the rage, the crack of pain that followed too close behind.

But it never came.

He had looked at me, eyes dark, jaw locked, every muscle

191

coiled like a storm. I saw the violence there. The inevitability of it. Fear spiked through me, sharp and absolute. And then he said, I'm going for a run.

And he left.

The silence he left behind was louder than his rage.

I pressed my palms into my thighs, trying to stop the trembling. Was this what change looked like? Anger redirected into the ground, into the pounding of his feet instead of the breaking of my bones?

God, I wanted to believe it. I wanted to believe he was becoming someone different. That he was learning control, the way Jerome always preached.

Still, I couldn't forget it, his choice not to hurt me. For the first time in a long time, his anger had terrified me, but it hadn't touched me. That should have felt like relief. Instead, it twisted. Because a darker thought whispered through me: If there was ever a moment I deserved it, it was this one.

But he hadn't.

That contradiction knotted inside me until I couldn't tell if it was mercy or just another move in a larger game.

The mug sat cooling, its damp ring spreading across the iron. Proof that he had been here. Proof that, for once, his rage had left no mark—at least not on my skin.

Inside, though, the bruise was already forming.

ALEXANDER

When I pushed the door open, the cool air inside hit me like a wall. I was soaked through, shirt plastered to me, shoes biting into the backs of my heels. My lungs still burned from the run I hadn't prepared for, but I couldn't stop until the fury bled out enough to face her again.

She was there in the sitting area, still in the robe, knees pulled up, fingers locked so tight around them the knuckles shone white. Her eyes were red-rimmed, lashes spiked with salt. She looked small, my wife, folded in on herself, like she was waiting for something worse.

The sight gutted me.

The anger flared again, sharp as glass, but not at her. Not this time.

It was all for him.

Marcus.

He'd wormed his way in while I was gone. Targeted her. Pursued her when she was vulnerable. He made me out to be the liar, the monster I'd been working to prove I wasn't anymore. He took the one place I thought I could rebuild from, the truth, and dragged her into his arms with it.

She flinched when I stepped further into the room. That cut deeper than her confession. I hated that she still thought I could break her, even when I'd run myself into the ground to keep from doing it.

"I'm not going to hurt you, Sammie," I said, breath ragged, voice low. "Not again. Not ever."

Her lip trembled, tears threatening again, but she said nothing. Her silence was heavier than any answer.

I limped past her toward the balcony doors, dragging a towel from the chair to wipe at the sweat. My reflection in the glass looked feral—hair matted, face twisted with exhaustion. But my eyes, when I met them, were clear.

The fury wasn't for her anymore.

It was for Marcus.

And her confession—that was proof enough she still loved me. Why else admit it? Why else tell me at all if not because she wanted me to know? Fear didn't break her loyalty; it tethered it tighter. Guilt bound her to me more surely than any vow.

He'd stolen what was mine. Lied his way into her trust. Made her believe I hadn't changed.

I turned back toward her. She was still sitting there, robe slipping off one shoulder, watching me like I might erupt in front of her.

Not her fault, I told myself. She didn't know. She was afraid. She was astray.

But Marcus—Marcus had done this.

And Tokyo was only four days away. Four days to play the dutiful husband, to remind her where she belonged. Four days to let Marcus think he'd won something. Let him feel safe.

When I got back, I'd take it all from him. Piece by piece.

And I'd make damn sure he paid for it.

SAMANTHA

After he stormed out, I sat frozen in the robe, my mind unraveling thread by thread. Regret clawed through me—regret for not seeing it sooner. Jerome's chessboard, Drusilla's whispers, and Marcus's steady presence when I was weakest. All of it had played me like a violin. And I'd let it.

But Alex...

He hadn't touched me. Not with his rage. He'd run himself bloody instead. The absence of his hand was almost louder than its memory. Mercy or menace, I couldn't tell, but it left me shaking.

When he stepped back in from the balcony, sweat cooling on his skin, his voice startled me. Low. Controlled. Too controlled.

"Do you still have the picture?"

My head snapped up. "The picture?" My thoughts scrambled.

"One of me. At the bar. With her." His eyes bored into mine.

For a moment, I almost lied—reflex, survival—but then I remembered: the envelope was still tucked in a drawer back home. "At the house," I admitted, wary.

"Good." His jaw worked, a muscle jumping. "I want to see it when we get back. And then I'm getting that fiend out of our house."

It took me a second to understand. Marcus. He meant Marcus.

The conviction in his voice made my stomach twist.

He arranged a late checkout, but by noon, we were on the road. The pine forests blurred past, but I hardly saw them. My hands itched against my thighs the whole drive, my heart climbing into my throat. What if the photo said something I didn't want to hear? What if he could explain it? What if he couldn't?

Back at the house, I retrieved the envelope with shaking hands. The paper felt hot, toxic. I handed it to him like it might burn me.

Alex tore it open, stared for barely a breath, then slammed his fist against the wall. The sound cracked through the room like a gunshot, and I jumped. But his face wasn't turned toward me—it was locked on the photo, his jaw hard, his fury aimed outward. He looked like a man cursing a broken machine, not like the monster I'd braced for.

"Sam." His voice was harsh, but steady. "That is the Reiki healer I've been working with. I assure you, she is not a prostitute. Her hand is on my arm because she stopped me from finishing the drink. When I said I had one drink, I meant one sip." He thrust the photo toward me. "She was there with her husband. She intervened."

I stared at him, unable to form words. The picture in my hands looked different now—less damning, more like a snapshot of something ordinary dressed up as scandal.

"I haven't stopped working to be better," Alex said, eyes locked on mine. "Not because I'm overseas. Not ever. I've been learning how to control this—" he gestured at himself, fists curling then opening, "—so I don't destroy what we might still have."

The photo shook in my hand. All this time, I had believed. Then I had doubted. Now belief and doubt tangled so tightly I couldn't tell one from the other.

And underneath that tangle came the sting. I had betrayed him, with Marcus. The words I'd confessed this morning still echoed between us. And now, by admitting the photo existed, by handing Alex proof he could dismantle, I had betrayed Marcus, too.

Because Alex would never stop at explanation, his fury wasn't spiraling at me.

It was spiraling toward Marcus.

And I believed with every ragged breath in me: Marcus was in danger now.

If Alex truly set his mind to it, Marcus's days under our roof were numbered.

ALEXANDER

The house was too quiet. Too clean. We circled each other in polite little exchanges—passing the salt, asking about the laundry—like strangers who had once shared a life. No fights. No intimacy. Just a distance thick enough to choke on.

I'd slept in the guest room. She hadn't asked me not to. Maybe that hurt more than if she had. A rejection in silence, in absence.

This afternoon, I dragged the ladder into the hall. The smoke alarm had been chirping for days, each high-pitched reminder of neglect grating at me until I couldn't stand it. The least I could do was fix something. Put something back in order. Prove I could still be useful.

The test button shrieked, a sharp, piercing cry that rattled the walls. Half a second later, Samantha came running, eyes wide, face pale as if she expected the house to be burning down.

For a moment, the fear in her eyes gutted me. Not fear of fire. Fear of me.

I covered it with a laugh. "Relax, Sammie. Just a battery."

She froze, then let out a startled laugh of her own. Small, raw, but real. And God, it knocked the air out of me. I hadn't heard her laugh like that in so long.

I climbed down the ladder, batteries clutched in one hand. When my feet hit the floor, I reached for her hand to steady myself. She stiffened instantly, the old recoil I had burned into her. The one I'd put there.

But she didn't pull away.

Her skin was cool against mine, her fingers tense. I let my thumb trace over her knuckles, slow and deliberate, as if I could erase the history written into her muscles. "I like seeing you laugh," I said. And I meant it more than anything I'd said in weeks.

She looked away, her face shadowed with something I couldn't read, guilt maybe, or just exhaustion.

I held her hand a moment longer before letting go. "I don't blame you, Sammie. Not for any of it."

And I didn't. Not anymore.

The blame belonged to Marcus. He had waited for me to be gone, circled like a vulture until she broke. He had slithered into her grief, her loneliness, her doubt, and called it comfort. Maybe she'd let him in, but he was the one who had pushed. He was the one who had crossed the line.

I could forgive her. I had to.

But Marcus?

No.

That bastard would be out of my house. Out of her life. Out of our marriage.

One way or another.

And when I finally made him pay, I'd make sure she understood: that confession meant she still loved me. And love, real love, wasn't fragile. It was a bond that could be reforged, if necessary, in fire.

SAMANTHA

I felt something I hadn't felt in months, a kind of steadiness. No pressing hands, no sharp edge hidden under tenderness. Just warmth. For a moment, I let myself sink into it.

He had been gentle, almost kind, since the night he poured the bourbon down the drain on New Year's. I could still see the bottles lined like soldiers across the counter, the smell of liquor sharp in the air as he emptied them one by one. That night had cracked something in me, not enough to heal, but enough to let hope slip in like water through stone.

Then came the symphony. He hated classical music, hated sitting still, hated crowds he couldn't command. And yet he'd taken me there, watched me light up to John Williams like it was something he could give me instead of take away. That memory still burned in me, dangerous and sweet.

Now this weekend. Pinehurst, lilies on the nightstand, laughter over bad golf and ruined gnocchi. Even after the wreckage of last weekend, even after Marcus, part of me wanted to believe. To believe Alex could be this version of himself and not the man who broke me.

But then, like a tide pulling back, something shifted in him. His shoulders tightened, the breath he released not soft but measured, purposeful.

It was subtle, but I knew him too well. I knew the difference between comfort and calculation. Whatever had passed through his mind just then, it wasn't about me.

A chill brushed down my spine.

I didn't move, didn't call it out. But I stored it, another red flag in a sea of them.

And God, I hated myself for how easily I'd believed Drusilla for how stupid I'd been. I should have known better—her honeyed voice, her well-timed lies. I should have seen the knife she was slipping between my ribs even as she smiled.

My throat tightened, guilt and shame rising like bile. "I shouldn't have trusted her," I murmured before I could stop myself.

He drew back just enough to look at me. "Her?"

I froze.

Drusilla's name hovered unspoken on my tongue. My stomach lurched. If Alex knew she'd planted the seed, spun the story, shown me the photos. What would he do with it?

I dropped my gaze instead, biting down hard on the inside of my cheek. "It doesn't matter," I said, too quickly.

But his eyes sharpened, catching the slip anyway.

So I breathed steady, tucked my expression into something practiced. I would not give him another thread to pull. Drusilla had taught me that much, at least—how to wear treachery like silk, how to make silence into armor.

I hated her for it.

But I would use it all the same.

ALEXANDER

Her words clung to me long after I let her go. I shouldn't have trusted her.

Her.

Not Marcus. Not me. Drusilla.

Something twisted cold in my gut. Of course. He hadn't acted alone. Drusilla's fingerprints were all over deception like this. She always played her games from the shadows, always feeding the right poison at the right time.

And Samantha, my Sammie, was caught in the middle, torn between lies and loyalty.

I forced my voice even, casual. "You'll be at the manor later this week, won't you?"

She nodded, hesitating. "Yes. I have to be up to speed on things before Drusilla goes out of town for Horatio's state championships."

"Good." I reached for my keys, masking the heat boiling under my skin.

But before I left, I crossed back to her. Her eyes lifted, wary, searching mine. I cupped her cheek, let my thumb graze lightly below her temple, and bent to press a kiss against her forehead.

Gentle. Steady. The way I knew she wanted me to be.

"I need to take care of a few things," I murmured. "Don't worry."

She blinked at me, surprise softening the lines in her face. That flicker of relief was almost enough to undo me. Almost.

Because even as I played the devoted husband, I savored the lie of it. That was the beauty of control, knowing I could be warmth one moment and steel the next, that I could calm her with a kiss while already sharpening the knife for those who dared touch what was mine.

"I'll bring back ice cream," I added. I caught her smile as the door clicked shut behind me.

The keys dug into my palm as I slid behind the wheel.

Drusilla. Marcus. Both circling her like carrion birds, both convincing her to doubt me, to betray me.

The engine roared to life. I steered toward the manor, rage and resolve braided tight in my chest.

It was time to remind them both.

Samantha was mine.

JEROME

The growl of an engine carried up the drive, too fast, too hard. Tires spat gravel as Alexander's car slid into place before the manor steps.

Jerome didn't rise from his chair. The late afternoon light slanted long across the study, cutting bars through the cigar smoke. He tamped ash into the tray, lifted his glass, and waited.

Moments later, the door opened without a knock. Alexander stalked in. His hair was mussed from the wind, his shirt skewed at the collar, but it was his face that betrayed him: flushed dark, eyes rimmed red, jaw clenched so hard Jerome thought he might crack a molar. The fury came off him in waves, heat clinging like a second skin.

Jerome slid several papers together and tucked them beneath a leather folio before his son could glimpse them. "Alexander," he said evenly, smoke curling upward. "To what do I owe the pleasure?"

Alexander didn't pace, didn't shout, though Jerome could feel it vibrating in him like a held storm. His words came clipped, sharp as cut glass.

"Marcus is out of my house. Out of Samantha's orbit. Out."

Jerome raised a brow. Calm, always calm. "And what has

prompted this sudden urgency?"

"He's been circling her. Pressing where she's weakest. I won't have it."

"Careful," Jerome said, exhaling a ribbon of smoke. "Assumptions have a way of making fools of even clever men."

Alexander leaned in, bracing his hands against the desk. His voice dropped low, lethal. "This isn't an assumption, Father. He put his hands on what's mine."

Before Jerome could respond, a knock split the air, and Marcus entered with a folder tucked under his arm, summoned for some errand. He froze mid-step, catching the tension like the smell of ozone before a storm.

"Sir," Marcus said carefully to Jerome, "these are the additional contracts you requested."

Alexander moved before the words settled. He pushed a chair aside, and in three strides, he was across the room. His hand fisted Marcus's collar and slammed him into the carved shelves. Wood shuddered, books rattling but holding firm. Marcus's breath left him in a grunt, papers scattering across the rug like snow.

Alexander's hand locked around his throat, his face inches away, eyes burning scarlet with rage barely held in check.

"You think you can crawl into my house, into my wife's bed, and I won't gut you for it?" His words came out as a growl, molten and raw. "You pathetic little parasite. I'll break every bone in your body before I let you near her again."

Marcus clawed at his wrist, a red welt blooming across his throat. His lips moved once, hoarse, strangled, "My fault, not hers."

It only inflamed Alexander further, his knuckles whitening as if he meant to finish it.

Jerome let it stretch, savoring the crackle of violence in the air. Then, at last, he tapped ash into the tray and spoke.

"Alexander." His voice was measured, unhurried, as though he were commenting on the weather. He didn't rise, only regarded the scene through the haze. "Release your brother."

The word landed like a spark in a powder keg. Alexander's grip faltered, parsing brother as metaphor—family, loyalty—but Marcus's eyes betrayed something else: fear that the word carried more truth than either wanted said aloud.

Alexander's teeth bared. "He's not my brother."

Jerome exhaled, smoke curling upward like a veil. "And yet, he is family. As is your wife. And see how you treat them both."

For a heartbeat, Jerome thought his son might disobey. Then, slowly, Alexander's hand uncurled. Marcus staggered free, coughing, his hand pressed to his throat, but he didn't flee. Didn't even move toward the door. That pause damned him more than any denial.

"Out," Jerome said softly.

Marcus nodded, his gaze lowered, shoulders squared as though bracing to take the weight of it all himself. He left without protest, papers still scattered on the floor, leaving only the faint rasp of his breath in the hall.

When the latch clicked shut, Jerome let silence reclaim the room. Then he set down his glass and regarded Alexander with something colder than anger.

"I had begun to think you were learning. Reports from Tokyo praised your restraint, your precision. Even Drusilla's accounts—Alexander Devereux, finally holding his temper." He studied the ember at his cigar's tip. "And yet, with a single grip, you undo months of progress."

His gaze sharpened, voice dropping like a blade. "You may think it matters that this time your violence wasn't turned toward your wife. But it proves the same thing, Alexander, you cannot be trusted near the things you claim to value most. Rage ruins everything it touches."

The disappointment wasn't loud. It didn't need to be. It pressed harder than fury ever could.

Jerome leaned back, letting the smoke veil his expression. Marcus's hesitation had already confirmed enough. One son is too weak to resist. One too volatile to trust.

The game had shifted. And Jerome, as always, would decide how both would be played, Samantha, the children she had yet to bear, even the family name itself. All precious things. All better kept in his hands, not theirs.

ALEXANDER

"I haven't undone anything." My voice came out low, clipped, but steady. My jaw ached from holding it there. "You think I don't know how close I've come to destroying everything with Sam? I've worked—God, I've worked harder than I ever have— to change for her. I've run until my lungs felt like they would bleed, I've gone dry for months, I've sat with healers who chant and breathe and tell me how to sit still when every part of me wants to rage."

I leaned forward, palms braced against his desk, fingers digging into the polished wood. "And it was working. She was starting to believe me again. Until Marcus. Until him. He circles her like a vulture, whispering in her ear, making me out to be the monster while he positions himself as her savior. You think that

209

doesn't undo everything I've tried to rebuild?"

Jerome didn't flinch. Didn't blink. Just sipped his scotch and let me spit fire.

I jabbed a finger toward the door Marcus had slunk out of. "And you—calling him family. Family. Don't think I didn't hear it." My teeth ground together, hot pressure behind my eyes. "Explain to me what you mean by that, Father. Because I sure as hell don't have another brother."

For a long moment, nothing but the crackle of the fire and the tick of the clock. My pulse thundered in the silence. Then Jerome leaned back, smoke veiling his face, his tone surgical in its calm.

"You do."

The words hit like a blade in the ribs.

My stomach turned, bile and heat rising. "You cheated on my mother."

"Most men falter in their youth, as you know." His reply was measured, delivered like a lecture rather than a confession. "The difference, Alexander, is that strong men rise above it. They build empires, protect what they love. Your mother had my loyalty. Always. But I am not immune to blood and impulse. Nor are you."

My nails bit into my palms. "You make excuses for yourself the same way you accuse me of making them." Even as I spat it, I knew the futility. You didn't argue with Jerome Devereux and win. Not in this house. Not in any house.

Revulsion burned hotter than the scotch in his glass. This was his game. Truth not spoken but weaponized, released like poison when it suited him. Marcus wasn't just some hanger-on. He was a piece Jerome had kept hidden until it cut deepest.

I forced my voice level, though my throat felt raw. "Does Drusilla know?"

His gaze sharpened, predator's cold. "It doesn't matter. What matters is this: steer clear of Drusilla. And go home to your wife. Marcus will be... relocated, in due time."

Dismissal. As though the revelation were nothing but a paper moved across his desk.

I swallowed the acid in my throat, shoved down the instinct to press harder. My father had revealed enough for one night, and I knew better than to push past his line. But as I turned toward the door, one thought burned, relentless:

Marcus wasn't only a rival. He was proof. Proof that this family was rot and that it had been spreading all along.

And when I faced him again, I wouldn't just be fighting for my wife. I'd be fighting to carve myself free of the sickness Jerome had tried to make me inherit.

I left the study without another word, the manor's corridors closing in around me like a mausoleum. Outside, the air was cool, damp with evening. My hands still trembled on the wheel as I drove, but the farther I got from Jerome's smoke and silence, the more the rage began to settle into something else.

Sammie. My Sammie.

I pulled into the little shop on the edge of town, the one she always begged for when we were still dating. The lights buzzed overhead, the smell of sugar and syrup clinging to the air. I ordered without thinking—her favorite: brownie sundae, two scoops, hot fudge, nuts, and an extra cherry. I could still hear her voice saying it.

As I carried the bag back to the car, my chest eased. This was what mattered. Not Marcus. Not Jerome. Not Drusilla and her games. Just her, and the things that made her smile.

By the time I walked through our front door, the weight in my jaw had loosened. She was curled on the couch, knees drawn up, wrapped in her robe. I crossed the room, set the bag down with deliberate care, and pulled out the container I'd ordered on the way back.

A brownie sundae—two scoops, hot fudge, nuts, and an extra cherry. Her favorite.

I set it on the table in front of her, a peace offering in sugar and chocolate. "Thought you could use something sweet," I said, steady, as if the world hadn't been cracking apart only hours before.

For a moment, she just stared at it like she couldn't decide whether to laugh or cry. "You remembered."

But when she finally reached for the spoon, when the first taste softened her face a fraction, something loosened in my chest. Proof I could still give her that—proof I could still make her smile.

Let Marcus think he had her ear. Let Father think he had the strings. They didn't know her, not like I did. They didn't know the little things.

This was my Sammie. And I'd keep her, no matter what it cost.

CHAPTER SEVENTEEN

The Bargain of Blood

"Men are not punished for their sins, but by them."

DRUSILLA

Alexander stormed from the manor, his car spitting dust as it tore down the long drive. A temper tantrum in expensive leather shoes.

On the landing, Marcus passed me, head down. The red mark blooming along his throat told me all I needed to know. He didn't meet my eyes—didn't dare—and I didn't stop him. Weakness announces itself without words.

"Sampson," I called softly.

The butler appeared as if conjured, wearing that politely blank expression he'd mastered over decades. "Madam. Mr. Devereux is waiting for you on the rear terrace."

Of course he was.

I found Jerome beneath the awning. The late afternoon light draining gold across the lawn, cigar smoke uncurling in lazy ribbons around him. He didn't rise; he merely tipped two fingers toward the chair opposite, a sovereign acknowledging a courtier.

"Alexander lost his composure," he said evenly. "It was handled."

I didn't need the sordid details; Marcus's throat had already supplied them. Still, Jerome's eyes carried a weight that said the matter wasn't to be dismissed with a quip and a drink.

"You'll avoid Alexander until he returns to Tokyo," he continued, voice low, measured. "It would be unwise to provoke him further. For your safety."

I inclined my head. "And Marcus?"

"He stays here at the manor until Alexander departs." A pause, deliberate. "Alexander wants him out of his house."

My lips curved, faintly. "Shall I make arrangements?"

"Not yet." He tapped ash neatly into the tray. His tone brooked no debate. "He'll leave for law school soon enough. Three years away from Samantha. More than enough time."

This smile I allowed myself was genuine. "Strategic."

"Always," Jerome replied, gaze fixed on the horizon as if the matter had been settled before I ever arrived.

I let the quiet draw out, then angled my head. "And the girl, Samantha? What of her safety?"

Jerome's eyes narrowed through the haze of smoke. "She is safe. Alexander's anger is directed elsewhere now."

He let the words settle, his tone carrying the weight of certainty.

Not reassurance, exactly, Jerome didn't deal in comfort but fact.

That answer pleased me more than the cigar seemed to please him.

Still, I knew the truth. Anger redirected was still anger banked—smoke smoldering, waiting for the right breath to fan it to flame.

MARCUS

My throat still ached where Alex's hand had been. Heat pulsed there, tender, angry, like the imprint of his fury had been branded into me. I should have fought back. God, I should have done something besides stagger and cough like a coward. But in Jerome's study, with those cold eyes on me, I froze.

Now the walls pressed in. It wasn't wood and stone; it was the weight of their name, of his gaze, of a life bent into obedience. Jerome had called me family. The word was meant to bind, not free.

But it wasn't my pride knotting my chest. It was Sam.

How did he know? What had she told him? The rage in Alex's eyes hadn't been wild; it had been honed. He knew enough to make a blade of it.

I paced the room, palm at my neck, replaying every word, every glance. I didn't care about reputation or the endowment or the future Jerome dangled. None of it mattered if Alex turned that rage on her.

Sam.

The thought of her alone with him, waiting for a storm that would come, made my breath go thin. She'd trusted me. She'd let me hold her. Let me love her. Now she is paying the price.

Humiliation faded under a darker burn: panic. Time stretched like a wire, every minute another mile Alex could cover, another moment she might be bracing for impact.

I grabbed my phone. Calling was reckless. He would not be there yet. If he heard—

Silence was worse.

I hit dial.

Too many rings. Then: "Marcus?"

Her voice nearly buckled me. "Sam, are you okay?" The words came raw, shredded by more than Alex's grip.

"I'm fine," she said too fast. Her breath hitched. "You shouldn't have called. He'll...Marcus, if he finds out..."

"I don't care," I snapped, then forced my tone down. "I just... I needed to know. Did he—"

Silence. Then: "He didn't touch me."

Relief hit so hard I had to sit.

"Marcus, what if everything I did, everything, was because of a lie?"

My stomach dropped. "What do you mean?"

"The photo," she whispered. "The woman. What if it was staged? What if I let myself believe something that wasn't even true?"

Damn Dru. Damn all of them.

I wanted to tell her I'd known the second I saw that glossy snapshot: too clean, too convenient. I wanted to say Alex's rage didn't need props.

But if I called it staged, she might run back to him. If I let her believe, she might finally run from him. I said nothing, and hating myself for both choices was all I had left.

"Even if it was staged," I managed, "it doesn't erase what he's done. What you've lived through."

She made a muffled sound, maybe a sob. "Promise me you'll be careful," I said. "Please."

"I don't know what to believe," she breathed. "Marcus, don't come here. He'll kill you if he sees you."

The line went dead.

I stood with the phone pressed to my ear, heart hammering. She was protecting me, when she was the one who needed saving.

SAMANTHA

When Alex finally came home, I braced for thunder. Rage. Accusations. Something violent.

Instead, he carried a paper bag. He set it down with quiet ceremony, drew out a small plastic container, and slid it across the table toward me.

A brownie sundae—two scoops, hot fudge, nuts, and an extra cherry. My favorite.

For a moment, I just stared at it, stupidly, like it was a trap. My throat was too tight to swallow.

Then I took the spoon, let the chocolate and cream melt on my tongue. Sweet, heavy, grounding. He watched me like the smallest shift in my face would tell him whether he'd won.

And damn him, a smile cracked through before I could stop it. Not joy. Not forgiveness. Just the reflex of being seen in some small, ordinary way.

He caught it instantly. Of course he did. His whole body eased, as though a sundae could rewrite the history between us. As though my favorite dessert meant I was his again.

He asked what I wanted for dinner. Complimented the flowers I'd arranged. Set a glass of water at my elbow like this was an ordinary evening.

But beneath the sweetness, unease lingered. Because it wasn't the sundae that scared me, it was how quickly he read my smile as proof.

It was disorienting.

He moved around me carefully. And I was tired of it. Everyone treated me like glass, my friends, Marcus, even Craig, with those sidelong looks. And now Alex, suddenly tender, suddenly careful, as if that could erase the pain. They wrapped me in softness; none of it felt like safety.

Everyone except Jerome.

Jerome never softened a word. No pity. No gauze. Just demands. It was terrifying. It was honest. A small, shameful part of me respected that.

Night after night, Alex didn't raise his voice. He held me without pressing. He laughed at tiny things, the flour I spilled, the neighbor's cat trying to scale the screen. He reminded me of the man I first loved.

"New beginnings," he said once, thumb brushing my hand like he could sand down all the edges. "That's what this is, Sam."

I wanted to believe.

But the current never stilled. And when silence stretched too long, he said it, casual, almost offhand:

"Would you rather it were him?"

The question pierced. He didn't name Marcus. He didn't have to.

I froze, breath caught in my chest, but before I could answer, Alex's voice softened—low, coaxing, almost gentle.

"Sammie, I understand. He is what I'm not. Soft, compliant. Clever at slipping into the cracks when you're weakest. He made you think I couldn't change, that I hadn't changed. And maybe I hadn't given you enough yet to believe me. That's on me. Not on you."

His thumb brushed the back of my hand, feather-light. "We have a lifetime to get this right. I don't blame you, Sammie. If anything, it's my fault. I left you room to doubt. I won't make that mistake again."

Something in me ached at the words. It was the Alex I had once loved, the boy who held me in hospital corridors, who whispered I wasn't alone. For a moment, dangerously, I wanted to believe him. To let that warmth cover the wounds.

But doubt twisted in me. What if he was right? What if Marcus had manipulated me? He'd been there every time Alex faltered, always steady, always waiting. Had I mistaken persistence for love? Had I let him trick me into crossing a line that never should have been crossed?

I said nothing. My lips wouldn't shape words, not yes, not no.

Alex smiled, but it didn't reach his eyes.

And the unease curled deeper, because I couldn't tell if I'd just been forgiven or claimed.

Then the nausea hit—sudden, brutal. Nerves, I told myself. Or maybe the sugary sweetness of the ice cream.

The thought flickered, mean and bright.

Pregnant.

I shoved it down. I'd deal with it if and when I had to.

ALEXANDER

The Uber idled at the curb, engine low, waiting. She stood in the doorway, eyes shadowed but soft enough that I let myself believe. I pulled her close, held her longer than I should have. Her hair brushed my cheek, and for a moment, it was like it used to be.

She didn't say much, just leaned into me, let me kiss her temple, her cheek. "I'll call you," I promised, murmuring against her skin. "New beginnings, remember?"

Her silence held. No words, no vow back. But she didn't pull away. She let me linger, let me leave on that note. And that had to be enough.

The Uber hummed east, tires chewing the road, pines blurring into gray streaks. I leaned back into the seat, replaying her in my mind. How she'd let me hold her, how she'd laughed at the smallest things, how she'd finally kissed me goodbye.

No declarations. No forgiveness. But something. Enough to keep trying. Enough to keep clawing at the man I was becoming.

Marcus.

Even now, the name burned through me like acid. I'd seen the flinch when I asked the question: Would you rather it were him? She hadn't answered. Her silence had screamed, but not against me. Not truly. If she'd wanted him, she would have said it. Instead, she chose not to wound me. She chose to stay.

Tokyo would fill my days—deals, dinners, the endless march of duty. But no ocean could blot out a man circling my house. Jerome promised he'd handle it, Marcus moved, pieces corrected, but trust in my father had limits.

This was my wife. My Sammie.

And silence or not, she'd chosen me.

I wasn't done fighting.

My thumb dragged slowly over the band on my finger, the gold warm from my skin. That ring was proof of vows spoken, of a bond she might doubt but could never erase. She still wore hers. I'd seen it catch the light when she reached for me, when she held my gaze too long to be nothing.

The metal pressed into my skin, solid and unyielding. A circle without break, without end.

Just like us.

SAMANTHA

I stood in the doorway long after the Uber turned the corner, the red taillights shrinking, then swallowed by the trees. The house was silent once again, but my mind screamed.

Inside, everything still smelled faintly of him—aftershave clinging to the bathroom, the faint trace of his cologne woven into the sheets. I drifted through the kitchen, the hall, until I reached the bedroom. The bed was unmade, sheets tangled from where we had slept side by side but miles apart.

I meant to smooth the covers, return the room to order, but instead I collapsed into it. The cotton was cool against my skin, the emptiness beside me vast. Nausea rolled through me, sharp enough to curl me inward. I told myself it was nerves. Exhaustion. The weight of weeks compressed into days. But deep down, in the marrow of my bones, I knew better. My body knew better.

And still, I denied it.

My thoughts spun without mercy. His words at the door: New beginnings, Sammie. A chance to start again. His soft assurances that Marcus had tricked me, manipulated me when I was vulnerable. The photos that Drusilla planted. The guilt I carried like a brand.

Had Marcus manipulated me? Had I used him? Was it both? The questions circled, clashing until I couldn't untangle them anymore. Love. Betrayal. Lies. Desire. I couldn't tell which was which. Was any of it real?

I pressed my palms against my eyes, as though pressure could still the noise. But behind the darkness came more: memories of my parents, their voices steady with conviction. Marriage is forever, Samantha. Divorce is not an option. Love bears all things.

And so I decided.

If this were my fate, I would walk into it with my eyes open. I would be a good wife, not the shamed girl who faltered at the first trial. I would learn everything I could from Drusilla and Jerome, no matter how sharp their lessons cut. If there were a child—God, if there were a child—I would learn how to protect it, how to protect us both, even if it meant surrendering pieces of myself.

Resolve hardened in me, thin and trembling, but it was something.

I curled deeper into the sheets, wrapping the silence around me like armor. My mind still screamed, my body still trembled, but I clung to the one thought that steadied me:

I would endure. Whatever it costs.

CHAPTER EIGHTEEN

Blood Tithe

"What is bred in the bone will not out of the flesh."

SAMANTHA

Six weeks bled together. Drusilla had me at the manor most days—names of staff, feed schedules, which corridor complained after dark. Routine steadied me.

Alex wrote almost daily. I answered weekly. Enough.

Marcus hovered at the edges, mostly gone, the air heavier when he wasn't. A brush of fingers, a shoulder too close—one heartbeat's warmth before guilt drowned it.

And my body betrayed me. Nausea. Crippling fatigue. A missed period, I kept calling stress.

By Thursday morning at the stables, I couldn't pretend. Drusilla rattled off times and tonnage; the floor tilted, heat snapped to cold—then outside, knees in the dirt, my stomach heaving until my ribs ached.

"Bill! Get the cart!" Drusilla's voice cut sharp. She knelt too close, perfume too sweet. "How long?"

"A month... maybe more," I whispered. "Not like this."

She smiled. It made me sicker. "Really?"

"No," I rasped. "No, Dru. I can't be."

Then Dr. Sinclair's kind voice greeted me as he entered the exam area.

"Mrs. Devereux. Congratulations. I figure you are seven to eight weeks along."

DR. ELI SINCLAIR

I stepped back from the bed, clipboard balanced against my arm. Samantha Devereux's vitals were steady now, though the dehydration had been severe enough that her veins had fought me for the IV. She looked pale, exhausted, the kind of exhaustion that went bone-deep.

"Mrs. Devereux," I said gently, though her eyes were already fluttering shut. "The nausea and fatigue you've been experiencing are common in early pregnancy. But left unchecked, they can be dangerous. Severe dehydration can throw your electrolytes out of balance, strain your kidneys, and even cause fainting. We'll keep you here a few more hours, make sure the IV fluids replenish what you've lost."

She stirred faintly, but it was the woman standing near the door—Drusilla Devereux—who held my gaze. Elegant, cold perfume was too sharp for a hospital room.

"She'll need prenatal vitamins," I continued, tone still professional. "I'll write a prescription, though folic acid is the most important early on. Small, frequent meals. Hydration above all else. Ginger tea, plain crackers, and broth—simple things to steady her stomach. If nausea worsens, there are safe medications we can try."

Drusilla's mouth curved, polite but unreadable. "Of course."

I let the pause stretch a fraction longer than necessary. "Rest is as important as nutrition. She'll need a calm, stable environment. Stress can worsen symptoms, sometimes significantly."

Her smile didn't shift. "Naturally."

I made a note in the chart, though my pen slowed. I wasn't sure my words would change anything once she left this room, but I said them anyway. Samantha Devereux looked too brittle, too fragile to be dropped back into whatever storm had made her flinch at shadows even in her sleep.

When I slipped out, I told the nurses to keep her IV steady, fluids running slow. She needed more than medicine—but medicine was all I could give her.

SAMANTHA

I woke in a small room—IV tugging at my arm—to Craig in the chair beside me, unreadable. "You're awake," he said, as if stating the weather. He adjusted my blanket. Poured water. Strange kindness from a man I'd only ever feared. Those were probably lies, too.

Then the door turned. Drusilla. Marcus. She swept in with coffee in hand, calm as though this were all routine.

She set the cup neatly on the tray beside my bed, her movements precise, deliberate. "Hospitals are dreadful without caffeine," she said lightly, as though we were gossiping in her parlor. Her eyes flicked to Marcus, then back to me, amusement tucked sharp behind her smile.

Only then did she draw the envelope from beneath her arm. She let it dangle between two fingers, a casual afterthought, before releasing it onto the blanket. The corner gaped open on impact, photographs spilling across the white sheet—our weekend, our skin, Marcus's hands. Proof.

Craig shifted in his chair, the faintest grimace flickering across his face before he schooled it blank. He hadn't known. He didn't approve. The realization hit me like a jolt. This wasn't orchestrated by them all. This was Drusilla's knife alone.

She sipped her coffee, unhurried. "I'm not cruel, Samantha. I simply gave you what you needed. Alexander has his distractions. Why shouldn't you? Such a pretty picture you two made," she murmured, almost wistful. Her gaze lingered on the images, then flicked toward Marcus, sharp as glass.

"And now," she continued, velvet smooth, "a child to prove it."

The nausea surged—sharp, sour, curling through me. I pressed a trembling hand against my abdomen, as if I could steady it. My throat burned, words torn raw. "You staged those photos."

"Oh, but not these." She nudged one with a manicured nail, sliding Marcus's hand against my skin back into the light. Her smile sharpened. "Always pull the curtains, love. These needed no staging at all."

Her smile widened, cruel and satisfied. "Go on, Marcus. Congratulate her. We both know whose blood she carries."

The air left my lungs. Marcus's silence burned louder than any denial, his face wrecked with guilt he couldn't hide.

"I'm not your broodmare," I spat, my hands trembling against the sheets.

Her smile sharpened, all teeth. "No. Mares are far harder to break—and more expensive."

I wanted to fling the photos at her face, to claw the smugness from her lips. Instead, I sat frozen, Marcus silent at the corner of the bed, Craig unmoving in his chair, the weight of it all collapsing onto my chest.

A baby. Maybe his. Maybe not. My stomach twisted violently, nausea clawing as if my own body mocked me. And now Drusilla held the rope and called it a ribbon.

MARCUS

I couldn't breathe.

"Go on, Marcus. Congratulate her. We both know whose blood she carries."

The envelope buzzed like a live wire. Proof. Leverage. Chains.

I should've denied it. Defended her. Something. But my throat locked, guilt written across me for Dru to read like book.

Sam trembled. Wide-eyed, searching for air that wouldn't come. I wanted to lift her out of it—tell them and the world to go to hell. But if I reached across those sheets, Dru's narrative would calcify into fact.

Still, the certainty burned hot and cold. I knew. In my bones, I knew. It terrified me—because if Alex learned this truth, it could kill us both.

And some twisted part of me clung to it, a spark of hope I couldn't stamp out. A child. Proof we weren't a mistake.

Drusilla saw all of it. "Lovers," she murmured dismissive, and glided out.

The door clicked. Silence roared.

My hand twitched—an inch of movement, nothing more.

Her eyes caught it. Saw the hope. Felt the danger. Something heavy settled in her expression. Not joy—gravity.

"Don't," she whispered.

I stood because I couldn't bear to sit and ache. "I'll give you space."

She didn't watch me go.

Craig did.

He rose from his chair slowly, his gaze flicking from the envelope to Sam, then to me. His mouth opened as if to speak, hesitation clawing at him, before he set the water glass within Sam's reach.

"You don't deserve this, Samantha," he said quietly. "Neither of you does."

His eyes met mine—no menace, no judgment, only the weight of what we'd both just endured. Regret, maybe. For the cruelty of it. For being part of a house where kindness was rationed and weaponry came dressed as love.

I left then, the silence between us saying more than words ever could.

CRAIG

The door shut behind Marcus, the latch catching soft, but the silence it left behind felt like a slab of stone dropped into the room.

Samantha didn't move. She sat small against the pillows, blanket pulled up like she could hide, eyes fixed on the envelope that still gaped open across her lap. The photos gleamed under the fluorescents, obscene in their neat arrangement.

I'd seen Marcus's hand twitch before he left, the way he looked at her like she was the only thing anchoring him. And I saw her turn away from it—too tired, too gutted, too tangled in guilt to meet that look.

He believed it. I could read it plain as ink across his face. Believed the child was his. And maybe it was.

Samantha's breath shook, not quite a sob, not quite steady. A jagged sound that cut sharper than if she'd wept outright.

I set the water down on the table within her reach and stayed standing, hands restless at my sides. For a second, I didn't know what the hell to do—me, of all people, in a hospital room with a woman I'd once thought a liability, now folded in on herself like she'd been gutted.

"You don't deserve this," I muttered.

Her eyes flicked toward me—just a glance, but sharp enough to say she'd heard. Then she pulled the blanket tighter, silent.

I broke before the silence did. "Samantha... I know the stories that get told about me. Hopefully, by now, you know stories and truth aren't the same, especially in this family. Everyone—I mean everyone—has a role. They made mine the bad guy."

I hesitated, words dragging, heavier than I liked. "I just want you to know, I'm not pushing an agenda. I want you and your child to be safe." Another pause. "I'll help you where I can."

The unspoken truth sat heavy in my chest: I had my own son, Horatio, to protect. And I didn't have the steel my wife or father carried.

She didn't answer. Didn't need to. She just stayed curled small against the pillows, her silence louder than anything I could offer.

I sat again, the scrape of the chair soft against tile, and kept watch. The kind of watch that felt half-useless. Half-late.

Even when I wanted to mean it, the thought crawled in anyway: maybe whatever I could offer her would always be too little, too late.

JEROME

Hospitals always smelled of beginnings and endings—both of which could be scheduled with the right hand. I walked the corridor with the unhurried stride of a man who owned the ground he crossed. Nurses dipped their heads; staff stepped aside.

At Samantha's door, I paused. Craig was inside, slouched in the visitor's chair, a cup of cooling coffee balanced on his knee. He looked up when I entered.

"That will be all, Craig," I said, tone mild but leaving no room for argument.

For a moment, his jaw worked like he might resist. Then he rose, set the cup aside, and left with a glance at Samantha—something unreadable flickering there. The latch clicked shut, and the room was mine.

Samantha lay against the pillows, eyes closed. Not sleeping. Tear tracks faint as chalk, her jaw set in that familiar line. Stronger than Elizabeth. The same softness, but threaded through with grit. Useful.

I cleared my throat. A courtesy dressed as command. She opened her eyes at once.

"You are a willful young woman," I said, taking the chair. Mild tone, verdict weight.

"Jerome," she whispered. "I really don't feel well."

"I know." The corner of my mouth twitched—sympathy performed. "And yet you're carrying what we've all been waiting for. A next-generation Devereux. Nothing pleases me more."

"You haven't told Alex," she said. Not quite a question.

"Of course not. That should come from you when the time suits. But don't insult either of us by pretending you didn't know. A woman always knows." Her hand drifted toward her abdomen, then stopped. I noted that too.

"I'm trapped," she said, voice shaking. "Tied to this family for life."

"Trapped, no. Bound, yes. There's a difference." I folded my hands. "You are bound to something larger than yourself. That child makes you invaluable. Do not mistake that for weakness."

Tears threatened. I allowed it. Tears soften; softened things shape.

When I rose, I smoothed my jacket. "Rest, Samantha. Take care of yourself. I will take care of the rest."

Outside the hospital, the patio air was warmer, tinged with burnt coffee. The no-smoking signs were for people I did not know. I lit a cigar and let satisfaction breathe.

The timing was exquisite.

Samantha—pregnant, compliant by necessity; her agency muffled by obligation. Marcus—cornered, guilt-ridden, and therefore moldable. Drusilla's theatre served my design; an heir was necessary, yes, but more valuable still was Marcus's appetite, guilt, and hope braided into a leash I could pull from three time zones away.

He would sign. Stipend. Tuition. A taste of power. A Faustian bargain like no other; boys seldom read the fine print when love spells it for them.

In a few weeks, he'd be across the country—"pursuing dreams." In truth: indebted, obedient, still tethered by his feelings for Samantha. Exactly where I needed him.

Timing is everything. The boy would be waiting. It was time to seal his fate.

MARCUS

The study pressed in on me—polished oak, brass lamps throwing long shadows, the faint tick of the clock loud as a gavel. Jerome's cigar smoldered untouched in the tray, a coil of ash leaning but unbroken. He didn't need the indulgence; he inhaled power.

The folder on his desk might as well have been breathing. Ink, clauses, coils—a contract dressed as future.

"It's simple," he said, steepling his fingers. "Law school. Stipend. Backing. A future carved clean of uncertainty. Or—" his gaze flicked lazily toward the door—"walk away and lose it all. No school, no money, no future. And Samantha?" His

238

smile thinned. "Left entirely to Alexander."

My jaw locked. He always knew where to press.

"You make it sound like I'm selling my soul."

"That's precisely what bargains are," he said, almost amused. "Souls for power. The trick is not to whine about the price."

The words curdled. The folder seemed to sprout tentacles, invisible coils winding tight around my wrists.

"Why?" The word tore out of me. "Why me?"

"Because you want her," he said, lamplight cutting his face into sharp planes. "And because wanting her makes you useful."

"Not an answer."

His gaze hardened, voice smooth as stone. "Because, Marcus... you are mine."

The air vanished. "Yours?"

"My son." He said it as if reciting a date. "Your mother was a diversion. You were the result. That makes you a Devereux."

"You're lying."

"I've no need." His face didn't flicker. "What matters is blood. My grandchild will not be raised outside this family. Whether it carries Alexander's name or yours is irrelevant. What matters is which father bends when I tell him to."

My fists dug crescents into the chair arms.

"Sign," he said softly. "Bind yourself to what you already are. Your child will carry our name, our protection. And you will be rewarded—if you remember where your opportunity comes from."

The folder pulsed. A trap, baited with promises.

How would Sam look at me when she learned? Hate me as one of them? Or understand that I did this to fight them from inside?

I told myself that lie until it nearly sounded like the truth. If I signed, I could protect her. Protect the baby. Maybe even buy us a future.

But as the pen touched the page, the brass lamp caught my reflection. Not mine. Not the boy who wanted her. The tilt of my jaw, the set of my eyes—it was Jerome's.

Each stroke of the pen wasn't freedom. It was surrender dressed as salvation.

The truth: I wasn't fighting Jerome's grasp. I was sinking deeper into it.

JEROME

I watched the signature settle. There is always only one outcome; the drama is for the boy signing.

Two sons bound differently—Alexander by rage, Marcus by yearning. Samantha is the key to both. The web tightened as designed.

I lit another cigar and let the smoke rise in slow rings. Marcus believed he'd purchased Samantha's freedom. In fact, he'd chained himself—and linked her—more tightly to the family than ever.

Still... Samantha, this unknown was the center of all.

Elizabeth once filled a room with music. Samantha does it without trying. A hum under her breath, a tune half-sung while her hands worked, the faint lift of her hand as though guiding unseen strings. People notice. They lean toward it. Staff, guests—anyone in her orbit bends, without realizing why.

She is not extravagant, not gilded. Simple in manner, but stubborn once her mind is set. Influence without effort. Authority shrouded in kindness, if not grace.

She is a marvel in her way. Two of my sons caught fast, unable to free themselves. And I—more than they—see the value of such gravity. Properly directed, it will serve the family.

Softness flickered. I crushed it. She wasn't Elizabeth. She was an asset.

She would stay. She would give this family its future.

Gravity bends everything toward it—but in this family, I decide where it lands.

SAMANTHA

They'd said I could go home by midnight, but the hours stretched, IV bags changed, monitors humming, electrolytes trickling back into me drip by drip. By the time the sun broke on Friday morning, I was exhausted, hollowed out. Marcus was the one they sent to fetch me.

Part of me was grateful. Part of me dreaded it.

The drive back was quiet, the kind of quiet that hurt your ears. I stared at the passing pines, nausea gnawing faintly but dulled by the meds. He kept his hands tight on the wheel, as if the wrong touch might careen us into a ditch. I suppose we were already in the ditch.

The house felt too clean when we returned, like a stage reset between acts. Marcus probably cleaned all night.

Marcus carried my things inside, shoulders tense. He set it down gently, like noise alone might break me.

I wasn't sure what he saw when he looked at me. A woman he'd loved. A mistake. A future.

I lowered myself to the couch. The IVs had steadied me, but the nausea still prowled at the edges. Marcus paced once, then sat opposite. His eyes were heavy with guilt, with a hope I couldn't afford.

He leaned forward. "Sam... I need to tell you something."

I tensed. "What?"

"I signed Jerome's agreement."

The words landed with the weight he intended: protection, plan, love shaped like leverage.

"For law school, the stipend, the future," he rushed. "I did it for you. For us. To take care of you. To take care of the baby."

Part of me wanted to believe that picture—escape, safety, a man building something for me instead of against me. But beneath the tenderness, I saw it: the gleam. Ambition dressed as devotion. Maybe both. In this house of Devereux, those two wore the same suit.

He swallowed. "He told me something else. About my father."

Time slowed. "Who?"

He hesitated, jaw tight. "My mom worked for the Devereuxs—"

"Jerome?" The word broke from me like a plea.

His silence was the answer. Then the word itself, ash-thick: "Yes."

We sat with it. The room tipped, rights becoming wrongs, wrongs becoming threads in a pattern I hadn't drawn. I wasn't just caught between Marcus and Alex. I was pinned beneath Jerome's palm. Another piece on his board.

Marcus lifted his hands, empty. "I leave for California in the morning."

I stared past him, at the spotless countertop. "Then this is easier."

He flinched. "Easier?"

"You said you'd protect me. Do it. If the child is yours, he can't know. You need to go. And not come back."

His voice cracked. "It is mine. I can't leave you with a monster and pretend—"

"You told me you'd do anything," I cut in, quiet, sharp. "Did you mean it?"

"Yes."

"Then go."

He stood, anger and grief warring across his face. "What am I supposed to do? Pretend I don't love you? Pretend it's not my child? This is—"

"—the consequence," I said, spine straightening, voice steady for the first time since the hospital. "Of our choices."

A long beat. His hands clenched, unclenched.

"When you leave tomorrow," I finished, "don't come back."

He didn't argue again. He just looked at me, eyes raw with all the things he couldn't say, then turned for the room he would vacate tomorrow.

I held myself rigid until he was behind his bedroom door. Only then did I let my hand drift to my abdomen, trembling. Not as an embrace. As a vow.

If I couldn't protect Marcus from this family, I would at least protect the child.

Even if it meant breaking myself to do it.

MARCUS

I leave for California in the morning. The bedroom door stacks my bags, lined up like gravestones for the life I thought I might have here. Law school, a stipend, a future—Jerome had dressed it up as an opportunity. But it felt like exile.

I'd tried since Alex left to care for her, to prove she wasn't alone. A blanket pulled around her shoulders, a chair pulled out, a hand hovering close enough to touch. But somewhere in the weeks after Alex left for Tokyo, a door closed inside her. Sam was polite, even kind, but her eyes no longer softened when they met mine. The warmth I'd lived on was gone.

And then tonight—her voice quiet but unshakable: "If the child is yours, he cannot know. You need to leave and never look back."

She said it to protect me, I know that. But it landed like something else—like being shut out of the only place I'd ever belonged. It wasn't just me she was asking to erase. It was fatherhood itself. My chance to claim what was mine.

The cruelest part? I'd already sold myself to Jerome, telling myself it was for her, for us. I signed his papers, bent my neck under his hand, and was convinced obedience could buy her freedom. And the first thing she did after was push me away. Even my sacrifices had turned into Alex's victories.

I pressed my palms against the counter until they ached, trying to ground myself. She was still inside that house, carrying a child I believed was mine, and I was leaving with nothing but a suitcase and a name chained to Jerome's ledger.

She said, 'Don't come back.'

And I will leave—because she asked it of me. But every mile

I put between us will only make the weight heavier because I know the truth she doesn't want to admit.

That child is mine.

And one day, I'll come back for both of them.

SAMANTHA

I stayed behind my locked door the next morning. Listening to the shuffle of luggage being hauled out. The knock came minutes later, Marcus's voice muffled through the wood, swearing he'd leave but never give up. I pressed my palms flat to the panel, breath held, and stayed silent until his footsteps retreated down the hall.

The quiet after was unbearable. My body still remembered him—how he steadied me, how he touched me without demanding. That memory throbbed like an open wound. Desire, shame, grief—they all tangled until I couldn't tell them apart. What I had done was wrong. He had been my best friend's fiancé. He is Alex's half-brother. My dearest friend. And still, some treacherous part of me wanted him near.

Alex's words whispered back: He tricked you, Sammie. He convinced you I couldn't change.

Was that true? Had Marcus circled me, waiting for me to falter? Or had I reached for him, knowing exactly what I was doing?

The doubt tore at me, but no answer came—only the weight in my chest and the pulse of something growing inside me.

I drew the blanket from the bed and wrapped it around my shoulders, holding myself against the shaking. My hands slid down, instinctively, to my belly. The only innocent in this ruin. The only life untouched by Devereux games.

"For you, little one," I whispered, my voice breaking, "I will do the hard things."

The vow steadied me even as it hollowed me out. My parents had believed in forever—that marriage was not something to escape but to endure, that faith was measured in sacrifice. I wasn't sure they were right, but their creed lived in me all the same. And so I chose.

If I were to be bound to this family, I would make it binding on my terms. I would learn what Drusilla knew, what Jerome demanded. I would make myself strong enough to protect the child I carried, no matter whose blood ran through its veins.

Tears slid hot down my face as the resolve settled. Fragile, yes. But real. This choice was mine.

It broke me even as it built me.

And I knew, with a finality that burned all the way through, that this was only the first step.

CHAPTER NINETEEN

The Weight of Small Things

"The invisible threads are the strongest ties."

MARCUS

The flight had been the longest of my life—North Carolina to California in a single stretch. By the time I stumbled through baggage claim, the place felt like another planet. Faster, louder, every horn a curse, every skyline stacked ambition made of glass and steel.

The driver took me through traffic that moved like a tide with teeth, spitting me out in front of a tower I didn't belong in. Jerome's tower.

The apartment swallowed me whole when the door clicked shut behind me. Open concept, glass walls, the city glittering beyond like it wanted to burn me alive. Marble counters, leather furniture, every surface sleek, expensive, and soulless. Except for one room.

The study.

I stood in the doorway, and for a moment, it felt like the manor had followed me across the country. Dark wood, shelves already lined with case law and legal tomes, the faint smell of paper and polish. Jerome's hand was everywhere in it, like he had carved a corner of himself into the space. Maybe he'd used it once, back when Silicon Valley was just another venture he toyed with. The thought made my skin crawl.

The rest of the apartment gleamed, sterile, but the study breathed like a cage dressed as legacy. I dropped my bag and traced a spine at random. Federal Procedure. Nothing here was by accident. He was already shaping me into what he wanted: his son, his lawyer, his weapon.

I poured water from the spotless fridge and stood at the window, the city buzzing below. But it wasn't the skyline I saw. It was Samantha. Always Samantha.

The way she looked at me the last time I held her. The way she told me to go. If the child is yours, he cannot know. You need to leave and never look back. The words replayed until they hollowed me out. She didn't even say goodbye this morning.

I wanted to fight them. Wanted to believe she'd only said it to protect me. But a deeper part of me wondered if she'd already chosen. If Alex's poison had worked—if she really believed I'd circled her, manipulated her, tricked her.

The ache pulled me toward the bar cart set against the wall, bottles gleaming. A Devereux touch. Scotch. His drink, not mine. I didn't pour. Not yet.

Law school started on Monday. Berkeley. Another Devereux investment, another stage already set for me. Casebooks stacked on the desk like waiting sentinels. Three years, Jerome said. Three years of work, of patience. Then New Year's. Always New Year's. The one summons no Devereux could refuse. The only guarantee I'd see her again.

Until then? Silence. Distance. Study.

I told myself it was a strategy. That if I built something here—money, power, a name—I could come back strong enough to break her free. But when I pressed my palms to the glass, the truth pressed back harder.

I wasn't building freedom. I was living in Jerome's shadow, in Jerome's cage.

And I wasn't sure I'd ever get out.

GENEVIEVE

By mid-October, Fayetteville had settled into the burnished edge of fall. Between classes at Methodist and my hours at the accounting lab, the coffeehouse down the street had become my favorite stop. Today, though, I wasn't buried in ledgers. I was waiting for Samantha.

She came in with that quiet composure she'd been wearing more lately, as if she'd rehearsed it in the mirror before

251

stepping outside. The bump under her sweater was impossible to ignore now, but she carried it well, shoulders back, all smiles.

We ordered, and she surprised me with her choice. "One affogato," she told the barista, almost smiling. "Decaf."

I raised a brow. "Affogato?"

"Drusilla's doing," she admitted, almost sheepish. "Espresso and ice cream. It sounds ridiculous, but it's... divine."

She leaned on the counter like a child caught in some small delight, and for a second, the shadows that usually clung to her seemed to lift.

When we sat, I stirred my coffee, studying her. "Have you heard from Marcus?"

She stiffened just slightly, then shook her head. "No. He's gone."

I kept my tone casual, as if I were only asking out of habit. "Just wondered. He was a friend once—for both of us."

Her eyes flickered, but she gave me nothing more. So I let it drop.

Instead, I nudged the conversation sideways. "I ran into Rachel the other day. Whatever happened between the two of you?"

Something shuttered in her expression. "Life," she said after a beat. "Life happened."

The food came then, and she insisted on paying, sliding her card down before I could argue. A small shift, but a clear one—Samantha wasn't the girl who counted pennies for lunch anymore.

Afterward, we drove across town to Tiny Town. Neither of us had set foot in the place when we were kids—too expensive, too far from what our parents could afford. Now, walking past racks of impossibly soft onesies and rows of tiny shoes, we both felt a little out of place.

We stopped at a display of christening gowns, silk and lace lined up like fragile ghosts. Samantha's fingers lingered on one, her throat tightening.

"My dad," she whispered, almost to herself. "Big man, rough hands—but he used to knit. Made christening coats for family friends. This little one will never have that. Will never know them."

Her eyes glistened, and I touched her arm lightly. "Maybe not coats, but stories. You'll pass them down."

She nodded, blinking back tears. Then, as if refusing to let the moment sink too deep, she forced brightness into her voice. "Names. I keep circling Scarlet. My mom and I—God, we loved Gone with the Wind. She always said Scarlet O'Hara was tough without being hard, feminine without being frilly. That name stuck with me."

I smiled. "Scarlet suits. But what if it's a boy?"

She laughed softly, relief in the sound. "That's the trouble. I don't know. Samuel? Benjamin? I'll figure it out."

We wandered on, touching soft blankets and tiny socks, letting the future feel real for a while. For the first time in months, I left her with hope threaded through her words instead of despair.

As we left the store, the late-afternoon light slanted gold across Raeford Road, painting everything softer than it really was. Samantha carried the bag of tiny things with careful reverence, as though it already held a future she could protect.

I walked beside her, smiling when she spoke of Scarlet, of resilience and beauty stitched into a name. I echoed her hope because she needed it. For her sake, I hope it is a girl.

But later, when I slid into the quiet of my own car, the smile slipped. Marcus's name hung in the air like smoke I couldn't fan away. I hadn't meant to ask about him, but I did because I suspected. Because some part of me knew the shadow between them was more than memory.

I pressed my palms to the wheel and exhaled. Whatever truth lay buried, Samantha was carrying enough already. I wouldn't add my suspicions to her load. Not now.

So I tucked the thought away, folded it tight, and drove home with only the image of her in the baby aisle—hopeful, trembling, but still standing—burned into me.

SAMANTHA

The streetlights blinked on along Raeford Road, halos of pale gold bleeding through the October dusk. Mid-October, and already dark so early—it made the day feel shorter, as if time itself was closing in. I started the engine, the low hum filling the silence, steadying me in a way my breath couldn't.

Tiny Town's bags rustled in the passenger seat, a christening gown wrapped in tissue, small tokens of a future I wanted to believe in. Scarlet. The name lingered with me still, the one my mother and I had always circled back to—Scarlet O'Hara, fierce and unyielding, feminine without being fragile, toughness without being hard. I whispered it once, just to hear how it sounded in the car's quiet.

Scarlet.

I clung to the thought, praying for a baby girl. Something about the idea felt like a whispered promise—soft yet strong, a promise, a hope I could hold in my hands.

But as I clutched that hope, Marcus flickered across my thoughts like a shadow. The way he'd hovered, the way his eyes held things he never said aloud. The truth I hadn't let myself name. For a heartbeat, I realized I thought of him more than I thought of Alex.

Guilt knifed through me. My husband was across the ocean, writing letters, promising new beginnings. He was the one trying. He was the one who had sworn to change for me, for the baby. What kind of wife still lets her thoughts drift back to Marcus?

Hormones, I told myself. That was all. An imbalance. A trick of the body. Nothing more.

And yet, beneath the guilt, resolve hardened. Alex was changing. He had been trying—for me, for us, for the child. He had poured out the bottles, taken me to the symphony, and learned to move carefully around me in a way he never had before. Whatever storms still circled, he was building something steadier.

I would believe in that. I had to. For the baby. For myself.

So I drove home, thoughts warring but hands steady on the wheel, clutching hope like prayer beads, telling myself it was enough—while somewhere deep inside, I still waited for the sound of the next shoe dropping.

MARCUS

December in California wasn't winter the way I knew it—no bare branches or frost on the glass. Just endless gray drizzle rolling off the Bay, slicking the sidewalks, making the city feel restless. I hadn't felt right in days. Couldn't put my finger on it.

Maybe it was the sushi from Telegraph Avenue, or nerves about flying home in two weeks. But today was the worst. My stomach knotted, head swimming, every nerve on edge like I was bracing for something without knowing what.

I told myself it was anticipation. Samantha is on bed rest before Thanksgiving—Craig had updated me, of all people. The irony wasn't lost on me. He'd been the one to say it gently: It's a girl. The words had gutted me and lifted me in the same breath.

A girl. My daughter.

I didn't let myself say it out loud, not even alone in the apartment. But the thought lived in me now, steady as a heartbeat.

On the desk—the one lined with law books Jerome had stocked like bait—sat the gift I'd bought and repacked a dozen times. A silver rattle. Old-fashioned, a little absurd maybe, but it gleamed with weight in the palm. Something real, something to hold. I pictured Sam's face opening it, softening for just a moment before the walls went up again. I pictured tiny fingers clutching it, my daughter's fingers.

The thought made me dizzy, the ache in my gut worse. Like somehow my body knew what my mind couldn't reach—knew that somewhere, something was happening to her. To them.

I laughed it off. Bad sushi, bad nerves. Nothing mystical.

Still, the unease crawled higher until I couldn't sit still. I crossed to the cabinet, poured two fingers of scotch. Jerome's scotch— the good bottle he had placed in the apartment study. The smell alone was him, filling the room with all the weight I'd spent months trying to shake.

I lifted the glass, sipped once. Heat slid down my throat, sharp and familiar.

Then I set it down, staring at the amber swirl.

Not that easy, Dad.

I carried the glass to the sink and poured the rest out. Watched it circle the drain until nothing was left but the smell.

My reflection in the window looked pale, unsettled. But under it, beneath the sickness, there was something harder.

I wasn't him.

And when I got back on the fifteenth, I'd prove it—to Sam, to the child, to myself.

CHAPTER TWENTY
Legacy

"Trust, once broken, leaves a fracture that never heals."

SAMANTHA

Months passed, and my body finally yielded to the rhythm of pregnancy. The nausea dulled as the weather cooled, though fatigue still clung to me like a second skin. I spent nearly every day at the estate now, following rules without protest. My world had narrowed to Jerome's commands and Drusilla's corrections.

Isolation pressed in. Rachel was a ghost from another life, Genevieve a voice on the phone, Marcus a soft memory, and my husband in Tokyo. My circle had been whittled down until it felt like I barely existed outside these walls. Sometimes I wondered if that was the plan all along.

And yet, small mercies surfaced. Mrs. Keene, the cook, had become a comfort. I sat in her kitchen, learning how to plan parties, what to serve and when. I confessed—half-apologetic— that I preferred my granny's instant banana pudding to her layered masterpiece. On a dreary day, she made it just for me. I nearly cried at the first bite.

Alex's letters arrived almost daily—actual letters, not just emails. His handwriting scrawled across paper, his words steady, careful. I answered only once a week. He never faltered. Not since his return had he shown me the old Alex. No anger at me. No bruising words. Every ounce of his fury he seemed to funnel elsewhere—into some secret furnace where Marcus's name burned. With me, he was gentle. Forgiving.

By late November, the doctor ordered bed rest. Jerome ordered Alex home. "For the baby and the holidays," he said, but I knew the truth: fewer scandals to bury if Alex was tethered close.

The door opened one evening, and for a heartbeat, I thought it might be Drusilla or Sampson with one of Jerome's endless instructions.

But it wasn't.

"Alex." My voice caught in my throat. "You're finally home."

The relief that welled up startled me—it wasn't supposed to be there, not after everything, not after months of trying to harden myself. But it rose anyway, warm and unbidden, before I could tamp it down. These damn hormones.

He left his luggage at the door and crossed the room in long strides. "Stay there," he murmured when I shifted. He knelt beside me, careful, almost reverent, like he thought I might break.

"You look tired," he said softly.

"I am. So much for that mommy glow people talk about." My laugh came brittle, but he smiled.

His hand hovered, then settled against the swell of my belly. I didn't pull away. Instead, I pressed his palm firmer.

"She's kicking," I whispered.

His eyes widened, sharp edges falling away as awe broke through. He stilled, waited, then I saw it—the flicker when she moved. His thumb brushed instinctively, coaxing another.

"She's strong," he murmured, wonder threading his voice.

"She has to be," I whispered.

And for a heartbeat, I almost let myself believe it—the gentleness, the awe. Almost forgot the leash Jerome had him on. Almost forgot how fragile trust was, how easily it could be snapped. The voice inside whispered that he was careful now only because someone else demanded it. Because Jerome's eyes were always on us, that thought left me trembling, half in wonder, half in unease.

For a moment, though, it was simple. No betrayals, no lies, no Devereux games. Just us, holding our daughter between us, feeling her announce herself.

* * * * * *

261

The dining room shimmered with silver and evergreen, every surface staged under Drusilla's perfection. Candles burned low, wreaths hung just so. It should have felt festive. Instead, it felt like theater.

Jerome sat at the head of the long table, glass in hand, surveying his empire like a king at court. Craig and Drusilla flanked him. Alex and I sat midway down, the picture of domestic unity, whether we wanted to be or not.

Alex had been gentle since returning, so careful around me, it unnerved me. He pulled out my chair, poured my water, and laughed softly at things I barely said. Best behavior. Not a trace of temper. Whatever darkness still lived in him, he funneled it somewhere else.

And I felt... relieved. That was the strangest part. Relieved he was home, relieved he hadn't lashed out, almost like I trusted him again. Almost.

Conversation hummed, but I barely joined. His hand brushed mine under the table, tentative. I didn't pull away.

At the height of the meal, Jerome rose. Glass lifted. The room hushed.

"Tonight we celebrate more than the season," he said, voice smooth as velvet. "We welcome Alexander back where he belongs. And we look ahead—to continuity, to legacy, to family.

Horatio, my grandson, already represents that promise. And soon,"—his gaze fixed heavy on me—"this child will carry it further. The next generation. Strong, unshakable. The true future of the Devereux name."

The air thickened. My chest constricted. I couldn't draw a full breath. Claustrophobia wrapped around me, every pair of eyes pinning me in place. My belly—my body—made into the axis of the room. I smiled, raised my glass, but inside I gasped for air.

Alex's hand covered mine. "She's strong," he said again, wonder lacing the words.

Across the table, Drusilla's lips curved, but her eyes chilled. Jerome had named Horatio, yes—but only as a prelude. It was my child he placed at the center. My child called the future.

Drusilla drank her wine, lips curved faintly. But it wasn't a pleasure. It was a warning.

* * * * * * *

That night ended politely—coffee, murmured pleasantries—but I barely made it upstairs before I doubled over, clutching the doorframe. Not just a kick this time. A tightening, sharp and low.

Braxton Hicks, I told myself. Too early. January, they'd said. Maybe Christmas. But not now.

I eased onto the bed, breathing slow until the pressure uncoiled. My heart didn't.

By dawn, the estate lay silent, gray light pressing at the curtains. Another tightening gripped me. Not sharp, but insistent. I braced against the dresser, breathing the way the nurse had shown me. False labor, I whispered. Just a rehearsal.

By evening, I almost believed it.

Until the world tilted at dinner, pain ripping through me like a current. My vision blurred. My hand clamped the frame to keep from falling.

CRAIG

"Samantha!"

Her name ripped out of me before I realized I'd moved. One second, she was steady in the doorway, the next she was folding in on herself, face ashen, hands clutching for purchase.

I caught her elbow, slid my arm around her back. She was trembling, her weight collapsing into me.

"Breathe," I whispered, low and sharp against the din. "Stay with me. You're okay. Just breathe."

The dining room erupted, chairs scraping back, voices colliding, silver clattering to the floor. They surged forward, but none of them were close enough. None of them mattered.

I kept her upright, her head tipped against my shoulder, her eyes wide and unfocused.

Then Alex was there—barreling through the noise like a storm. He ripped her from my arms with the desperation of a man who couldn't afford hesitation.

I didn't fight him. I couldn't. My eyes tracked them both, the way her head lolled against his chest. Wrong. Very wrong. For the first time, real fear knotted in me—not for myself, but for her.

"She's bleeding," I said, my voice flat, deliberate. The stain spreading across her dress was proof enough. No one could spin this as false labor.

The words hit him like ice water. His jaw snapped tight, his grip hardening around her. But he didn't bark at me, didn't try to shove me aside like always. He just moved—fast, relentless— shouldering through the door like the world might split apart if he stopped. That was dissonance I hadn't seen before. Alexander never yielded control. For once, he didn't fight me. That told me how afraid he was.

Out in the night air, cold hitting my lungs, I saw him fumbling for his car. Instinct took over. "Keys," I barked, and before he could argue, I snatched them from his pocket and slid into the driver's seat.

He didn't hesitate. He climbed into the back with Samantha still in his arms, cradling her across his lap, his face ghost-white in the shadows. For once, Alexander had no choice but to let me drive.

She looked so small against him. Too small. Too light. The sight pulled a memory sharp as glass—the weight of my mother at the bottom of the stairs, her blood seeping across the wood, Alex kneeling beside her like a boy caught in something he couldn't undo. My throat closed. I should have fought harder, even then. And now here we were again—different stage, same damn play.

I shoved the car into gear, tires spitting gravel. My hands locked around the wheel, white-knuckled. The manor lights shrank in the rearview. For once, I had the reins. For once, Alexander's silence in the backseat told me everything: he was terrified.

ALEXANDER

Craig's voice cut clean through the noise: She's bleeding.

The words hit me harder than a fist. I tightened my hold, felt the heat of her against my chest, the limp weight of her body. No hesitation. No time to think.

I stormed out into the night, Sampson throwing the front doors wide. Cold air hit me, but all I felt was her breath faltering against my collarbone.

Then Craig was suddenly beside me. "Keys," he barked, not waiting for an answer. He snatched them from my pocket and slid into the driver's seat.

For once, I didn't argue. That was the measure of my terror: I let him lead. I climbed into the back with Sammie still in my arms, knees braced against the seat, clutching her as though my grip alone could keep her tethered here.

Her head lolled, her lips parted. Too pale. Too still. "Stay with me, Sammie. Just breathe. That's all you have to do," I whispered, my voice breaking at the edges.

Craig's hands were steady on the wheel, eyes fixed on the black ribbon of road ahead. He drove like the devil himself was at our heels, threading the car through gaps in traffic with terrifying precision.

"She's slipping," I muttered, panic chewing through me.

Craig flicked a glance in the mirror, jaw tight. "Then don't let her. Talk to her. Keep her here."

I pressed my forehead to hers, whispering her name like a prayer. "Samantha. Sammie, come on. We're almost there. Just a little longer."

Her fingers twitched weakly against my chest. It was nothing—and it was everything.

Craig didn't speak again, but he pushed harder, red lights snapping past, tires screaming at every curve. The irony wasn't lost on me: the brother I'd spent years hating was the one carrying us toward salvation while I clung to her in the back, powerless. For once, we wanted the same thing.

When the hospital lights split the dark, relief punched through me so hard I nearly sobbed.

The car fishtailed into the bay, brakes shrieking. Craig slammed it into park, but I didn't wait. I had her in my arms before the engine even shuddered quiet, her weight hot and limp against me.

"Help!" My throat tore as I shouted it. "She's bleeding—she's—"

Hands met us at the door, nurses rushing forward, voices sharp and overlapping. Questions I couldn't answer. Samantha's head lolled against me, a smear of blood already bright on my shirt.

They pulled her from me, too fast, too rough, and the emptiness where she'd been cut me raw.

"Sir, we've got her—please, let go."

I didn't want to. God, I didn't want to. But my hands unclenched, trembling, and she was wheeled through double doors that banged shut behind her.

I was left in the hallway, drenched in sweat and blood, my chest heaving like I'd run miles.

Craig's hand landed on my shoulder, firm, grounding. "She's in their hands now," he said quietly.

But I barely heard him. All I could hear was her voice, faint in the car, whispering my name before she went slack.

I looked at Craig—steady, controlled, the one who had driven us through fire to get here—and felt the sick twist of dissonance. He had always been painted the villain, and yet here I was, helpless, undone, while he stood anchored. For once, I was the weak one, and I hated him all the more for it.

CRAIG

Hospitals had a way of stripping everyone bare. The light was too white, the air too cold, silence waiting like a held breath for bad news to fall.

Alex paced the waiting room like a caged animal, his shirt stained dark, his face gray with panic. I stayed in the corner, hands folded, forcing myself still. Stillness had always been my shield.

But inside, my thoughts churned.

Samantha didn't belong in this story. She was too kind, too

human. She remembered people's names, asked questions no one else bothered to ask. Even Sampson—old stone wall that he was—had smiled, even laughed, because of her. That was Mom all over again. And it terrified me.

Mom had been kind too. And kindness, in this family, always ended in ruin.

The doors opened. A doctor stepped out, tugging down his mask. "Mr. Devereux?"

Alex was on him in an instant, nearly grabbing his coat. "That's me. Tell me—how is she?"

The doctor steadied himself. His voice was calm, practiced, but I caught the faint crease at his brow. "Your wife is stable for now. She lost more blood than we'd like, but we have her on fluids. She's strong."

Alex sagged against the wall, a sound breaking from his chest— relief and fear tangled tight.

Then the doctor's tone shifted. More direct. "The placenta has separated—placental abruption. It's serious. We need to deliver immediately. She's being prepped for surgery now."

I saw Alex flinch, as though the word surgery carried more weight than any blade.

"And the baby?" His voice cracked.

The doctor hesitated just a beat, then: "Your daughter is small but strong. The team is ready. We expect her to do well."

Alex's breath caught. For the first time that night, his face cracked into something raw, boyish. "My daughter," he repeated, like he had to say it aloud to believe it.

The doctor nodded. "We'll bring you word as soon as she's out." Then he moved on, leaving us with the white light and the waiting.

Alex folded back into pacing. I stayed seated, my hands locked together. Relief warred with dread inside me.

Samantha was alive. The baby was alive—for now.

But all I could think was of the weight of my mother at the bottom of the stairs, Alex kneeling beside her, powerless to stop it. I should have fought against being cast as the villain while his sins were buried.

I closed my eyes, whispering a prayer I wasn't sure I believed anymore: Don't let her be another ghost.

ALEXANDER

The hall reeked of antiseptic and old coffee. Too clean, too sharp for anything with my name attached to it. My legs felt like they didn't belong to me, still trembling from the rush, but I followed the nurse all the same.

And then I saw her.

Through the glass—rows of tiny strangers in glowing boxes. But I knew instantly which one was mine. The card read Devereux, Baby Girl, but I didn't need it. I followed the nurse to my daughter.

She was impossibly small, a bundle of pink and wires, her chest rising beneath the rhythm of a machine, fists jerking like she was already fighting. A shock of dark hair curled against her head.

My hand pressed flat to the glass before I realized it, my breath fogging the surface. My daughter.

The nurse's voice was soft, practiced. "She's stable. Breathing on her own, though the monitors help us keep watch. You can put a hand in, if you like."

I swallowed hard and slid my palm through the porthole. My fingers brushed her skin—warm, fragile as paper—and her tiny hand flexed, curling against me.

Something cracked in my chest.

"Hey, sweetheart," I whispered, voice breaking. "It's your daddy."

Her fingers gripped weakly, but it was enough. Like she already knew not to let go.

Tears blurred my vision. For once, I didn't fight them. All the fury, all the shame, all the lies—none of it mattered in that second.

"She's strong," I murmured, more to myself than anyone else, almost in wonder.

* * * * * *

Hours blurred. A hard chair. Fluorescent hum. Coffee that tasted like ash.

And then a rustle of sheets pulled me upright.

"Alex?"

Her voice—hoarse, raw—shot me to my feet.

I was at her side in two strides, leaning close. "I'm here. You're okay. You scared the hell out of me."

Her eyes fluttered, unfocused, until they settled on me. "The baby?"

"She's perfect," I said, swallowing the burn in my throat. "Small, but strong. She's waiting to meet you."

Relief softened her face, just for a second.

Minutes later, the nurse wheeled her—IV still in her arm, pale but upright—into the NICU. I followed close, afraid that if I blinked, she'd vanish.

When she saw the incubator, her breath hitched. Her hand trembled as she reached through the port, and when Scarlet's tiny fingers brushed hers, her shoulders curved protectively, her lips parting with a sound that was half a sob, half a laugh.

"She's... beautiful," Sam whispered.

I stood behind her, my hand slipping over hers through the glass. Together, we looked down at the tiny face fighting in her box. Scarlet blinked, mouth working in a restless pout, as if she knew she'd been born into chaos and chose to fight anyway.

"She has your hair," Sam said, brushing one fingertip gently over the strands.

"And your stubbornness," I whispered, smiling through tears. "I felt it the second she grabbed me."

For once, the silence between us wasn't heavy. It was full. Scarlet sighed, her chest rising steady under the monitor's glow, and something shifted in me.

No rage. No suspicion. Just awe.

"She's ours," I said softly, my lips brushing Sam's temple. "Everything's different now."

Sam nodded, her eyes never leaving the incubator. "Everything," she echoed.

And for the first time in years, I let myself believe it could last.

CRAIG

The NICU hummed with machines—steady beeps, low whirs, the occasional alarm that made every parent in the room stiffen. It wasn't chaos, not like the dining room had been. This was worse. This was order. Control. Lives measured in numbers on screens.

I stood outside the glass, half in shadow, watching them.

Alex, with his hand braced over Sam's, guided it through the porthole to touch the baby's fist. Sam was leaning forward, shoulders curved, her face lit with something I hadn't seen in months—hope, fragile as frost on a windowpane, beautiful but ready to vanish with the slightest heat.

For a second, they looked almost normal. Husband, wife, child. Like all the blood and lies and screaming had never happened, like peace was possible.

But I knew better.

Peace in this family was a costume. Worn when convenient, discarded when it wrinkles.

The baby—so small I could barely believe she was real—shifted against the blankets, her chest rising under the glow of the monitor. Alex's face cracked open at the sight, raw awe where I'd only ever seen rage. He kissed Sam's temple, whispered something I couldn't hear.

And Sam let him.

That stung in a way I hadn't expected. Not because I wanted her for myself, but because I'd seen the lies that covered bruises, the silences that followed her into rooms. Because I knew what it meant when people lowered their voices in houses like ours.

Now she was sitting beside him, her hand in his, their daughter between them.

Maybe that was the cruelest part: sometimes the monster could look like a man.

A nurse passing by slowed, noticing me at the glass. She gave a small, polite smile, the kind meant for family hovering on the edge. "She yours?" she asked softly, nodding toward the isolette.

My throat caught, but I managed: "My niece."

Her smile warmed, a flicker of something kind. "She's strong. Fighters usually are."

I only nodded, because words would have betrayed too much.

When she moved on, I stayed in the shadows, the glass between us holding me where I belonged.

The shadow did not touch Samantha, not tonight.

SAMANTHA

She was perfect. Too perfect. Even beneath the wires and the faint hiss of oxygen, Scarlet's tiny body moved with a strength that shouldn't have been possible. The rise and fall of her chest, the restless shift of her fists—it was everything.

I pressed my palm against the isolette, as close as I could get. Her warmth didn't reach me through the plastic, but the sight of her—alive, fighting—settled into me like something I hadn't known I was missing until now. For the first time in months, I thought I could breathe.

Alex stood close, his hand warm at my back, his head bowed toward the glass as though in prayer. And I thought: this is family.

But then the thought came—sharp, unwanted, crawling through me like ice.

What if she's Marcus's?

The shape of her eyes, the way her mouth puckered—it was too soon to tell. Too soon for anyone to know. I hated myself for even looking, for letting doubt creep into a moment meant only for awe.

I forced it down, smothered it before it could take root. I chose Alex. I chose my husband. And now I have chosen my daughter.

Scarlet deserved a family, not a battlefield.

My eyes blurred as I watched her kick weakly against the blanket, fighting, always fighting. Alex's hand lingered steady against me, anchoring me in place.

I would not let anything ruin this.

Not Jerome's games.

Not Drusilla's lies.

Not even the truth.

ALEXANDER

She didn't want to leave. I could see it in the way her fingers clutched the armrest of the chair, her eyes locked through the glass like the distance might swallow our daughter whole.

Scarlet.

The nurses spoke softly, promised they'd watch her, that Sam could come back in the morning, but she didn't move. Her voice cracked when she finally spoke. "I can't. Not while she's in here."

I tightened my grip on the handles. "You'll be back tomorrow. Every day until she's strong enough to come home. Four weeks, maybe less if she keeps fighting like this."

Four weeks felt like forever. I knew she was hearing it the same way—an eternity measured in feedings and weight checks.

"Sam," I said again, quieter this time. "She needs you to rest. That's how you fight for her now."

At last, she let me push her from the nursery, but her head turned until the last possible second, eyes dragging over every inch of our daughter like she could memorize her into permanence.

The hallway lights felt too bright, the wheels too loud on the tile. She didn't look back at me once. Only toward the place we were leaving her.

Back in her room, I eased her into bed, pulling the blanket high, pressing the call button for the nurse. She folded in on herself, small against the sheets, hands trembling as they settled over her stomach. Empty now.

I lowered into the chair beside her, elbows braced on my knees. She still leaned toward the door, her whole body tilted toward the NICU as if her heart had been left behind in that glass box.

"She's strong, Sammie," I said, forcing my voice steady. "Just like you."

Her eyes flickered, still wet, but she didn't answer.

So I sat there in silence, watching her fight sleep, watching the worry tighten every line in her face.

Scarlet was alive. Sam was alive. That should have been enough.

But in the quiet, I realized the truth: nothing about this would ever feel like enough.

I leaned closer, brushing a stray strand of hair back from her cheek. It clung, damp with sweat and tears. "Your hair's in tangles," I murmured, softer than I meant to.

She tried to smile, but it broke. The tears came faster, spilling silent down her temples.

I reached for the brush on the table, pulling it gently through her hair, careful not to tug. Each stroke smoothed the knots, slow and steady, until her shoulders loosened by inches.

She wept quietly, her breath hitching, and I told myself it was the weight of the day—the baby, the NICU, the fear of leaving her behind.

I told myself that was all it was.

And I kept brushing, steady, certain, as though order could be restored one strand at a time.

If this were what it took to keep her close, I'd do it every night.

SAMANTHA

The nurse folded the discharge papers into a crisp packet, her voice steady, rehearsed. "No heavy lifting. Plenty of rest. Keep your incision clean and dry. You'll come back in two weeks for a wound check, sooner if you notice fever or unusual bleeding.

Do you have help at home?"

"She'll be with us at the manor," Drusilla answered smoothly before I could speak. Her hand touched my arm, light as silk. "We'll see that everything is handled. A nurse has already been arranged to oversee your recovery—and to assist with Scarlet when she's able to come home."

Her words hovered somewhere between kindness and claim. *Back to us*, she seemed to say, as though I'd been on loan to the hospital.

The nurse nodded, unconcerned. "Good. Support is important, especially after a cesarean. You'll need time to heal."

I nodded, though the words barely landed. My mind was already two floors up, behind glass walls and beeping monitors. "And my daughter?" My voice cracked. "When can I see her?"

The nurse softened, the clinical lines of her face easing. "As soon as you're discharged, you can go straight to the NICU. She's doing very well."

I nodded, though relief felt fragile, like a thin thread stretched too tight.

They settled me into the wheelchair, efficient hands drawing the blanket across my lap. Policy, they said. Liability. To me, it felt like surrender. Alex walked beside me, Drusilla behind, their silence its own kind of weight.

Only when we reached the NICU doors did something loosen in me. The air changed—hushed, reverent, full of beeps and whispers. They rolled me to her crib, and there she was: so impossibly small, her chest rising beneath wires and tape, a knitted cap pulled low over her dark hair.

"Scarlet," I whispered. My hand trembled as I reached for the opening in the incubator, brushing the back of her tiny fist. She stirred, fingers curling around mine with more strength than I thought possible.

My throat closed. "She knows me."

"She does," Alex murmured, close enough that I felt his breath against my temple. He pressed his palm lightly against my shoulder, steady, almost reverent.

Drusilla, of all people, leaned in beside me. "She's beautiful," she said softly. For once, I couldn't hear the menace I expected. Only truth.

The nurse gave me minutes, not hours. Time moved too fast, and soon she was urging us on, explaining monitors and feeding tubes, the plan for three more weeks if Scarlet stayed strong. Christmas, maybe. New Year's, at the latest.

I clung to that hope with both hands. "She'll be home by then," I said, more to myself than to them. "She has to be."

Alex steadied me again as I rose from the wheelchair in the lobby. His arm wrapped around my waist, guiding me as though I were breakable. I hated how easily I let him.

Outside, the air was too sharp, the sky too wide, the world too loud. But behind my ribs, a new rhythm beat steady and fierce. Scarlet's.

And I swore I'd hold to it, no matter what waited at the manor.

DRUSILLA

Christmas Eve draped the manor in soft lights and hollow cheer. Carols played faintly through the hall, but their sweetness felt brittle, like sugar left too long in the damp.

The nurse met me in the corridor outside Samantha's room, her clipboard held like a shield. "She's healing," she began cautiously. "Stitches are clean, blood pressure normal. But she isn't eating enough. Sleeps more than is ideal. She should be walking a little each day, rebuilding stamina. Instead..." The woman hesitated, lowering her voice. "She spends hours at the NICU and little strength anywhere else. It may just be exhaustion, recovery—but I'm concerned about possible postpartum depression."

I inclined my head, filing the information away. If anyone had cause to collapse beneath the weight, it was Samantha. Beaten, betrayed, pulled into a family not her own—and now her child dangled in an incubator, a prize just out of reach. Yes. If anyone had earned despair, it was her.

But despair was not useful.

I carried the update to Jerome. He sat by the fire, cigar smoke trailing lazy in the glow. His gaze sharpened when I mentioned Samantha's condition, then cooled into calculation.

"And the child?"

"The doctors are optimistic," I answered smoothly. "They expect her home within the week. Perhaps Monday. In time for the new year."

His lips curved, faint and satisfied. "Good. And there is no possibility she remains at the hospital longer?"

I allowed myself a small smile. "Already asked. They say no. The child is thriving. She will be released."

He nodded once, as though moving pieces into place.

Later, I checked on Samantha myself. She lay curled on the bed, pale in the lamplight, Alex at her side. His hand rested on hers, his posture rigid with vigilance. Watching him watch her, one might almost mistake it for devotion. But I knew better. His care was not born of love—it was fear of losing what he believed was his.

"Samantha needs rest," I said lightly, standing just inside the door. "Alexander, a word?"

He bristled, reluctant to move, but at last stood and followed me into the corridor. His eyes glinted, sharp with suspicion. "She's finally sleeping. Why drag me out here?"

"Because you must see it too," I replied, tone soft but weighted. "The fatigue. The emptiness. Postpartum shadows can linger if they aren't addressed. If she falters, the child suffers too."

He stiffened, as though I'd struck a nerve. "She's strong. She'll manage."

"Strength doesn't shield the mind," I murmured. "You've seen her drift. Withdraw. You need to help her anchor. Otherwise, the nurse will take notice, and then the world will."

For a moment, he said nothing, his jaw tight, his gaze darting back to the door.

I let the silence stretch, then added gently, "Think of the child, Alexander. This family cannot afford weakness—not now."

His breath left him sharp, but he nodded once, clipped. Agreement or dismissal, it didn't matter. I had planted what needed planting.

As I watched him return to Samantha's side, I felt a flicker of relief that I had never subjected myself to such ruin. My son had come into this world by way of another woman's womb. A body spared. A mind spared.

Let Samantha bleed and ache. Let her unravel, if she must. I had already learned: a child passing through you rips both body and mind. Better to stand apart, untouched, and manage the pieces once the breaking is done.

CHAPTER TWENTY-ONE

Homecoming

"Every man is the son of his own works."

ALEXANDER

The car seat clicked too loudly in the silence of the drive, Scarlet bundled in lavender and cashmere like she was royalty. Sampson had stood stiff-backed while I'd checked and rechecked the straps, his eyes giving nothing away. Only when I lifted her free at the manor steps did he murmur, "Ms. Samantha is waiting. She's been anxious all morning."

I nodded, throat thick, and climbed the stairs with Scarlet tucked against me.

When I pushed open the suite door, Samantha stood in the middle of the room, coat in hand, her face taut with nerves. She thought I'd come to take her to the hospital to see Scarlet.

Her eyes dropped to the bundle in my arms. For a heartbeat, she froze, disbelief stealing her breath. Then tears broke, fast and unstoppable.

I crossed the room, set my hand gently at her elbow, and guided her down into the rocking chair by the window. She sank into it like her legs might give out. My hands trembled as I placed Scarlet into her arms.

"She's home, Sammie," I whispered, voice raw. "Our daughter's home."

SAMANTHA

The world blurred the moment he lowered her into my arms. Scarlet. My baby. Warmth against my chest, breath soft as a whisper, the faintest weight and yet heavier than the whole world.

I traced a fingertip across her cheek, afraid she might vanish if I blinked. Lavender fabric brushed my skin, cashmere softer than anything I'd ever owned, but none of it mattered—she was what mattered.

I'd dreamed of this moment every night in the manor, every day in the hospital. Now it was real, and the flood broke through me—grief, joy, terror, love—colliding until all I could do was weep.

Alex knelt beside us, his hand stroking my arm, steadying me. "She's perfect," he murmured. "Just like her mother."

I bent my head and breathed her in. My daughter. My Scarlet.

For the first time since the fire, since the photographs, since the lies that had almost broken me, hope took root again. Fragile, trembling, but alive.

And I clutched her closer, whispering against her hair: "You're home now. You're safe."

ALEXANDER

I couldn't look away from her—Samantha bent over Scarlet, the baby tucked against her chest like she'd always belonged there. Sammie's tears still streaked her face, but her shoulders had softened, her body curved protectively around the tiny bundle.

I didn't remember there ever being this much love in this house, not even when my mother was alive.

But tomorrow would come, and with it, expectation. Jerome had already made it clear: the child should be presented. Legacy on display.

"I'll carry her down at the gala tomorrow," I said softly, careful not to jar the moment. "From the grand staircase landing. No one but family close enough to touch her."

Samantha's eyes lifted, wary. "I don't want so many people around her. Not yet."

I touched her shoulder gently. "She'll be safe. I promise. They need to see her, Sammie. Our daughter. Our future."

Her mouth tightened, but she didn't argue.

"Will you try to attend?" I asked hopefully.

Her answer came flat, stripped of emotion. "No."

I hesitated, then tried again, softer. "Maybe it's time to start getting back to normal."

She shifted Scarlet closer, rocking once, eyes never leaving the baby's face. "She is my new normal."

I swallowed the protest, let my hand linger on the back of the chair instead. Tomorrow, I'd stand alone at the landing with Scarlet in my arms. For now, Sammie's world was small, and it was hers.

And I'd have to be content with that.

MARCUS

The ballroom glittered the way only Devereux money could make it—crystal chandeliers, champagne towers, an orchestra playing as though the fate of the world hinged on every note. I was a ghost drifting from corner to corner, shaking hands with men who didn't matter and smiling at women who smiled back too easily.

Craig had told me everything: Samantha on bedrest, the emergency, the early delivery, the fight to stabilize her. He'd spared no detail, but details were different than being here—different than seeing the hollow where she should have been.

She wasn't here. Not anywhere.

I told myself it was to protect me, to protect the baby. But standing in that ballroom, surrounded by glitter and lies, her silence felt like the blade slipping deeper.

Movement at the far doors stilled the hum of voices. Alexander appeared—not swaggering, but solemn—with a bundle swaddled in lavender satin and cashmere against his chest. He didn't descend into the crowd. He climbed the grand staircase and stopped at the landing, framed by chandeliers, every eye turning up to him.

Jerome didn't need to speak. This was theater, and Alex knew his cue.

"My friends," Alexander said, projecting that practiced confidence Jerome had drilled into him since childhood, "allow me to introduce the future of this family."

He shifted the bundle just enough, and a murmur swept the room.

"Scarlet Elizabeth Devereux."

The name cracked like a bell through glass.

Elizabeth.

Across the room, Jerome's lips curved—not the broad mask he wore for politics, but something smaller, rarer. Pride veined with memory. Elizabeth's name spoken aloud, tethered to the family again through this child.

Beside him, Drusilla smiled, her expression as polished as ever, but I caught it—the faint twitch at the corner of her mouth, the narrowing of her eyes. Displeasure, buried deep, but there all the same.

Applause swelled. Champagne glasses clinked. The orchestra struck up a brighter refrain.

And me? I stood rooted, gut twisting.

Last New Year's, Samantha and I had huddled in her house, the smell of smoke still in her hair, the night heavy with all the things we didn't say. Now Alexander cradled her child—their child—presenting her like a prize to the world.

I should have felt relief. Joy, even. She was alive. The baby had survived. By all appearances, she was well. Instead, I felt the hollow cut of distance, the ache of being severed clean from her world.

I slipped away as the applause swelled again, leaving my untouched glass on the tray of a passing waiter. The kitchen stairway was quieter, darker, and not meant for guests. My hand skimmed the rail as I climbed, the music below muffled to a dull thrum.

If Alexander staged Scarlet for the world from the grand landing, I would find my own way to her, out of sight, out of Jerome's spotlight.

Scarlet Elizabeth. My daughter. My maybe-daughter. My never-daughter.

And the music rose behind me like laughter.

CRAIG

From the shadows of the landing, I watched them all.

Alexander, holding the baby like redemption. Jerome, smiling as if the universe had bowed to him. Drusilla, her expression carved from porcelain but cracking at the edges. And Marcus, Jerome's other son, though the room didn't know it, was adrift in the crowd with pain written plain across his face.

I knew that look. It was the same one I wore most nights. The expression of a man who didn't belong, who could feel the game tightening around him but didn't yet know the rules.

Scarlet Elizabeth.

The name struck harder than I expected. Elizabeth had been my mother, too. To the world, she was Jerome's perfect, tragic wife. To me, she was warmth, laughter, a gentleness that this family stamped out of everyone else. Samantha reminded me of her, kind even when it cost her, kind to Sampson and Mrs. Keene, kind to me despite the whispers.

And now she'd given Jerome what he wanted most: another Devereux heir. The cost of that gift was written all over Marcus's face, and though he didn't see me, I saw him.

Three brothers. One holding the prize. The other was watching it slip away. Me, always out of place.

Then, he did see me. His gaze lifted, searching the crowd, and found mine across the room. For one still moment, the noise of the gala blurred, muted.

No words. No gestures. Just recognition.

The kind that said we both knew the truth, and neither of us could speak it aloud.

I looked back at Scarlet in Alexander's arms—my niece, and thought of Horatio asleep upstairs.

Two children. Both Devereux. Both needed protection from the very name meant to crown them.

Movement tugged at my eye. Across the floor, Marcus slipped toward the rear of the hall, his head down, his shoulders rigid. Not the front doors—never that. He was angling for the service corridor, the narrow stair that ran up from the kitchens.

My jaw tightened. He wasn't leaving. He was going upstairs.

MARCUS

My hand skimmed the rail as I climbed, the music below muffled to a dull thrum. Each step carried me further from the gala's glitter and deeper into the quiet where truth waited.

At the landing, the corridor stretched hushed and still, lined with doors that all looked the same. But I knew which one was hers. Even before I saw the sliver of lamplight spilling beneath the frame, I felt it—like gravity pulling me forward.

Inside, the air was warm, touched faintly with lavender. She lay propped against pillows, her frame smaller now, fragile in a way that twisted inside me. Her hair shorter, her face bare. No polish. No mask. Just Sam.

For a moment, I couldn't move. My chest constricted, awe and ache knotted together. She was still the most beautiful thing I'd ever seen.

She stirred, blinking, caught halfway between dreams and waking. And then she smiled, soft, unguarded—like she thought I was someone else.

"Alex," she whispered.

The name gutted me.

I should've left. Should've spared us both. But the words I'd carried like a stone for months forced their way out.

"She's mine, isn't she?"

It came out raw. Not an accusation. Not even a demand. Just the desperate edge of hope.

Her breath caught. Panic flickered in her eyes. She was too weak to argue, too worn down to soothe me.

"Marcus..."

"You cut me off, Sam." I said, the hurt breaking loose. "Not one word. Do you know what that's done to me?"

Something shifted in her gaze then. Not fear. Recognition. Like she saw in me the same blood she'd been fighting all along.

Her voice steadied, gentled, careful as if she were holding fire. "My husband will be back soon—with my daughter. It would be best for you to go."

The words split me open. My chest hollowed, but I didn't move. Couldn't move.

My hand still clutched the doorframe, my body taut with the need to reach for her, to plead one more time. She sat propped against the pillows, pale and trembling, tears brimming as if the fight had already drained from her.

"How can you do this to me?" The words tore out before I could choke them back. Not an accusation, not even a demand—just the raw ache I couldn't bury anymore.

She flinched, eyes darting away. I thought she might answer, but silence filled the room instead, heavy as heart in my chest.

I stepped closer, desperation clawing at me, the air too thick to breathe. My fists opened and closed at my sides, like motion alone could keep me from breaking.

Then footsteps echoed down the hall—measured, steady.

The door swung wider, and Alexander stepped in, a small bundle cradled against his chest. Scarlet. His voice came low, even, but edged like glass:

"She was busy with her family, Marcus."

Scarlet stirred, her tiny fist pressing against his shirt, and my chest twisted so hard I thought I'd choke.

I backed away, the truth cutting clean—I'd lingered too long.

Her gaze flicked past me, tears spilling as she reached for the child in his arms. Toward him. Toward them both.

The message was clear.

Alex ushered me, the sound of her soft weeping and Scarlet's breath replacing me in the room.

Her family. Not mine.

ALEXANDER

Marcus's voice bled into the hall before I even stepped through the door: raw, jagged, desperate—"How can you do this to me?"

Inside, Sam was pale and trembling, tears brimming. Marcus was too close, his presence in the room a weight pressing down on her.

"She was busy with her family, Marcus." My voice cut across the room. Not loud, but sharp enough to break the moment.

He jerked back, startled, his eyes dragging to the bundle in my arms. Scarlet stirred, her fist curling tighter against my shirt. My girl. My family.

I crossed to the bed and bent low, lowering her into Samantha's waiting arms. Sam's tears spilled, but the moment Scarlet touched her, something steadied. She curled protectively around our daughter, whispering to her like Marcus and I didn't exist.

I kept my eyes on him. Everything in me screamed to drag him out by the throat, but Scarlet was here now, breathing between us. I wouldn't let a fight steal this from her.

"Time to go, Marcus," I said, voice even, though my jaw ached from clenching. I hovered a hand near his shoulder, guiding him toward the hall, ready if he made me.

At the threshold, Sam's voice broke through—hoarse, soft, but clear.

"Alex."

Not Marcus.

The word tightened something deep in my chest. I turned back to her, to Scarlet, to them.

My family.

MARCUS

I stumbled into the corridor, my pulse hammering like I'd been gutted.

I was not the one she called out to.

The words echoed, jagged and unrelenting. For a moment, I thought I might collapse right there against the wall. But then something inside me snapped back—cold, sharp. A whisper of resolve through the cracks: It isn't over. Not yet.

She was exhausted, confused, drowning in the tide of her own fears. She couldn't see clearly. Not now. But I'd help her see. I'd remind her of what we were—what we still could be.

I gripped the banister, forcing my feet down the stairs. My chest was splintered open, but beneath the ache, my mind began to shape something else. A plan. A path. She would come back to me. She had to.

At the bottom of the steps, Craig was waiting, arms folded, his sharp eyes cutting through the dim light of the foyer.

"Where are you coming from?" he asked, voice casual but heavy with implication.

I hesitated. Dodged. "Just needed some air. Place feels crowded."

Craig's gaze lingered too long, like he could peel the truth off me. And then—just for a flicker—his eyes lifted toward the upper landing before snapping back to mine. He knew. He didn't say it, but he knew.

He stepped closer, his tone dropping low, deliberate.

"She's made her choice, Marcus. And you need to respect it. Because if you don't... it won't just be Alexander you're up against. Jerome's 'backing'—the stipend, the apartment, law school—it all disappears the second you cross the line. You'll find yourself cut off, and the whole damn family standing in your way."

The words landed like stones in my gut, but I only nodded once, curt, not trusting myself to answer. Respect it? No. Not when every part of me still burned for her.

I pushed past him, the promise hardening in my chest.

This was far from over.

CRAIG

Marcus pushed past me, his shoulder brushing mine, his steps clipped and fast like he needed to outrun something gnawing inside him. He didn't answer, not really. Just that tight nod—the kind you give when you're cornered and refuse to admit it.

I didn't need him to speak. His silence told me everything.

He loved her. Not with Alexander's violence, not with Jerome's cold strategy. Marcus's love was different—protective, stubborn, almost naïve. He wanted to shield her, to shoulder the blows for her. But in this family, even love like that could be weaponized.

And Scarlet—God help us all—there was every chance she was his. You could see it in the way his eyes lingered, in the way guilt and longing pulled at him like undertow.

Maybe that's what twisted me up most. Samantha was either the most careful woman I'd ever met... or the most careless. Maybe a little of both. Careful in the way she wrapped silence around herself. Careless in letting Marcus close. Careless to believe anyone in this house could love her without Jerome finding a way to turn it into leverage.

For the first time, I almost felt sorry for him. Because wanting to protect her—that was the one weakness Jerome knew how to exploit best. Marcus thought he was making choices for her, for the baby. But really, he was already tangled in Jerome's net, just like the rest of us.

The party below was thinning, laughter slipping into farewells. A few stragglers clung to the champagne, reluctant to leave the glow of Devereux money. But the tide was turning. Soon it would be time to join the others in the study—Father with his cigars, Drusilla with her polished smile, and me, the shadow in the corner, listening to every word while pretending I was meant to be there.

Debrief. Always a debrief. Nothing in this family ended with applause; it ended with analysis. Who bowed, who lingered too long, which rumors needed to be planted, which snuffed out.

I straightened my cuffs, letting the last echoes of the ballroom die behind me. Upstairs, Samantha was cloistered with her child. Down here, the game never stopped.

And Marcus—he was about to learn that love, in this house, was the most dangerous role of all.

JEROME

The dining room had been stripped bare, candles snuffed to stubs, the echo of music silenced. The staff melted into their corners, leaving the house still for the first time all evening. The quiet after the spectacle was always his favorite moment—the place where power was measured, weighed, and banked for later.

In the study, Jerome poured himself a scotch. The peat curled warm through the air, richer than the perfume of the gala. He wasn't surprised when Drusilla appeared moments later, brandy in hand, her entrance as deliberate as the tilt of her wrist. She never crossed a threshold without calculation.

Craig followed a beat after, jacket slung over his shoulder, posture loose, but the lines around his mouth betrayed the concern he hadn't yet managed to bury. Unusual—the three of them together without Jerome demanding it.

"She's a beautiful baby," Drusilla began, her tone faintly wistful, though her eyes glittered with something harder. "Scarlet Elizabeth. Of course, she'll be spoiled, but she has the right name for the family she's been born into."

"She hardly fussed," Craig added, leaning on the mantle. His voice was even, but his eyes flicked to Jerome with something protective underneath. "Alex carried her like she was the only thing that mattered. If I didn't know better, I'd say fatherhood suits him."

Jerome smirked and sipped, savoring the burn. "He has been... well-behaved. A surprise, but a useful one. Perhaps Tokyo isn't where he belongs anymore. A wife struggling, a child needing her father—better for him to play family man here than cost me fortunes covering his outbursts overseas."

"Struggling is one word," Drusilla murmured. She swirled her brandy but didn't drink, her sharp eyes glinting with private amusement. "Fragile, yes, but I see more. Postpartum may be part of it, but not all. She hasn't untangled herself from Marcus. That is where the cracks are."

Craig's jaw worked, the muscle twitching. "I caught Marcus coming down the stairs tonight," he said, voice low. "He looked unsettled. Guilty. He'd been somewhere he shouldn't have been."

Jerome's brows lifted slightly, filing the detail away. Before he could respond, the door swung open.

Alexander strode in, sleeves rolled, hair mussed, fury clinging to him like static. His voice was flat, iron under strain.

"We have a problem. Marcus disturbed Samantha. She was crying when I came back upstairs."

Drusilla tilted her head, sipping at last, savoring the scene. "And what exactly do you intend to do about it?"

Alex's jaw locked, shoulders squaring, voice rough and shaking at the edges.

"If I take care of it, Sam will never forgive me. But hear me— he so much as looks at her again, I won't stop myself."

The room went still. Jerome let the silence draw taut, then swirled his scotch. The clink of ice was punctuation.

"Cut him out," Alex pressed, pacing once, fists flexing. "Get him out of our lives. He's a threat. I won't have it."

Jerome's reply was calm, carved from iron. "Marcus is a

Devereux. He will not be cast out. But distance can be arranged. His path is law, not home. And there he will remain."

Alex froze, fury vibrating beneath his skin. Slowly, he turned his eyes to his father. The look was cutting, absolute. He did not agree. He never will.

Jerome lifted his glass, unshaken. Drusilla drank. Craig's silence thickened.

Without another word, Alex left. His silence was louder than any outburst, a promise waiting for the right fuse.

Jerome let the quiet settle again, tasting the scotch on his tongue. Marcus would still be useful—more so now that guilt had its hooks in him. Distance would temper him, sharpen him. And when the time came, that yearning would drive him straight back into Jerome's hand.

He thought of Elizabeth then, pale and listless after Craig's birth, her songs silenced, her laughter gone to dust for weeks. Postpartum, the doctors had called it. Nasty business—what childbirth could do to the mind of even the strongest women. Samantha carried the same softness, but also grit. A dangerous blend—but one he knew how to shape.

Scarlet was here now. An heir. A tether. And Jerome would see to it that none of them—not Alexander, not Marcus, not Samantha herself—ever escaped the web.

ALLISON

The bell above the salon door chimed as my last customer left, scarf wrapped high against the January wind. I locked the door behind her, turned back—and there was Marcus, slouched in the waiting chair like a storm cloud had followed him in.

I didn't need to ask what brought him. His eyes said it before his mouth ever could.

"Happy New Year," I said softly. I crossed the room and wrapped him in a hug before he could protest. He didn't hug back at first, but then his shoulders dropped, just a fraction, like he'd been waiting for it all along.

When I pulled back, I studied his face. "Alright. Tell me."

He sat forward, elbows on his knees, words tumbling low. "It's a girl. She's named her Scarlet."

I smiled faintly. "How's the proud daddy?"

"Alex seems very happy."

"I was talking about you." I touched his arm, steady, grounding him. "How are you holding up?"

"Ally... she wouldn't even talk to me. She never even really looked at me."

I set the broom aside, locked the shop door, and sat beside

him. My hand stayed on his arm, quiet pressure. "She has to be struggling with all of this, too. What about the family?"

His jaw worked, the words catching. Then finally: "What if she's given up? Decided to just be a pawn in whatever game they're playing?"

My chest tightened. There it was—the desperate terror beneath the bravado.

I slid my hand down, lacing my fingers briefly through his. "Then you've already lost her. Sam's strength has always been knowing her own mind. If she's surrendered, nothing you do will undo that. But Marcus..." I held his gaze. "Be careful not to force what you want on her. She's getting that from everyone else already. You're only beginning to understand what it's like in that house. In that family."

He let out a low, bitter laugh. "They pushed us together. Once Jerome knew we were close, Dru picked up on it, put us in situations. The photo, the fire... none of it was chance. They wanted Sam pregnant with a Devereux child and leverage to control her. Something about Alex can't have kids."

My hand slipped back into my lap, stiff. "Not likely, no. Alex had the mumps—I once heard Mom and Jerome saying it damaged him. Maybe not infertile, but close. Jerome was furious. Called it weakness."

Marcus pressed his palms to his eyes, fury tangled with revelation. "So he doesn't even know?"

"Not the truth, at least not then. Mom kept it from him. She worried what Jerome would do if he thought Alex couldn't carry on the line."

Marcus sagged, voice breaking. "I don't care what Alex can or can't do. I care about Sam. Tell me what I can do, Ally. Anything."

I reached for his hand again, squeezing once, firm. "Nothing. You can't do anything now. You've tied yourself to Jerome, and now you've got to let the hand play out."

His voice sharpened. "He's my father—biologically, at least. Why shouldn't I let him pay for law school, set me up?"

"Because you're selling your soul to the devil." My tone stayed quiet, but steel threaded through. "Before this is over, you'll be helping the very people you swore you'd stop. The money's too tempting. The leverage is too great. You're not strong enough to resist it. I've loved you like a brother since we were kids, but you're not good at resisting temptation."

He stared at me, stung. He reached for humor instead. "Technically, I am your brother."

Silence stretched, heavy. I broke it first. "Speaking of brothers—how is Craig?"

Marcus frowned. "I don't keep in touch with Craig." He hesitated, then added, quieter, "Though... he was kind enough to let me know what happened when Sam went to the hospital. With the baby. Not immediately, but otherwise I would've been in the dark. Otherwise, I have kept distance from creepy Craig." Relief flickered at the shift away from Samantha, but the weight of gratitude lingered in his voice.

"Don't call him that." My voice snapped sharper than I meant. I caught his sleeve, forcing him to look at me. "He doesn't deserve it."

"From all I've heard—"

"Stop." I cut him off, my pulse hot in my throat. "Craig is probably the best of all of us. He hasn't had it easy. The rumors, the lies... The family has enough real demons without turning Craig into one."

He shifted, unsettled. "Ally, there was a story about a maid being... assaulted by Craig. That's not what happened, is it?"

My throat tightened, but I forced the words out. "No. That was Alex. Mom pulled him off the girl, slapped him, and screamed at him. Minutes later, she was at the bottom of the stairs. Jerome blamed Craig. Made him the scapegoat. And Craig's lived with that stain ever since."

Marcus sat frozen. "Jesus."

I pressed my palms together, grounding myself. "Jerome punished Craig for being gay. He used the rumors as leverage. Craig's played the role ever since—to survive."

He leaned forward. "How did you ever get away from it?"

"I ran when I was sixteen. Turns out I'm not Jerome's daughter. Elizabeth was already pregnant when she married him. Jerome saved her from scandal by putting his name on my birth certificate. But I was never his." I took a breath, "So legally I would be your sister, but biologically—no DNA match."

Marcus exhaled, bitter. "Lifetime would pay millions for this script."

"Too many secrets," I said, my tone sharp. "Jerome built a world on appearances. Drusilla, I hear is even worse. She can weave a façade out of smoke and make you choke on it."

Silence settled. He rubbed his temple, heavy with everything I'd told him. "Ally... what if I'm no better? Obsessed. Calling it love. Just another Devereux man choking on it."

I reached out one more time, squeezing his shoulder. "No. You're different, Marcus. But only if you stop letting them write your story for you."

He looked at me, eyes hollow. I pulled him into another hug, fierce this time. "I mean it. You're family. And I won't let them destroy you, too."

CHAPTER TWENTY-TWO
The Distance Between

"Absence diminishes little passions and increases great ones,
as the wind extinguishes candles and fans a fire."

MARCUS

A year. Scarlet's first birthday.

I hadn't set foot in North Carolina since last New Year's. This year, I wouldn't either. COVID gave me cover—classes remote, flights risky—but truth was, I didn't want the fight it would spark if I showed up. Not yet.

The pandemic turned Berkeley into ghost halls. Lectures streamed from living rooms, exams proctored by glitchy cameras. I sat in my apartment, books stacked high, and let the days bleed together. I barely saw anyone. Didn't care to. The vaccine came fast—too fast. Maybe it was fine, maybe I was wrong, but it all felt rushed. Better to stay shut in, stay untouched.

Craig called sometimes. Mostly business properties, Jerome had me tracking in California, deals that stalled under lockdowns, tenants behind on rent. But under the numbers, there were always fragments about Sam. About Scarlet. He never gave much, but enough that I wasn't completely in the dark. Enough to imagine her growing, changing.

I wondered what her first birthday would look like if Jerome staged it like a coronation. Suppose Sam found a quiet corner to light a single candle, just for her. I wondered what Christmas would be like at the manor, with Scarlet wide-eyed at the lights, maybe grabbing at ribbons. And I wondered if she would know me at all.

The mail piled high. I sorted through bills, flyers, the usual clutter—then froze. My name, written in a hand I knew too well.

Samantha.

I tore it open, breath held, and read.

Marcus, I owe you an apology for how I reacted on New Year's Eve. I've wanted to write or call, but this pandemic has kept us all quarantined at the manor. Life feels untouched here compared to what I see on the news, but still—I think of you. I want to know you're okay. Regardless of what transpired, we were friends long before I was married, and I hope our friendship remains. Now I suppose you are family. That still feels strange to write, but it's true.

Scarlet... she is my joy. Being her mother is what was missing in my life. She's healthy and strong, beautiful. She turns one soon. I can't believe it's been a year—since I became a mom, or since I've seen you. Genevieve asks about you.

It's probably not wise for you to write back. I'm not sure Alex will ever be comfortable with you being part of our lives. But I want you to know you are missed. You'll be missed during the holidays.

Love, Sam

I read it twice, three times. The words blurred, steadied, blurred again.

Love, Sam.

It wasn't a promise. Wasn't even hope. But it was more than I'd had in a year.

I poured a drink. Bourbon. His drink. I hated myself for reaching for it, hated myself more for liking it.

The burn slid down my throat, and I sat in the half-dark, the letter open on the table.

Finally, I folded it carefully, too carefully, and slid it between the pages of a heavy law book. Buried but close.

For the first time in months, I let myself imagine it again. Not just law school. Not just the stipend or the leash Jerome had me on.

Samantha. Scarlet. A family that could still be mine, somehow.

The bourbon burned, but the thought burned hotter.

SAMANTHA

Scarlet's first birthday.

It was supposed to be a small dinner, but nothing in this family was ever small. The dining room gleamed—candles flickering low, china set as though heads of state might walk in, a cake big enough to feed a dozen, though it was only us. Scarlet didn't care for any of it. She wanted the paper, tearing it into strips with chubby fists, squealing when it crinkled.

Drusilla, of all people, was the one who indulged her most—lifting her high, letting Scarlet tug her silk hair, even smiling when frosting smudged across her sleeve. I caught it, that rare softness, and held it close.

Craig poured wine, Jerome his scotch, and Alex his water. "Finally sleeping through the night, it is worth a toast." Alex said, leaning close enough for only me to hear. His eyes were tired, but the smile was real.

I laughed quietly, remembering the colic nights, the endless rocking. "I wasn't sure we'd ever survive those months."

Across the table, Jerome cleared his throat, and Scarlet, as if sensing her cue, reached for him. He lifted her, unpracticed but sure, and for once the stern lines of his face shifted into something lighter. Almost tender.

Alex watched, then tipped his head toward me. "Look at that. My father, smiling." He squeezed my hand under the table, a brief flicker of unity I didn't want to lose.

After dessert—Scarlet was more interested in smashing the cake than tasting it—I excused myself. She was heavy against my shoulder as I carried her upstairs, her laughter dissolving into little hums of exhaustion.

The nursery was dim, moonlight spilling across the crib as I eased her down. She curled instantly around her stuffed pony, cheeks flushed, curls damp against her forehead. My chest tightened.

I thought of Marcus then. California. Empty apartment. Online classes flickering on a screen while the world shut its doors. I thought of the letter I had sent, the one I had agonized over, every word pared back until it was safe enough, distant enough. I wanted to say more that I missed him. That I hated he was alone while we were here, together. But it would not have been kind. He needed to move on, find happiness. I had chosen my life, and—for now—it was good.

I didn't hear Alex until he was behind me. His hand slid around my waist, his chin resting on my shoulder. We stood there a long moment, both watching Scarlet breathe, listening to her soft baby snores.

"She's an angel," he whispered, his breath warm against my ear. "Like her mother."

He kissed my cheek, gentle, fleeting, and turned away.

The guilt swelled sharp in my chest, heavier than any joy.

CHAPTER TWENTY-THREE

Unicorns

"The innocent and the beautiful have no enemy but time."

GENEVIEVE

Scarlet met me at the door, curls bouncing, her little hands clutching the hem of her party dress as she squealed, "Gen!" She barreled into my legs, and I scooped her up, inhaling the faint scent of cake batter and baby shampoo.

"You know," I murmured against her hair, "the whole manor bends to you. Even the old man."

Scarlet giggled, wriggling in my arms until Samantha appeared behind her, smiling despite the dark smudges beneath her eyes. "She has them all wrapped around her finger. Sampson wears crowns now. Jerome wore a unicorn horn for ten whole minutes."

I laughed, setting Scarlet back down to race off toward the kitchen. "Even Jerome can't resist her."

We walked together down the hall, arms loaded with glittering unicorn banners and pastel streamers for the ballroom. Scarlet's second birthday—unicorns everywhere, Samantha's idea, though I knew Drusilla had orchestrated the shine and polish.

As we worked, Samantha broke the silence. "Marcus will be here."

I glanced at her. "You're nervous about seeing him, aren't you?"

Her hands stilled on the ribbon she was tying. "Is that weird? So much has happened. I'm a mom. The pandemic... he's finishing law school, you're an accountant, and me still clawing at this bachelor's degree I'll probably never use. And for Marcus—California feels like another world."

"Not weird," I said softly. "Just human."

She smiled faintly, but her eyes slid away.

By the time the guests gathered, the ballroom shimmered with unicorn balloons and a cake taller than Scarlet herself. Sampson wore his crown without complaint, Jerome settled into his seat with a paper horn cocked at an angle, and Alex hovered near Samantha like she was a rare jewel.

Then the lights dimmed, and the cake was carried in. Two tiny candles burned against the frosting, golden points reflected in Scarlet's wide eyes. Samantha leaned close, laughing—really laughing—as Scarlet tried to blow them out all at once, cheeks puffed, curls shaking with effort. She managed a weak gust, then squealed as Sam helped her, their laughter tangling together.

From the corner, Marcus watched. He stood beside Jerome and Craig, head bent as though discussing business, but his eyes flickered once—just once—toward Samantha. She caught it. Their gazes brushed like fingertips before breaking apart.

I saw it. And I knew Marcus had too.

Later, when the room thinned and coats were gathered, Marcus found me by the door. He looked older than the boy I remembered, his face sharper, eyes heavier, but still Marcus beneath it all.

"Almost done," he said, half-smiling. "Graduation in May. Bar in July. Then Jerome's firm waiting."

"Big steps," I said. "Congratulations."

His smile faltered. "How's she?"

I didn't ask who. We both knew. "She's... devoted to Scarlet. To Alex, too, I suppose. They seem happy." I hesitated, then admitted, "Sometimes it feels a little fake. Maybe that's just me being jealous."

His gaze sharpened, hungry for more, but he said nothing.

"I'll see you at the gala?" I asked.

He shook his head. "I'll be back in California before Christmas. But... good to see you, Gen."

When he left, the cold rushed in, and I wondered if Samantha had noticed the way his eyes had lingered. The way hers had softened, if only for a flicker.

MARCUS

The party glittered around me—balloons, frosting, paper horns perched on heads I never thought I'd see them on. Jerome, with his posture still regal even in a child's crown, Craig playing pirate at Scarlet's command, Alex hovering at Samantha's elbow like a shadow that couldn't detach.

I kept my distance, standing with Jerome and Craig when business crept into the conversation, nodding where expected. But my eyes... they betrayed me. Every time Scarlet squealed, every time Samantha laughed with her, the sound reached me. I'd almost forgotten that laugh.

When the candles came out, I stayed back, hands in my pockets. Scarlet puffed, cheeks red, curls shaking. Samantha bent close to help, and for a second the two of them glowed in the flicker of candlelight—mother and daughter, whole. My chest tightened.

She looked up then. Just a flicker. Our gazes touched. And in that breath, I remembered everything we'd buried. Then she looked away. Of course she did.

Later, as guests pulled coats from the racks, I lingered near the door. Genevieve passed, and I asked after her—after them—pretending it was casual. It wasn't. Her words gave me nothing and everything at once. "They seem happy."

Seem. Not are.

I walked out into the cold, knowing I'd carry that flicker of light back to California.

SAMANTHA

The day blurred into laughter, streamers, and unicorn horns crooked on heads that should never have worn them. Even Jerome submitted to Scarlet's insistence, his paper horn cocked. His dignity could survive crepe and glitter, after all.

I should have been exhausted—classes, Scarlet's energy, the endless tightrope of keeping peace—but instead, I felt light. My little girl was two. She squealed at the balloons, tore paper with more joy than the gifts inside. She had Alex twirling her to silly kid songs, Genevieve fixing ribbons in her hair, and Craig pretending to guard the cake like treasure. Even Drusilla laughed when Scarlet shoved frosting at her.

The house felt... full. Warm.

I caught him, though. Marcus. Standing off to the side, too composed for a party like this. His eyes brushed mine across the room—brief, unguarded, a flicker that tightened my breath. I looked away before Alex noticed, but the echo of it stayed.

That night, after Scarlet collapsed in her bed, still clutching a plush unicorn, I lingered by her bed. She'd ruled the house today, bending even Jerome to her will. Who was I kidding? She ruled the house every day. She was joy itself.

And yet... my mind slipped where it shouldn't have, to Marcus.

To the way his gaze had found me in that crowd, the way memory pressed at the edges of the life I'd chosen.

Alex stepped into the nursery.

"Is she already out? She said she wanted a story." Alex gave an almost pout. His slight disappointment was playful, but honest.

I left her bedside and met him in the doorway. "You can read a story tomorrow night." I paused and shot him a grin, "If you are a good boy."

He raised an eyebrow, "Why, Mrs. Devereux, are you flirting with me?"

I put my hand on his chest and I passed through the doorway. He took my hand and pulled me back. He leaned toward me and kissed me. This had been our life the last two years—taking care of our daughter and sharing tender moments like this. For a heartbeat, I let myself sink into it, into the warmth of what we'd built. But even there, in his arms, I felt the ghost of another gaze—the brief flicker from across the room that afternoon. Marcus. The echo of it lingered, uninvited, pressing at the edges of my mind, reminding me how fragile even happiness could feel.

CHAPTER TWENTY-FOUR

Family Alignment

"We are never so defenseless against suffering as when we love."

CRAIG

The ballroom shimmered in pastel again—streamers, balloons, and a cake crowned with yet another unicorn. For the third year running, Scarlet had gotten her way.

Drusilla suggested princesses, Horatio pushed for pirates, but Samantha just laughed at us trying. "You can't negotiate with a terrorist," she'd said, and she was right. Scarlet was the sweetest little dictator to ever run a house, bending all into line.

Marcus stood beside me at the buffet, taking it in. He'd been back in North Carolina since passing the bar, buried in Jerome's real estate holdings. He fit neatly enough into the family machine, but I could see the strain in him sometimes, like gears grinding too hard.

"Unicorns again," he murmured, almost to himself.

"Third year in a row," I said. "She doesn't bend. Not even for Drusilla."

That pulled the faintest smile out of him, but it didn't last. His eyes tracked across the room, landing where Samantha stood laughing as Scarlet tugged a party hat over Sampson's head. For just a second, the whole manor bent around them.

Marcus kept his voice even, too casual. "She seems... better. Stronger."

I caught the angle immediately. "She's managing," I said. "Scarlet keeps her moving."

He hesitated, then tried again. "Still reading? Still finishing classes?"

I set my glass down with a click. "Marcus. She's your sister-in-law. If you want to know how she's doing, ask her yourself."

He didn't answer, only nodded and looked away, pretending interest in the cake. Across the room, Scarlet squealed as the candles flared, all twelve lit for a girl who was only three.

I let the silence hold. In this family, questions were never just questions.

SAMANTHA

The children's laughter filled the ballroom, high and bright, echoing off marble and crystal. Scarlet darted past me with Horatio at her heels, both sticky-fingered from too much frosting, her curls bouncing under a crooked paper crown. She squealed, the sound sharp and joyous, and even Jerome's mouth twitched like he was resisting a smile.

I stepped toward the cake table, reaching for a clean plate, when I nearly collided with him.

Marcus.

He shifted back quickly, murmuring, "Sorry," as if the space between us hadn't already been electric for years.

I forced a smile, fingers fussing with the stack of plates. "So... how are things? Now that you've got your fancy law degree?" The words sounded stilted, lighter than I meant, but at least they broke the air.

His mouth quirked, almost amused. "Fancy, sure. Mostly just long hours and thicker files."

The awkwardness cracked then, just enough, and we found an easier rhythm. He told me about property disputes Jerome had thrown his way, about how half of real estate law felt like translation work—contracts no one human should be expected to read. I told him about Scarlet's latest obsessions: unicorns, twirling until she fell dizzy, the way she could command Sampson with a single pout.

"She runs this house," Marcus said, watching her dart across the floor. "No one stands a chance."

I laughed, soft. "She even has Jerome bending to her will.

That's power."

The conversation drifted—school, Scarlet's future, the endless balancing act of Devereux expectations. But in the pauses, the silences that stretched too long, there was something else. A weight neither of us acknowledged.

Our eyes met once, then again. A glance held too long, broken too quickly. Nothing was said, but everything was humming just below the surface.

Scarlet's shriek split the air again, dragging me back. I turned toward her, heart easing at the sight of her spinning across the floor, frosting smeared at the corner of her grin.

When I looked back, Marcus had already stepped aside, giving me space.

The cake knife gleamed in my hand. My smile stayed fixed, polite, but inside... I felt the ache of everything unspoken.

MARCUS

At least we were talking again.

The cake table exchange was nothing—light, awkward words about degrees and unicorns—but it was more than silence. More than the way she'd turned her face from me last year. I told myself I could live on scraps, that staying where she asked me to—just a friend—was enough. And for the first time, I believed I might actually manage it.

Because I'd learned.

Isolation during the pandemic had been its own schooling—long days without distraction, months of distance from the house, the family, from her. My mind had always run wild, reckless with what it wanted. But solitude taught me how to master the chaos. How to cage it. How to wait and plan. I studied the stoics, learning from the masters.

The chaos still came where Sam and Scarlet were concerned—always. The tug was unavoidable.

Scarlet's laughter ricocheted across the ballroom, curls bouncing under a crooked crown. Everyone in the Devereux line carried sleek, straight hair. Alex, Jerome, even Sam's auburn strands fell smooth when she didn't wrestle them into waves. But Scarlet's curls... they were like my mother's. Spirals soft and defiant, impossible to tame, like her spirit.

It hit me deep in the chest, recognition rooted in blood.

I forced my eyes away before they betrayed me. She didn't need my longing—not anymore. What she needed, though she didn't know it, was protection. And I could give her that, even from the sidelines.

Later, after the laughter had ebbed and the guests drifted home, I slipped into Jerome's study. The familiar smells hung heavy, the shelves looming with their usual weight. I leaned against the desk, steadying myself.

The door opened. Jerome stepped in, removing a paper unicorn hat from his head. For one absurd moment, he looked almost human. Then he caught my eye and smiled—an expression so rare on his face that it unsettled me more than any frown.

"Project Unicorn appears a success," I said evenly, careful to let no more than wry humor show.

His composure slid back into place. "Yes."

The moment vanished. Reports unfurled across the desk—commercial properties clawing their way back after the pandemic, warehouses devoured by logistics firms, hotels on the coast filling again. "Opportunity is always born from crisis," Jerome said, tone as smooth as the scotch he hadn't yet poured.

I nodded, flipping pages with deliberate care, listening but keeping most of my thoughts behind my teeth. That was another lesson learned: never give everything away.

Then his tone shifted, quiet, calculated. "I'm glad to see you and Samantha reconnecting after all this time. It was unnatural for you two not to be friends."

Our eyes locked. He lingered a fraction too long, as if waiting for me to flinch.

I didn't.

"Yes," I said at last. My face betrayed nothing, my voice even. "Friends."

But my gaze held his. Just long enough to say the thing I would never voice.

Time hadn't dulled what I felt. Not for her. Not for Scarlet.

And if Jerome thought otherwise, he underestimated me.

I might be standing at the edge of their lives, but that didn't mean I couldn't shield them.

Even pawns could guard a queen.

ALEXANDER

Scarlet was limp with sugar and excitement by the time I carried her to the SUV. She half-murmured something about unicorns before her head lolled against my shoulder, curls sticky from frosting. I buckled her into the car seat, kissed her hair, and closed the door softly so the latch wouldn't wake her.

Samantha was laughing as she tried to wedge the last of the gift bags into the back. "We may need a second car next year," she said, brushing her hair out of her face.

"Or fewer unicorns," I muttered, earning a quick, tired smile.

Together we managed the load, the two of us moving with the rhythm of parents who'd had practice by now. For a second, it felt simple. Almost normal.

We both lingered on the same memory as we slid into our seats—Jerome and Sampson wearing their party hats because Scarlet insisted. She achieved that every year and it never got old, or less shocking.

Samantha reached for my hand as I pulled onto the long drive back to Cumberland River. Her palm was warm, her grip steady. "It was a good day," she said quietly.

No bluster, no performance. Just observation.

"Yeah," I murmured. I lifted her hand to my lips, kissed her knuckles. For a heartbeat, I wondered how long we could stay in this bubble—three years of peace with our daughter, three years of carefulness, and the rhythm of family life holding us together.

Then I heard myself say it before I could stop: "You and Marcus. I saw you talking."

Her shoulders shifted, a pause. "We laughed," she admitted. "And it felt... good. We've all changed so much these past couple of years."

I swallowed, my eyes on the road. "I don't love it," I said, honesty heavier than accusation. "Just—be careful. My father's going to keep him close now."

The words hung there. Not menace. Not warning. Just the raw truth of how little trust lived in this family.

She didn't argue, only nodded once, her thumb brushing against mine.

I forced myself to shift the subject, to let it go before it poisoned the quiet between us. I glanced at the mirror—Scarlet was slumped sideways, mouth open, her tiny crown still on her head.

"She's out for the night," I said, softening. "That sugar crash will carry her till morning."

Samantha's smile returned, faint but real, and we drove on in silence. The car hummed, the road stretched ahead, and for now, I let myself rest in it—the sweetness of my daughter asleep, my wife's hand in mine.

But Marcus would do well to remember his lane. This was my family.

CHAPTER TWENTY-FIVE
Kill Me Softly

"Hell is truth seen too late."

SAMANTHA

Time moves quickly when you're happy. Or at least when you've convinced yourself you are.

Motherhood gave me something real, something unshakable. For a time, I even believed Alex had found the same.

I still thought of that weekend—the one where so many truths spilled loose. He had learned of my betrayal, I of Drusilla's poisonous games. I braced for the storm that once would have followed, but his rage never touched me. Since Scarlet's birth, it never had. He still flared, still bristled, but it was bark more than bite. Something in him shifted when he poured out the bottles and laced his shoes instead—rage turned into running. Sometimes, when the house was quiet, I almost believed the bruises, the hospitals, the shame had been nothing more than a nightmare.

Marcus once told me I'd look back and see it all as memory. I wasn't sure if he meant it as comfort or as a curse. I still saw him, even during the years he was in California, once or twice at family gatherings when he flew home under Jerome's command. After he graduated and returned for good, Marcus was back at the manor but always working, always vanishing for weeks at a time on Jerome's errands. When our paths did cross, civility had been restored, but it felt strange, like we were both pretending at a distance that had once been intimacy. That distance was its own safety, and I clung to it.

After Scarlet was born, Alex sold our old house in Fayetteville. "She won't grow up there," he'd said. "Too many ghosts." I agreed. Goodbye to walls that remembered too much. Goodbye to the house where Marcus' hands had once known me—where the walls still whispered it back with shame.

I was grateful to leave it behind. An exquisite kindness from my husband.

We were not on the manor's extensive property—I had refused—but close enough to please both Jerome and me. It gave me the distance I needed, while keeping our lives tied neatly into the Devereux orbit. Somehow, I found contentment there. Marcus stayed at a distance, true to Jerome's word, and though I thought of him every day, especially when I looked at Scarlet, I buried that longing deep. My daughter was happy, and that was enough.

Piece by piece, I built something of my own. A double major— psychology and accounting, of all things. Jerome scoffed, Alex frowned, but I pressed forward. Accounting pleased Jerome. Psychology belonged to me. Genevieve tutored, encouraged, and reminded me that my mind still belonged to me even in this gilded cage. With one class left, I could almost touch the finish line.

Scarlet's fourth birthday would be ribbons and laughter, horses in the paddock, children shrieking in warm December air. It would be nice to have the party outside for a change. Before the celebration started, I needed a word with my father-in-law.

JEROME

The terrace air was soft with unseasonable warmth, the December sun gilding the paddock where Horatio chased Scarlet across the lawn. Their laughter carried faintly, bright against the hush of the house.

Jerome sat, cigar balanced loosely between his fingers, eyes narrowed not against the light but in thought.

"Unicorns again?" he asked without turning.

Samantha joined him at the rail, her smile faint. "Not this year. Pegasus. Wings, not horns."

"She loves horses," Jerome observed. "Time she learned more than make-believe. Lessons. Horatio began before he was five."

"Isn't she too young?" Samantha countered.

"Nonsense. A Devereux learns to master the reins early."

They fell quiet, the children's shouts carrying across the lawn. For once, Jerome thought, the manor sounded alive.

Samantha's voice shifted, softer, careful. "Alex doesn't know yet. But somehow, it felt right to tell you first."

Jerome didn't speak. He let silence do the work.

"I'm pregnant," she said at last, steady despite the flicker in her eyes. "It seems your assumption about Alexander was unfounded."

Jerome's face was stone. Only the faintest incline of his head betrayed acknowledgment. "Bravo, my dear. Alexander will be thrilled."

A quick laugh slipped out of her. "So will Scarlet. She's been asking for a baby brother or sister."

They stood in companionable silence for a beat, the air touched with lavender from the gardens.

"Jerome," she added quietly, "please don't say anything yet. I want to tell Alex myself, but not today. This is Scarlet's day."

He only nodded once, but his mind ran sharper than the cut of any blade.

So, another child. If true, it upended certain previously assumed certainties. He had long believed Scarlet belonged to

Marcus—the curls alone whispered it, those spirals borrowed from the boy's mother, nothing Devereux about them. But if Alexander could father a child, then what of Scarlet? Chance? Coincidence? Or had Samantha been more clever than he thought?

Jerome's gaze followed Scarlet as she darted across the paddock, her hair blazing auburn in the sun. Spirals, untamed. The curls that did not belong.

SAMANTHA

Pregnancy plays tricks with your mind. Scarlet's eyes were ocean-deep blue—neither Alex's cold steel nor Marcus's warm green, somewhere between, wholly her own. And still, I searched. I always searched. The stubborn tilt of her chin that could have been Marcus's, the restless tapping of her fingers that echoed Alex's impatience. I studied her so much that sometimes I could hardly see myself in her at all.

And now, with another child growing inside me—one that could only be Alex's—I wondered if Scarlet had been his all along. If the guilt and the shame I carried, the belief that I was keeping Marcus from his daughter, had been for nothing.

But guilt doesn't vanish just because logic suggests it should. I carried it silently, like a private ghost that clung to me in the quiet hours. I smiled, I clapped, I passed out napkins and drinks, all while counting the ways Scarlet might belong to one man or the other. However she resembled them, however the questions whispered in the dark, she was mine. My daughter. And no one—not Jerome, not Alex, not Marcus—would ever take her from me.

Scarlet darted from one delight to the next, hair streaming like a banner, cheeks lit crimson with joy. I smiled through the nausea curling in my stomach, though the ache was sharper than I let anyone see. My body and pregnancy had never been friends. The memory of Scarlet's birth—blood, surgery, the cold rush of fear—rose unbidden. For a breath, it nearly pulled me under. But then I looked at her, laughing, alive, and I forced the memory back into its cage. Today was hers, not mine.

Alex stayed close, always a step behind her. He steadied her on the swings, lifted her so she could reach the candles. He beamed at her as though she were his whole world. And part of me—watching from the edges, my hand resting unconsciously over the swell of new life—felt both a sharpness and a strange peace. Because for Scarlet, Alex was always a loving daddy.

Yet even in that tenderness, a flicker of unease threaded through me. What happened when his devotion turned into demands? When Scarlet grew older, would his love soften her world or suffocate it, the way it once had with me? I swallowed the thought before it could root, holding tight to the image of him laughing with her now, the kind of father she deserved.

For tonight, I let it be enough.

JEROME

The table had settled into that lull I favored—candles burned low, wine nearly gone, laughter softened with fatigue. Scarlet was curled against Samantha, eyelids drooping, a child's kingdom of gifts already conquered. It was the precise moment to strike.

I set down my glass. "Beginning next fall, Scarlet will attend an international kindergarten in Tokyo. Craig will accompany her."

I did not raise my voice; I never had to. The words landed as intended—clean, unassailable—like a stone cast into still water.

Predictably, Alexander reacted first. His palm cracked against the table, silverware rattling like frightened birds. "She is not going without us. If she goes, I go."

The heat rolling off him would have unsettled a lesser man. I let it wash over me, exhaled slowly, and lifted my glass again. "Your place, Alexander, is here. The family requires your presence."

He bristled, fury vibrating under the skin, and for once, he had no immediate retort.

I turned then, deliberately, to Samantha. She stiffened before I spoke, clutching the child closer. "But you, my dear, of course, you would be welcome to accompany Scarlet. There are excellent programs in Tokyo. You might even expand your own studies while she begins hers. A fine mother-daughter arrangement."

I watched the calculation flicker in her eyes: longing, fear, defiance. She knew I was baiting her, offering an escape that was also a tether.

Scarlet shifted, murmured against her shoulder, unaware of the storm tightening above her head.

Alexander's hand had curled into a fist on the table, trembling with the effort of restraint. He looked at me the way his mother once had—like he knew he'd already lost the argument before it began.

I hid my satisfaction behind a sip of scotch. Plans required pressure. And pressure required just the right moment.

Tonight, I found it.

ALEXANDER

Jerome's words sat heavy in the dining room, like smoke you couldn't clear. Tokyo. Scarlet in Tokyo. My father smiled as though it were already settled, as though my daughter were just another line item in his empire ledger.

"No," I said, my voice louder than I intended. "You are not sending my little girl to the other side of the world. Certainly not my wife and my daughter." My hand came down on the table. Hard. A glass rattled, tipped, and fell.

Jerome didn't even flinch. He never did. "Children learn languages best at this age. She will be educated, refined. A true Devereux. Drusilla attended a similar program as a child. The immersive experience will enhance how quickly she learns."

"She is my daughter." My chest was tight. My voice is sharp, dangerous. "You are not turning her into another Drusilla."

Jerome's gaze slid past me to Samantha. Calm, deliberate. "Our legacy is not yours to stunt, Alexander. You'll thank me in the end."

The rage burned through me, but before I could unleash it, Marcus spoke. His voice was carefully measured, indifferent on the surface, but I heard the slip underneath—the wanting.

"Jerome, perhaps it's not wise to separate Scarlet from her parents."

I snapped before I could stop myself. "This doesn't concern you, Marcus."

Jerome's look silenced the whole table. "The decision is made." He rose, slow, smooth. "What you and Samantha choose from here... is up to you." And with that, he left.

The others followed. Drusilla murmured something sharp in his ear, Craig quiet, unreadable, eyes flickering to Scarlet before he disappeared.

I gathered my daughter's things, tucked her small coat around her shoulders. My hands shook. Samantha gathered her purse. We left.

But outside, at the edge of the drive, I stopped. I'd forgotten the keys inside. Cursing, I turned back toward the manor doors—just in time to see Samantha slip into a shadowed corner with Marcus.

I froze, heat rising in my chest.

"...what can I do?" she asked him. I could only catch fragments, muffled words.

"You or Alex would have to request passports," Marcus continued. "Jerome can't force it. Probably why he offered for you to go with her."

And then—then she hugged him. Quick, grateful. Not longing. Not romantic. Just... relief. But I saw the way Marcus looked at her. After all this time. The hunger was still there.

Scarlet's laughter carried from the car, muffled but bright. My hand curled into a fist at my side.

Samantha pulled back, turning to meet my gaze across the dark. Her eyes widened—caught, maybe, or just exhausted. There was no romance in her face. But Marcus—Marcus couldn't even hide it.

The world tilted. For years, I had clawed my way back to her trust, her affection. Over four years, I had kept my rage buried. And yet here he was—still circling, looking at her like she was his to claim.

Something cracked inside me. A door that had stayed shut for over four years, was stressing to open.

* * * * * * *

The drive wasn't long—ten minutes, maybe less—but it felt like hours. Scarlet chattered in the backseat, half-asleep already, her arms curled around the stuffed pony she'd refused to leave behind. Samantha's voice filled the car, low but urgent, running through possibilities, strategies.

"...passports are key. Jerome doesn't have guardianship. He can posture all he wants, but legally—legally, he can't move her without us. We can shut this down. He can't separate our family, not now."

Her words should have steadied me. She was thinking clearly, protecting Scarlet. But all I could see was Marcus's eyes when she hugged him. Not her—him. The hunger, the possessive glint he didn't even bother to mask.

I gripped the wheel tighter, knuckles straining white.

"...and if Craig's involved—Alex, are you even listening to me?"

"I'm listening." My voice was flat, a lie.

Because in my head, all I could hear was Marcus. Jerome can't force it. Saying it like he belonged in the conversation, like he belonged between us. Like he was the answer she needed, not me.

Samantha kept talking—about guardianship, about standing firm against Jerome—but her words blurred.

What if she still wanted him? What if every look she gave me was measured, chosen, not real?

By the time I pulled into the driveway, I wasn't thinking about Jerome anymore. My father could be beaten back. No, what twisted in my gut, what burned in my chest, was the same old rage I thought I'd buried.

Marcus.

Scarlet bounded out of the car the second the door unlocked, pony clutched tight in one hand, giggling down the hall toward her toys. Samantha called after her, gentle, patient, the way she always was. "Scarlet, you're supposed to stay with Mommy or Daddy."

"I'm gonna play!" came the inevitable reply, defiant but sweet.

"Bath, then bed," Sam answered, and she shot me a tired little smile over her shoulder. A mother's smile.

I closed the door harder than I needed to. Locked it. Bolted it. Every sound echoed too loud in my head.

Sam disappeared down the hall with Scarlet, the sound of water running and their voices rising in soft, playful rhythms. I didn't follow. Instead, I poured a drink. One glass slid down too fast, the second slower, heavier, the bourbon burning a trail that only sharpened the fire already building in me.

By the time Sam came back, she carried the quiet weariness of the bedtime ritual. "She's waiting for you," she said softly. "She wants you to come say goodnight."

I set the glass down harder than I meant and stood, crossing the hall to her.

Scarlet was curled beneath her blanket, the stuffed pony tucked under her arm. I bent down, pressed a kiss to her temple, and whispered goodnight. Her small hand reached for mine, then drifted back into dreams.

I slid the child-proof cover over the handle before closing her door. Securing Scarlet in her room for the night.

My hand lingered on the knob longer than it should have, knowing, on some level, what it meant. She was safe in there— locked away, unable to wander, unable to see.

Safe from me.

It also meant I was free to turn elsewhere.

* * * * * *

My hand slid off the knob. The bourbon still burned in my throat.

Sam was waiting, arms folded tight, eyes flicking to the half- empty glass on the table. Her voice was steady, too steady. "Alex... where did that come from?"

"A gift from the office," I said flatly. The lie tasted bitter, but I didn't flinch.

"You promised me—"

"Maybe Jerome's right." I cut her off, "Children do learn languages younger. Maybe it wouldn't be so bad for her."

Her eyes widened, disbelief flooding her face. "You can't mean that. You'd send our little girl across the world without us? Let them shape her into another Dru? Alex, we..."

"Not likable," I muttered, reaching for the bottle again, "but

346

Drusilla is a force to reckon with."

"You don't believe this," she said, stepping closer, her voice shaking now. "This isn't you."

But it was. Or it had been. The bourbon loosened the dam, and the image of Marcus—his face when she hugged him—seeped into every corner of me.

"You pretend so well," I hissed.

Her brow furrowed. "Alex—"

"Dutiful wife. Doting mother. Is there any role you can't play convincingly?"

"Babe, where is this coming from?" Her voice broke, soft, hurt.

"Marcus." His name came out like venom. "You're back with him, aren't you? My bastard brother. Is that what you want? To play his whore again? Maybe you want another baby."

Her hand flew to her belly, color draining from her face. "Alex, no. No. I'm—"

"Always there," I cut in, a bitter laugh clawing out of me. "And still he looks at you like that. And you—you let him."

She touched my chest, gentle, pleading. "Alex, don't do this. You and me—we've been good. So good. I love you."

"As much as you love him?"

"Stop it. I've kept my promise, and you've kept yours. Don't throw that away over a look you think he gave me."

Promise. The word scraped raw inside me.

"I know," I whispered. "I know I'm not Scarlet's father."

The silence screamed. Her lips parted, but no denial came.

Control snapped.

The first strike blurred, a flash of heat and sound. She cried out, clawed back at me, nails catching skin, her scream rising high enough to rattle Scarlet's door. The child-proof cover rattled against tiny hands tugging from the other side, her sobbing voice calling out, muffled, desperate.

"Mommy! Mommy!"

Sam's pleas tangled with Scarlet's cries. I shoved harder, rage and shame twisting tighter, every picture on the wall shattering as she crashed into them, blood smeared across wood and glass. She fought like she never had before, teeth, nails, everything, but I was stronger. I dragged her down.

When I came back to myself, she was crumpled on the living room floor. Blood striped the wall, pooled across broken frames. Her chest moved shallowly, raggedly—but she was silent now.

My knuckles throbbed. My arms burned from where she'd clawed me. My hand ached from where I'd twisted her hair too tight, pieces of her hair still knotted in my fingers.

Scarlet's cries still echoed, locked behind her door. Sammie grasping for life on the floor.

I staggered back, the sight of her—my wife, my Sammie—splintering something in me. For the first time in years, I couldn't stand to look at what I'd done.

So I left. The front door slammed against the frame, and I walked into the night without looking back.

SAMANTHA

Cold. The floor was cold against my cheek. Sticky. My hair was wet—blood? Couldn't move. Couldn't breathe without knives sawing at my ribs.

Door slam. His footsteps are gone. Gone.

Scarlet.

Her cries bled through the house, muffled by the distance. "Mommy! Mommy!" Little fists rattling. I tried to move, tried to drag myself down the hall. My arm gave out. My body stayed.

Dark pressed at the edges of my sight.

The baby. A hollow ache spreading low in my belly, sharper

than anything I'd ever known. Something wrong. Gone wrong.

Scarlet's laugh—birthday ribbons, cake, her curls bouncing as she ran. The sound replayed, too bright against the ringing in my ears.

Don't let her see. Don't let her see me like this.

My chest hitched, shallow breaths scraping air. Blood tasted copper on my tongue. My left eye swelled shut, the other blurred, ceiling spinning.

Scarlet's voice again, sobbing now.

My hand twitched forward, inches only, the floor slick. My body screamed, but I couldn't stop reaching for her.

For her. For them both.

The world narrowed to sound—the cry of my child, the faint rattle of the door.

My last thought before the dark swallowed me whole was a prayer.

Scarlet.

The baby.

Please.

DRUSILLA

The morning had begun as always. Horatio's uniform was pressed, his satchel waiting by the door. My plan was simple: drop him at school, collect Scarlet on the way, and listen to her chatter fill the car. Those little rituals had grown on me—her eagerness, his patient nods as though he were the older brother she begged for.

But when I turned into their drive, the picture shattered.

One car is missing. The front door was ajar. Glass was scattered across the porch like teeth.

My stomach dropped.

I didn't think. The phone was already in my hand, my voice sharper than I'd ever heard it as I called the manor, then 911. "There's been a break-in," I told the operator. "My sister-in-law and niece may still be inside." The words felt foreign in my mouth—sister-in-law—but my chest was tight with something real. Fear.

Craig and Marcus arrived with the police. Relief flooded me at the sight of more bodies, more hands. Anything but standing alone in that yard.

The officer swept inside, weapon raised. Silence stretched. Then—his voice, cutting and terrible.

"Found a woman—injured. And a child, locked in a bedroom."

The words stole the air from my lungs.

I didn't move until Scarlet was carried out, her little arms flailing toward me, her voice hoarse from crying for a mother who didn't answer. I caught her against me, pressing her tight to my chest.

"It's all right, darling. Aunt Dru's here." The words tumbled out raw, trembling, stripped of polish. "You're safe now. You're safe."

Her small fists clung to my blouse, sticky with tears. Her sobs shook through me until I nearly broke with her.

Behind us, Marcus stood pale and stricken on the steps, his throat working like he might be sick. Craig's fists were clenched so tightly the knuckles had gone white.

And me? I buried my face against Scarlet's curls, whispering empty reassurances, because I couldn't bring myself to look at the house.

I'd seen blood before, plenty of it, but never like this— never someone I shared dinners and secrets with, someone I'd grown to almost trust.

If I was shaken, then I knew—Samantha might not survive.

EMS

By the time we rolled up, the place was already crawling with uniforms. A patrol officer met us at the porch, his radio still crackling.

"Child's accounted for," he said quickly, jerking his head toward the driveway. A blonde woman stood there, clutching a little girl tight to her chest. The child's face was blotched from crying, but she was safe. "Victim's inside. Heavy bleeding."

We grabbed our bags and went in.

She was on the living room floor, sprawled among shattered frames and blood-smeared hardwood. Mid-twenties. One eye swollen shut, possible jaw dislocation, blood matting her hair where it had split at the scalp. Her chest rose unevenly, ribs fighting her with every breath.

"Airway clear," my partner checked fast. "Respirations shallow—ten, maybe less. Oxygen now."

"Pulse?"

"Thready. One-fifteen."

I slid a collar around her neck, the blood tacky against the plastic. Pressed quick along her ribs—crepitus, broken for sure. Abdomen is rigid, wrong.

"BP's tanking—seventy over thirty."

"Get the line," I snapped. IV wide open, fluids flowing. We cut away her blouse, bandaged what we could, but there was too much red for any of it to hold.

"Ma'am, can you hear me?" My hand squeezed hers. Nothing but a groan, faint, lost.

We rolled her to the board, locked her down, each strap sticky with blood.

Out on the lawn, the family hovered—men pale and tight-jawed, the blonde woman rocking the child, whispering against her hair. Their faces told us what our monitors already had: this was bad.

"She's circling the drain," my partner muttered. "If we don't move, she won't make it."

"Let's move!"

We pushed her out fast, boots crunching glass, gurney rattling as we loaded her into the rig.

Siren ripped the morning as we tore from the drive. The monitor screamed with us—pressure still plummeting, pulse wild.

I pressed a hand firm to her shoulder, holding her steady. "Stay with us," I murmured, low, like maybe she could hear through the dark. "Don't quit now."

MARCUS

The shriek of sirens split the morning, red lights washing over shattered glass and the yawning doorway. I didn't even remember moving until I was at the curb, fists locked, chest so tight it hurt.

They brought her out fast—strapped to the gurney, oxygen mask fogging, blood streaked into her hair. Tubes, wires, monitors shrilling. Her skin looked waxen, foreign. Not Samantha, not the woman I knew. For a heartbeat, I thought she was already gone.

"Jesus—" The word tore out of me before I could choke it back.

Her hand slipped from the blanket as they loaded her, limp, boneless. The same hand that once clutched mine like it could hold back the whole world. I lurched forward, ready to climb in with her, but Craig's grip locked on my arm.

"Don't," he said, voice low and flat. "Let them work."

I froze, useless, while the doors slammed shut. The siren screamed again, and she was gone.

Beside me, Drusilla had Scarlet crushed against her chest. The girl was sobbing, hiccupping, but Dru whispered, soothed, and rocked her as if sheer force of will could keep the world upright. Her fingers trembled. I'd never seen that before—not from her, not even with her own son. That scared me more than the blood, more than the ambulance vanishing down the street.

DR. ELI SINCLAIR

The trauma bay always moved the same way—bright, brutal light, clipped commands, the chorus of monitors chiming their warnings. But this morning the sound was sharper, the weight heavier.

"BP dropping—seventy systolic!"

"Two large-bore IVs, wide open fluids. Crossmatch four units, move!"

The ultrasound probe skated across her abdomen, and my eyes locked on the screen. Black where there shouldn't be black. Free fluid pooling. Internal bleeding.

"She's bleeding out," I said flatly. "Page the OR, let them know we may need a laparotomy. And draw a serum hCG—pregnant until proven otherwise."

A nurse's hand hovered. "Family says nothing about a pregnancy."

"Test anyway."

They nodded, already moving.

I bent low, my hand pressing gently against the side of her neck. Pulse thready, fading. She was young. Too young for this.

"Intubate," I ordered. The jaw injury meant to intubate a

cricothyrotomy had to be performed. Her breath replaced by the mechanical rhythm of the vent. A mask of tubing and tape over her face. Her voice silenced.

We were already running toward the elevators, monitors wheeling beside us, my palm still braced on her shoulder as though I could anchor her here.

* * * * * * *

The OR was waiting—lights blazing, instruments gleaming like teeth.

"Scalpel."

The first incision parted her flesh, and the suction whined, blood welling faster than we could pull it away.

"Massive hemoperitoneum," the resident murmured, awe and fear bleeding through his voice.

"Clamp," I snapped, my own hands steady. "Stay with me, Samantha. Stay."

We worked quickly, cautery hissing, clamps biting shut. The bleeding slowed, but not enough.

"Sir—" the anesthesiologist's voice broke in, low but urgent. "Lab's back. Serum hCG positive. Early pregnancy."

The words cut sharper than any scalpel. My jaw tightened as I stared down into the open cavity. Blood, torn vessels, tissue that had given life and now was losing it.

I closed my eyes for the briefest second. Damn it.

"Page OB. They'll scrub in. But she's unstable—priority is saving her life."

I felt the team shift around me, the rhythm altering as the news sank in. Another life threaded into this one, and slipping away just as fast.

"Keep moving," I ordered, my voice steel. "She has a daughter waiting at home. She doesn't get to leave her today."

I dug deeper, chasing the bleeding to its source, hands red to the wrists, the hum of suction and the hiss of the vent our only music.

Not on my table. Not if I could stop it.

MARCUS

Hours bled together under fluorescent lights. Craig sat rigid, leg bouncing in a steady rhythm, eyes nailed to the clock like he could force the hands forward. Drusilla paced the tiles, Scarlet finally asleep on her shoulder, though every so often Dru's hand smoothed the blanket with that same nervous twitch.

I stayed planted, knuckles white around the chair's wooden

arms. Every time the double doors swung open, my chest lifted, ready—then sank again when it wasn't him.

Finally—scrubs, a clipboard, and the look of a man about to cut us open with words.

"Family of Mrs. Devereux?"

We all stood.

Drusilla adjusted Scarlet's blanket, then passed her carefully into my arms—my arms—before stepping forward. "I'm her sister-in-law. How is she?"

The doctor—Sinclair. I knew him. He'd been there years ago, another time Sam was carried through hospital doors because of Alex. His face was older now, wearier, but the recognition hit like a blow.

He didn't rush. His tone was calm, practiced, but the lines around his eyes gave him away.

"Your sister-in-law sustained extensive injuries," he began, voice steady. "She arrived with significant head trauma, multiple rib fractures, and massive internal bleeding. She coded once in the trauma bay, but we were able to stabilize her for surgery."

My chest clenched. Coded. Died. Even if just for a heartbeat.

Drusilla's lips parted, but no sound came.

Sinclair continued. "She is in a medically induced coma. For now, she's stable, but the next twenty-four hours are critical. We'll be monitoring for swelling on the brain, watching her oxygenation closely."

The words dropped like stones in water, each one pulling me further under.

He paused, then cleared his throat. "I need to tell you the full extent of what we found. Mrs. Devereux was in the very early stages of pregnancy. The trauma caused her to miscarry. And due to uncontrolled bleeding, an emergency hysterectomy was required to save her life."

The room seemed to tilt. My ears rang.

She lost a baby. And she would never carry another.

Drusilla's hand went to her mouth, eyes wide with something that almost looked human. Craig closed his eyes, jaw flexing hard enough to crack.

I stood there, Scarlet heavy against my chest, her small hand fisted in my shirt like she belonged there. And all I could think—through the shock, through the devastation—was that Samantha would wake to a world where everything had been taken from her. Her child. Her body. Her choice.

"Can we see her?" The question tore out of me, rough, before I even knew it was mine.

"One or two at a time," Sinclair said gently. "I can take you back now. Prepare yourselves."

Drusilla cut me off, stepping forward like it was her right. "Craig and I will go. Marcus can wait. Let Scarlet sleep."

I swallowed hard. Nodded. Couldn't do anything else.

Scarlet stirred against me, warm, heavier than I expected. Four years, and I'd never held her. Not once.

The weight of her undid me—wonder and devastation in equal measure. Samantha is fighting for her life behind sterile doors, and me standing here holding the child who bound us together, whether anyone else admitted it or not.

CRAIG

When Sinclair finally let us back, I steeled myself. I'd braced for bad, but nothing prepared me for the sight of Samantha.

Her face was swollen, mottled with purple and blue. One eye sealed shut, her jaw set unnaturally tight beneath a gauze wrapping. Dried blood crusted at the corner of her mouth, and bruises marbled the line of her throat. Tubes and monitors kept a steady rhythm around her, but the stillness of her body made her look less like the woman I knew and more like a shell left behind.

She didn't look like herself. She looked broken.

361

For a moment, I couldn't breathe.

Drusilla asked questions with her usual precision—what her oxygen levels were, how much blood she'd lost, how long she'd remain in the coma. Calm on the surface, her tone cool, but I saw her knuckles blanch around the bedrail. For all her steel, she was rattled. Samantha had been brutalized. Not an accident. Not a fall. Rage had done this. Controlled in some ways, savage in others.

And I knew the pattern.

The ribs. The head wound. The blood loss. Whoever did this hadn't stopped until they stripped her down to bone and breath. My chest clenched with a memory I could never shake— my mother at the bottom of the stairs, blood pooling like ink across the wood, Alex kneeling beside her, his young face twisted with something I didn't want to name. Jerome had pointed the finger at me, painted me as the monster. I'd carried that stain for decades.

Now here was Samantha. Nearly destroyed, likely the same monster.

By the time we returned to the waiting area, Drusilla had retightened the mask. Scarlet was dozing in Marcus's arms, her curls pressed into his shoulder. For once, he looked like he belonged there. Maybe he did.

Marcus stood when he saw us, ready to demand his turn. I stepped into his path.

"Dru, go ahead. I need to ask Marcus something."

She gave me a look but didn't argue, sweeping outside to wait for her husband.

I turned back to Marcus and held out my arms. "I'll take her. She'll be safe at the manor tonight."

He hesitated, like handing her over cost him something physical. Then slowly, reluctantly, he shifted Scarlet into my arms. She stirred but settled quickly against me, small and warm, the only innocent thing in all of this.

Marcus's voice was hoarse. "Well?"

"Do you think this was Alexander?" My words were low, but they landed hard.

He blinked, like the thought hadn't solidified until I said it aloud. "Things had been going well for them, right? Why would you suspect?"

"Because my brother always snaps at some point." My tone was even, but inside I burned. "Do you know if they were arguing last night at all?"

"Not that I know of. They were both upset about Jerome wanting to send Scarlet off to Japan with you."

"Can't say that I blame them." I gave a humorless laugh. "It's a ridiculous notion, but Dru was sent abroad very young for similar reasons."

Marcus's jaw flexed. "Did Jerome cause this? Did his plan to send her away—break up that little girl's world—push Alex over the edge?"

Across the room, a detective leaned in close to Sinclair at the nurses' station. My stomach turned. This was already moving past family whispers.

"A detective is talking to Sinclair," I told Marcus quietly. "My guess is it's about Samantha. If you hear anything, let me know. Please."

His face softened just enough for me to believe he meant it when he said, "First call I'll make."

We shook hands—two men bound by the same wreckage, but in different ways. Marcus hadn't yet learned the other truth: once the family marked you as weak, you never got free—unless you forced open the cage.

Marcus looked like he wanted to say more, but Scarlet stirred, her little hand tightening in my jacket as if she knew the tension was about her too. I adjusted her against me, holding her closer. Such a petite girl for her age.

"She'll be safe with me," I said firmly. "At the manor. Jerome will want an update, and Drusilla's already in the car."

His jaw tightened at the name, but he only nodded. He didn't have the power to stop me, and we both knew it.

I turned, carrying Scarlet out into the cold night air. Through the glass doors, I saw Marcus sink back into his chair, his shoulders bowed. He looked every bit like the man left behind.

Drusilla was waiting curbside, calm restored, though her eyes flicked instantly to the bundle in my arms. I settled Scarlet into her lap, and only then did she exhale, like control returned with possession.

Jerome would want answers. And I would give him the facts. But the picture of Samantha—bandaged, bloodied, swollen beyond recognition—was one I would carry into that room with me. Because even in this family, there were things no amount of power could disguise.

MARCUS

I watched Craig walk Scarlet out, her little hand tucked into the crook of his arm, Drusilla waiting in the car. The lobby felt too quiet without her. For the first time all day, I let myself sit, collecting what was left of my composure.

That's when Dr. Sinclair reappeared.

"She's stable," he said, voice calm but lined at the edges. "We're moving her to the ICU. You'll have to wait until she's transferred before you can see her."

Wait. The word thudded in my skull.

I nodded, but the second he turned away, I was on my feet, pacing. The sterile hum of the vending machines filled the silence, every second stretching longer than it had a right to. The ICU doors swung open and shut, swallowing other families while I stayed stranded on the wrong side of the line.

How long was I supposed to sit here, useless?

Her hand still burned in my memory, limp, cold. If words could reach her in that coma, someone who actually loved her should be there to speak them.

When an orderly pushed a bed through, the door stuck open wider than usual. No one stopped me. My feet carried me forward, past the signs warning "Authorized Personnel Only."

A nurse caught sight of me in the corridor, brows pulling tight. For a second, I thought she'd call me out, send me back to the waiting area. But then her eyes softened, the faintest nod toward the room where Samantha had been wheeled. She let me pass.

The ICU was worse than the ER, whispered worry and hopeful dread. Machines hummed, lights blinked, everything measured in heartbeats and oxygen flow.

And then I saw her.

Samantha lay pale against the sheets, her face swollen beyond recognition. One eye swollen shut, gauze wrapped around her head. Dark bruises marked her throat and arms like fingerprints no one could scrub away.

I lowered myself into the chair at her side, slid my hand under hers, and felt the faint warmth of her skin. Thank God there is warmth.

"Alex went too far this time," I muttered, low enough for only her to hear.

A girl in a candy-striper uniform poked her head in. "Sir, you can talk to her. My brother was in a coma—doctors told us talking helps, even if they can't respond."

I nodded, and she slipped out as quickly as she came. My throat burned. I bent close.

"I love you, Sam. I can't lose you. Not again."

The door opened behind me. I turned—and there was Alex.

"What the hell are you doing here?" he snapped.

"Checking on her," I shot back, pulling my hand away from Samantha. "Where the hell were you?"

He frowned. "How did you hear about it?"

"I stayed at the manor last night. Jerome and I worked late. Drusilla called."

Alex looked unsettled but pressed, "Have they figured out what happened?"

"Dru said it looked like a break-in. Guess she startled them. They beat her badly. Did you talk to the doctor?"

I bit the inside of my cheek because I knew damn well what had happened. It wasn't strangers. It was him. No break-in, no intruders. Just Alexander finally snapping the way we all knew he would.

"That doc was questioning me like I had something to do with it. Bastard. I wasn't even home."

"Alex, they always question the spouse first. It's part of the procedure." I stood, giving him space. "I should leave you with your wife. Call the manor or me, if anything changes. Jerome will want updates."

"Are you still going hunting with us this weekend?" he asked, too casual, like Samantha wasn't lying broken in front of him.

"Doubtful there will be a trip..." I said tightly. "Your wife is in a coma. I don't think anyone should be going anywhere..."

"I think you underestimate us," he sneered. "If she's in a coma, she'll never miss us. Dru can check in. Might be the perfect way to blow off some steam."

My jaw clenched. "We'll see, Alex." I brushed past him, forcing calm I didn't feel. He was too detached. Too cold. If Samantha survived, it wouldn't be because of him. It would be in spite of him.

I left the ICU, the smell of antiseptic still burning my throat, and pushed through the hospital's sliding doors. The cold air slapped me hard, a sharp contrast against the warmth of the day before.

I wasn't drifting aimlessly. Not this time.

I was going back to the manor, back to Jerome, my father.

JEROME

Craig and Drusilla had only just left, their voices still echoing faintly in the corridor beyond the study. They'd given me the facts, the shape of things as the doctors presented them. I weighed it all in silence, scotch untouched, the familiar command of the room pressing heavier than usual.

The door opened again.

Marcus.

Not storming like Alexander, not pacing or trembling. Composed. Razor sharp. On mission.

"Marcus," I said evenly, gesturing toward the chair across from me. "Come in."

He stepped inside but didn't sit. His eyes never left mine.

"You did this."

I said nothing. Met his gaze.

"If she dies, the blood is on your hands too." His voice was controlled, but the strain bled through, taut as wire. "If she makes it through, you will never put her in danger again. Never."

My jaw tightened, a small bristle breaking through the mask. "Alexander was always going to snap. None of us could have imagined it would go to this degree."

Marcus took a step closer, his voice low but unyielding. "Jerome, she will never be knowingly put in danger again. Even if you don't care about Samantha, I know you care about Scarlet. And she needs her mother safe."

For the first time in years, my facade wavered. Only a fraction— but enough.

I exhaled slow, deliberate, each word carrying weight.

"Samantha will never be in danger again. Of that, you have my word."

He held my gaze a beat longer, then turned and left, the echo of his steps sharp against the marble.

When the study door clicked shut, silence pressed in. My hand closed around the untouched glass, the amber catching firelight. For once, the ritual didn't soothe. It sickened. With a sharp snap of my wrist, I hurled the glass into the fireplace. Crystal shattered against stone, shards scattering across the hearth. Scotch hissed in the embers, a bitter vapor rising.

The vow sat in my chest heavier than the wreckage at my feet. I had not said the words to reassure Marcus. I had said them because they were true. I was complicit in this ruin, though unintentionally so.

The door eased open again, so quiet I almost missed it. Sampson. He paused on the threshold, his eyes flicking once to the shards glittering on the floor. No words passed. He disappeared as silently as he'd come, returning with a brush and pan.

Precision defined his every movement—sweeping the glass, tending the hearth, restoring order without intrusion. He never glanced at me, never broke the rhythm of his work. When he was finished, he carried the fragments out and closed the door with the same quiet efficiency.

Alone again, I let out a breath I hadn't realized I was holding. I was grateful—not just for the cleanup, but for the discretion of a man who had always known who he worked for, and what to ignore.

ALEXANDER

The machines clicked, hissed, breathed for her. I sat in the hard chair by her bed, seeing nothing of my beautiful wife. She looks like someone who went a few rounds with death. I did this to her.

God, Sammie... I hadn't meant to hurt you like this. Not like this.

My hand hovered above hers, finally settling over her fingers. Cold. Too cold. I squeezed lightly, whispering into the stillness.

"I lost control. I know that. I justified it—told myself it was your fault, Marcus's fault, anyone's fault but mine. But it shouldn't have been you, Sammie. It should never have been you."

Her face was swollen, gauze wrapping her head, one eye sealed shut beneath bruises. It hurt to look at her, but I couldn't look away.

"I was angry," I murmured, my voice trembling then sharpening. "Angry at him. Always him. Circling. Watching you. Wanting you. I told you he was poison, didn't I? I told you."

I leaned closer, my words spilling, hot and frantic.

"You don't need to worry anymore. I'll fix this. Marcus won't be a problem, not after the hunting trip. Hunting season, guns everywhere—accidents happen. Even happened to a Vice President, remember? No one would ever question it. One shot. Clean. He's out of our lives."

My thumb brushed the back of her hand, tender and obsessive in the same breath.

"Once he's gone, you're safe. Scarlet's safe. We all are. I'll never hurt you again. Just the three of us. Family, whole, unbreakable. Sammie, wake up, I'll fix everything."

I bent closer, my lips grazing her temple, lingering on the edge of prayer and threat.

"I love you. I'll always love you. Enough to do whatever it takes."

The machines hummed on, indifferent to my vow.

I stood, every joint stiff, my chest tight with the storm I'd swallowed back down. I brushed her hair from her bandaged forehead one last time, then forced myself toward the door.

The hallway's fluorescent lights burned too bright after the dim hush of her room. I nearly walked straight into Sinclair.

He steadied his clipboard, his expression composed but not unkind. "Mr. Devereux. She's stable for now. We'll keep monitoring the swelling, but she's holding."

I gave a sharp nod, my voice rough. "Thank you."

He hesitated, adjusted his glasses, then added carefully, "I'm sorry for your loss."

The words hit like a rifle shot. I blinked, my throat going dry. "Loss?"

His gaze flickered, measured. "The pregnancy. We couldn't save it."

I froze. The words hollowed me out, gutted me where I stood. My mind scrambled, refusing to process. "I didn't... I didn't know."

Sinclair inclined his head, tone even but weighted. "I thought you should."

I turned away, the floor tilting under me. My lungs wouldn't fill, each breath scraping raw. By the time I pushed through the sliding doors, the night air felt like knives.

Shock gave way to grief, grief to a burn that spread through my chest until I thought it might tear me in half.

A child. My child. Gone before I even knew about it.

And then the grief twisted, sharper, darker. Marcus. If he hadn't been circling her, whispering doubts, stealing her loyalty, would she even have been pushed this far? Would we have fought at all?

The hollow inside me hardened into something jagged.

This wasn't just a loss. This was theft.

And Marcus would pay for it.

DR. ELI SINCALIR

I flipped through her chart, scanning the latest labs, vitals, and imaging notes. Hemoglobin holding steady after transfusion, intracranial pressure controlled. Sedation deepened to keep her from fighting the ventilator.

Then the brutal text of the trauma summary. My God, whoever did this to her was a monster.

Extensive facial injuries: left orbit swollen shut, ecchymosis spreading across the cheek like spilled ink; nasal bridge fractured and splinted; jaw reduced but grotesquely swollen with edema; scalp laceration stapled along the occiput. A face distorted by trauma, mottled with every shade of damage the

375

human body can muster.

Thoracic injuries: multiple left-sided rib fractures, some displaced; pulmonary contusion; shallow ventilation thanks only to the cricothyrotomy we'd placed.

Abdominal and pelvic trauma: blunt-force impact severe enough to shear vessels; internal bleeding that took her uterus and her pregnancy with it; emergent hysterectomy performed before she coded on the table again. Tissue notes say "non-viable" and "catastrophic" in the same sentence, words you never want to write. You certainly never want to say them aloud.

Occipital fracture with mild edema. Contusions trailing along the zygomatic arch and mastoid. Soft tissue swelling everywhere it shouldn't be. Internal bleeding controlled post-op. Ribs stabilized, airway secured, and vitals stable.

The monitors hummed their steady lullaby, machines doing the work her body wasn't strong enough for. Samantha Devereux was alive, but only just.

I adjusted the IV line and glanced up—someone in the corridor. Not family. Broader shoulders, olive skin, a cop's stance even before he pulled the badge.

"Excuse me, sir," I said, my voice clipped. "She needs rest. No more visitors tonight."

"She's in a coma," he answered, tone dry, edged with authority. "That's restful, isn't it?"

"Sir—"

"It's Detective." He flipped the badge. "Ciro DiSanti. I'll stay as long as necessary."

I held his gaze a beat, then nodded slightly. "Dr. Sinclair." I tugged my glasses up the bridge of my nose. "If you're investigating, start with the man who just left this room."

His brows lifted. "You're saying—?"

"I'm saying what I can." My tone softened, but I let the edge stay in my eyes. "Her injuries are consistent with blunt-force trauma, controlled and deliberate. Not random. Not a stumble. North Carolina law obligates me to report suspected domestic violence, and I've already done so. You'll have my statement on record."

His jaw tightened. "So you believe—"

"I don't state beliefs, Detective. I treat wounds. And these wounds," I let my hand drift toward the chart, "don't lie. This was unfettered rage."

He absorbed that in silence.

I sighed, lowering my voice. "This isn't the first time I've treated her. Years ago—different excuses—but I saw the pattern then, too. Tonight confirmed what I suspected back then."

DiSanti's gaze sharpened, but I lifted a hand before he pressed further. "That's all I'll say without a subpoena. You'll know where to find me when you have one."

I stepped past him, chart tucked against my chest, irritation prickling under my calm. HIPAA might gag me from speaking freely, but the report was filed. The law would force its way in now, as it should.

And as I walked toward my rounds, one thought gnawed at me: if this family closed ranks the way I'd seen them do before, Samantha might survive the beating—only to be buried alive in silence.

THE DETECTIVE

It had been two days, and the subpoena was still pending. Judges hesitated when the name Devereux was stamped across the top of a file. Too much reach. Too much money. But whispers already pointed in one direction: Jerome Devereux's son.

I stood outside the ICU, waiting for Alexander to emerge.

And while I waited, the memory of the crime scene details replayed.

378

The house had stunk of rage. Not just the metallic tang of dried blood, but of a violence that wanted to mark every surface. Bloody handprints smeared along the hall, the child's door, and the frame of the living room. Furniture wasn't looted—it was shredded. Robbery wasn't the motive.

I'd pulled a small vial of cotton balls from my pocket, vinegar stinging my nose—my grandfather's trick, better than Vicks—to keep from gagging.

Cataloging details: the alarm is unset. Rear doors locked. Windows sealed. Entry wasn't forced. Someone had been let in—or never left.

The photos stopped me cold. Dozens of the little girl. A handful of Samantha. None—none—of her with Alexander. Not even a wedding photo. A man proud of his family made damn sure there were portraits. The absence said as much as the blood.

And that blood—caked into the floorboards where she'd been found—told its own story. She'd tried to crawl. Tried to reach her child. Whoever attacked her hadn't been a stranger. They knew the house. They knew her.

Rage, yes. But rage sharpened by control.

And that narrowed the pool to one name already pounding in my head: Alexander Devereux.

The ICU door clicked, pulling me back. Alexander stepped out, face set, movements taut as a wire.

"Mr. Devereux—a word."

"Who the hell are you?" His tone was pure disdain.

"Detective Ciro DiSanti." I offered a hand; he ignored it. "I'm investigating what happened at your home."

"Then find the bastard who did this to my wife. Breaking in, locking up a child, destroying property—what were they thinking?"

I watched him carefully. The words were right, but the delivery was off. No grief. No fear. Just deflection. In a few clipped sentences, he told me more than he realized.

* * * * * * *

Two weeks later, she still hadn't woken. The medically induced coma had ended days ago, but Samantha lingered somewhere between worlds. Sinclair's updates were always the same: no swelling, no bleed, scans clear. Her body was healing. Nothing medical stood in the way.

She simply hadn't chosen to wake.

The subpoena had finally been signed—allegedly at Jerome Devereux's request. A man covering tracks, or a man playing a longer game? Either way, I'd have access to records. What I'd already gleaned painted an ugly picture: head trauma, multiple fractures, internal bleeding, pregnancy loss. A hysterectomy. She'd never carry another child.

Early interviews with staff and neighbors only reinforced the picture: Samantha had been known as a warm, attentive mother. Gentle with her daughter. Kind in ways that stood out against the Devereux reputation. And now she was reduced to this—a broken body behind sterile glass, denied the choice of more children. Shame burned at the edges of the report, even though it wasn't mine to carry.

This wasn't just violence. It was ruin.

I paced outside the ICU, restless. Forensics would drag. DNA, lab work, all of it. But I needed more than paper. I needed a witness, and the only one who'd been there was lying silent in that bed.

Or maybe not.

The door opened. A young man stepped in with a child in tow. I recognized him—Marcus Underwood, the family friend, from the night she came in. The little girl clung to his leg, wide-eyed and watchful. Scarlet.

"Excuse us," Marcus said quietly. "She just wanted to see her mother. Should we come back?"

The girl burrowed closer to him like she belonged there. His hand on her shoulder looked more paternal than anything I'd seen from Alexander.

"Do you think that's a good idea?" I asked carefully. "For the child?"

Marcus crouched. His voice gentled. "Little Ms. Scarlet here is on a hunger strike. Refuses to eat until she sees her mother." He smoothed her curls. "If Samantha wakes up and finds her daughter starved... there'll be hell to pay."

The girl finally spoke, tiny but firm. "I want Mommy."

I squatted down, making my voice soft. "Scarlet—that's a beautiful name. My name is Ciro. I'm a police officer, and I'm here to help your Mommy."

She giggled at the sound of my name, then leaned into Marcus. He nodded at me, granting permission without words.

"Scarlet," I asked gently, "can you tell me... do you remember when Mommy got hurt?"

She nodded. Whispered: "Daddy."

My ears sharpened. "Daddy?"

Her little mouth tightened. "Daddy was mad."

Frustration flickered across her face, like she'd said this before and no one listened. She huffed, louder now: "He said bedtime story and closed my door. Mommy was crying, but the door won't open. Then the fire truck took Mommy away."

Matter-of-fact. A child's mind piecing the unthinkable into simple cause and effect.

The air thinned. Marcus lifted her, carried her to the bed. She wriggled free just enough to set a small stuffed dog on Samantha's chest. "Patches will give her sweet dreams." Then she climbed carefully beside her mother, coached by Marcus to sit very still.

Scarlet nestled against Samantha, twirling her own hair, whispering nonsense to a woman who couldn't yet answer.

My gut twisted. The bruised woman, the loving child, the man who looked like he'd give his own arm to protect them—pieces falling into place, suspicion thickening.

Scarlet had given me something raw, unfiltered. A child's testimony wasn't courtroom-ready, but it was often the closest thing to the truth.

And I'd just heard the name of my prime suspect fall from a four-year-old's lips.

Daddy.

I straightened slowly, every detail etched sharp in my mind: her tone, her sequence of events, her lack of hesitation. Children didn't invent trauma. They repeated it.

And now I had enough to push harder. Not proof, not yet—but enough to argue for another warrant. Enough to start pulling at the threads of Alexander Devereux until the whole façade unraveled.

MARCUS

Her hand felt too light in mine. Scarlet perched on the edge of the bed, whispering to her mother about Christmas trees and presents, like Samantha might stir at any second and smile. My throat burned.

It hit me then—this was only one of a handful of times I had ever held Scarlet in my arms. All of them since Sam was rushed to the hospital. Not at her birth, not at a holiday or a quiet family dinner. Four years wasted on distance and secrets, while Alex played her father. And here she was, clinging to me like she knew. Like she saw something no one else did.

For a dangerous moment, I let myself imagine it: what it would be like if things had been different. Suppose she were mine, not just in blood or belief, but in truth. A family. Our family.

But the machines hummed on, indifferent. Samantha didn't stir. Scarlet rested her head against my chest, trusting me to be what I had never been allowed to be.

I bent close to Sam's ear, careful my voice didn't break.

"You have to come back to us. She needs you. I... I need you."

Scarlet tugged at my sleeve. "Uncle Marcus, can Mommy hear me?"

"Yes, sweetheart. She hears every word."

The little girl wriggled, voice stubborn. "Then tell her about the cookies."

I tried to smile, for her sake. "All right. Scarlet and Mrs. Keene made sugar cookies this week. She had flour all over her cheeks, proud as anything. But when she took a bite, she frowned and said, 'Mommy's are better.'"

Scarlet giggled softly at the memory, her curls brushing against Sam's arm.

I leaned closer to Samantha, letting the words spill low and steady. "She even roped Jerome and Sampson into cutting a few out. Can you imagine that? The old man and the butler in aprons, following her orders like she was queen of the kitchen. She has them all wrapped around her little finger."

Scarlet's small hand smoothed over her mother's blanket. "See, Mommy? You gotta wake up. Cookies are no good without you."

Her whisper was tiny, trembling. "Uncle Marcus... when will

Mommy wake up?"

I swallowed hard. "Soon, sweetheart." The lie scraped my throat. "Sometimes Mommies have to rest a long time when they're hurt. But she's strong. Stronger than anyone I know."

She considered that her brow furrowed the same way Sam's did when she was trying to solve a problem. "Did she get hurt 'cause of me?"

The question nearly broke me. "No," I said quickly, fiercely. "Never. You didn't do anything wrong. None of this is your fault."

Scarlet's eyes shimmered, but she nodded, leaning back into my chest.

I swallowed again, pressing my lips to Sam's knuckles. "She's right. Nothing is the same without you. Please... come back."

THE DETECTIVE

I lingered in the doorway, arms folded, watching the picture unfold. Scarlet curled into Marcus like she belonged there, his hand splayed across her back with the instinct of someone who'd done it a thousand times. Not an uncle's hold. Not a family friend's.

Something more.

And the way he bent over Samantha—gentle, reverent, whispering into the silence as if she might answer him—looked a hell of a lot more like a husband keeping vigil than a bystander.

I scuffed my shoe deliberately against the tile. He straightened fast, like a kid caught stealing from the cookie jar.

"Mr. Underwood, right?" My tone stayed even, conversational. "We crossed paths the night she was admitted."

His jaw flexed, but he nodded. "Yes."

"Remind me—what's your relation to Mrs. Devereux?" The question floated casual, but I didn't blink.

His throat worked. "Close to the family."

"Close how?" I tilted my head, letting silence do the work. "Cousin? In-law?"

The pause dragged. Too long. Finally: "Family."

Scarlet chimes in, "He's Uncle Marcus."

"Thank you for clearing that up, Ms. Scarlet." I considered her words and surveyed the man before me. "And yet that little one won't leave your side. And here you sit, hour after hour, like this is your cross to bear." My gaze slid between him and Samantha. "That's a lot of devotion for an uncle."

His eyes flashed. Defensive, but he swallowed it back.

I gave him a faint smile, nothing sharp. Professional warmth, just enough to set him off balance. "Don't worry, Mr. Underwood. I'm not here to pry where it doesn't matter." Then I leaned in slightly, let the weight drop. "But when it comes to what happened to Mrs. Devereux... everything matters."

I stepped back, let the words hang between us, then left him there with the machines.

The hallway felt colder when I stepped into it. My chest is tight, heavier than I wanted to admit. I'd seen Samantha's chart. Skull fracture, broken ribs, internal bleeding, hysterectomy forced by the damage—at twenty-seven years old, her chance for more children was ripped away. The family reiterated that she was a devoted mother who lived for her little girl.

Which made this uglier. Crueler.

The house had already told me its story—rage on the walls, control in every strike. Now her body told me the rest. This wasn't random. This wasn't a stranger. Whoever did this wanted to silence her, maybe destroy her, but leave her just enough alive to keep her tethered here.

And the more I looked at Alexander Devereux, the more he fit that mold. The way he deflected. The way grief never shadowed his eyes. Why wasn't he the one caring for his child, bringing her to see her mother?

But Marcus—he was another problem entirely. Too close, too devoted, too entangled. He was hiding something, too. They all were. Everyone except the woman in that bed and the little girl clinging to her.

I pressed my palm flat to the cool wall. "She has to wake up," I muttered.

Because she was the only voice that could cut through the lies.

And then, I prayed. Not a church prayer, not a polished one. Just a man's plea.

Seven years ago, booze nearly stripped me of everything. Badge, future, soul. An old chief had dragged me into AA, into church, into fighting for something better. Since then, I'd done this job for one reason only: to protect the people who couldn't—or wouldn't—protect themselves.

I thought of my mother, her bruises, her silence, the day she never got back up. Thought of Scarlet whispering Daddy was mad.

"Don't let me fail her," I whispered to the wall.

Then I straightened, squared my shoulders, and walked on.

JEROME

Twenty days. That's how long Samantha had lingered between worlds while my granddaughter faced her first Christmas without her mother.

The hunting trip had been delayed, then cancelled. No one dared question it aloud—not with Samantha broken in a hospital bed—but I knew the truth. Alexander had pressed too hard, too fast. He wanted that trip. He wanted Marcus isolated, alone in the woods where accidents happen and questions fade. Perhaps he intended to target me as well. His plan was transparent, as his always were, rage outpacing wit.

And now Detective DiSanti circled closer every day. He prowled the manor grounds that afternoon, pulling staff aside, listening with that quiet intensity of his. He smelled blood in the water. He hadn't yet asked the question outright—Did Alexander do this to his wife?—but it was in his eyes. It was only a matter of time.

That was the weight on my shoulders when I heard it:

"Where the hell is he?"

Alexander's voice cracked through the house, too loud, too raw. Drunk.

The oak doors rattled as he stormed inside, reeking of bourbon.

"I want to see the man that fucked my wife, whose kid I've been raising! Come on, Marcus—I know you're here!"

Marcus shifted in his chair beside the fire, tense, but I raised a hand. "Stay. I'll deal with him."

Craig was already in the hall, trying to slow him down. "Alex, don't do this. Not here."

But Alexander shoved past him, spit flying. "Where is he, Dad? I want the bastard now!"

Then the knife flashed. He drove me against the library door, steel biting shallow into my neck.

"I'll kill you and Marcus to take back what's mine," he hissed, breath hot with whiskey. "I'll kill that little girl and end your line. Shove you down the stairs like my mother. Samantha is mine."

Pathetic. Unhinged. Yet in his eyes, something rawer: grief. "I lost my child. My child," he choked, half-rage, half-confession.

"You'll lose everything," I spat. "You are weak. Weak men always resort to violence."

He drew back for the plunge—

—and the crackle of a Taser split the air.

Alexander's body seized, then crumpled, knife clattering across marble.

Detective DiSanti stepped from the shadowed corridor, Taser raised, the sergeant at his side. "Secure him."

The officer rolled him, cuffed him, and searched his leg. Came up with a snub-nose .38 strapped to his calf.

DiSanti's voice was calm, but his eyes were knives. "You took a hell of a risk standing him down, Mr. Devereux."

I pressed my hand to the sting at my throat, blood smearing my cuff. "My son craves attention. And approval. He wouldn't shoot me."

Marcus and Craig appeared in the doorway, faces pale as they watched Alexander being dragged away.

I sank into my chair at last, finally lifting the glass I'd ignored. The scotch burned, steadying.

"I told you she would never be in danger again, Marcus" I said, my voice iron. "He assaulted me, confessed to his mother's death, and nearly murdered Samantha. The girls are safe. For now."

Through the window, the December sky hung gray and cold. I turned my chair toward it, letting my sons see only my back.

I swirled the scotch in my glass, the ice catching the firelight. Marcus and Craig still lingered, pale in the doorway.

"Go," I said simply. "Both of you. I've had enough theatrics for one afternoon."

They hesitated, then they left, the heavy doors closing behind them.

Silence settled.

I leaned back in the chair, the sting at my throat reminding me how close steel had come. Alexander's words rang sharper than the blade. Your wife... I pushed her.

Elizabeth.

For years, I had allowed the word accident to stand. It was cleaner, more palatable for the family, for the world. But I think I had always known it was Alexander. My son's temper had driven her down those stairs. Her blood on the marble, her eyes wide with betrayal—he'd killed her as surely as if he'd held the knife he threatened me with.

And yet, for all his bluster, he would never kill Scarlet. He might rage, he might break Samantha, but not that child. Even Alexander wasn't capable of extinguishing his only tether to the family's future.

Still, the thought hardened in me: Samantha would never again be left vulnerable to him. Not in my house. Not under my name. If her wishes aligned with safety, she would have them. If they didn't, I would decide. It was protection, yes, but protection on my terms.

I raised the glass, scotch curling like memory. Elizabeth had been lost to me through his rage. Samantha would not be.

Not while I breathed.

ALEXANDER

The cuffs bit deep into my wrists, metal grinding against bone. Hands shoved me down the steps, through the front door, into the cold air that hit like a slap. I stumbled, head still twitching from the jolt of the Taser.

The patrol car loomed. They forced me inside, a steel cage, a glass partition. My chest heaved like I'd run miles.

What have I done?

The thought spun, jagged. The knife. My father's throat. His eyes—sneering, daring me. For a moment, it hadn't even felt like a choice. Rage had moved through me, unstoppable.

I slammed my head back against the glass, breath fogging the window. Scarlet's laugh rose unbidden, bright, then warped into her cry. My baby girl. I'd threatened my baby girl.

She's yours, I told myself, clinging hard. She calls you Daddy. She runs to you, not him. That's the only truth that matters.

Sam's face flickered—the hospital bed, her skin pale and broken, lips moving in pain. Those eyes. Wide with horror.

She'll never forgive me.

The thought came back hard, slicing deep. And then another followed, colder, steadier: She already left you. You saw it. The way she looked at him. The way he looked at her. Marcus.

My hands curled, cuffs biting deeper. Marcus thinks he can take her, take Scarlet, steal the life I built. But he won't. I'll tear him out of it before I ever let that happen.

And Jerome—my father, my judge, my executioner. He'd invited the detective in, let him see me fall. He'd sided with Marcus, chosen him over me. The betrayal burned hotter than the Taser ever could.

Marcus and Jerome. Both of them. They'll pay.

The words churned in me, not whispers, not voices—just my own thoughts, discordant and relentless, overlapping until they sounded like truth.

Scarlet is mine. Samantha is mine. Whatever it takes. Whatever it costs.

My throat worked, the same words circling, heavy as stone. What have I done?

And somewhere inside, the answer: Only what had to be done. And more to come.

CHAPTER TWENTY-SIX

Ashes of the Phoenix

"The boundaries which divide Life from Death are at best shadowy and vague."

DR. MIRIAM PATEL

We gathered in the small consultation room—too bright, too polished, the kind of space designed to soften blows that never softened. I set the chart down carefully, aware of the faces waiting for me: Jerome Devereux, composed; Drusilla, arms folded with that air of calculation; Craig, silent, watchful; and Marcus, his posture tight, eyes restless.

"It has been twenty-one days since Mrs. Devereux was admitted," I began. "Her body has stabilized. Her fractures are healing, her vitals are steady. But neurologically..." I exhaled. "She remains unresponsive. She came off sedation almost two weeks ago, and yet she hasn't woken. Medically, there is no reason she should not."

Craig's jaw twitched. Drusilla only tilted her head, waiting. Jerome's gaze stayed fixed on me like I was giving testimony under oath.

"This is what we call a prolonged disorder of consciousness," I continued. "It may resolve, but we cannot predict when. Days, weeks, months—or longer. At this stage, we recommend transfer to a long-term care facility. They're equipped for extended monitoring and rehabilitation attempts. It will be safer than keeping her in acute care indefinitely."

The word facility hung in the air. Clean. Professional. Final.

I paused, giving them the space to respond. "We'll, of course, respect the family's wishes. But I have to be clear—the longer she remains unresponsive, the more uncertain recovery becomes. A specialized facility would give her the best chance to stabilize long-term."

Jerome finally nodded once, dismissing me as neatly as one closes a book. Drusilla's lips pressed into the shape of agreement. Craig's hands tightened on the armrest of his chair, but he said nothing.

I gathered the chart, left them to it. The decision was theirs now.

MARCUS

The word facility hit like a hammer. A neat word for exile. For giving up. For locking her away where she couldn't be reached.

She had survived Alexander. She had survived all of it. And now they wanted to tuck her into a sterile place with strangers because it was easier?

I watched Jerome's face as the old man dismissed the medical staff. Watched Drusilla's cool calculation, even as she cloaked it in practicality. To them, Sam was an asset, a responsibility.

To me, she was... everything.

I flexed my hands behind my back, jaw tight. If she went to the estate, at least she would stay close. But if Jerome controlled who got in, who she saw... She'd never get free.

And yet Jerome always left the door open for me. Why? I was useful as counsel, sure, but there were plenty of other lawyers, more experienced ones, who could do the work. I was his bastard son. Only the family knew for certain, and still Jerome let me orbit close. Encouraged it.

Jerome and Drusilla had worked before to put Sam and me on a collision course. Would we have ever crossed the line if they hadn't orchestrated access? Was this round two? A second push?

The thought made me restless. Because underneath the strategy, underneath the unspoken arrangements, was the gnawing truth: I may never talk to her again. I may never hold her again. She may never hold Scarlet again.

Her daughter. My daughter. The lines blurred, bent, tangled. None of it mattered right now.

What mattered was that Samantha woke up. That her eyes opened, her voice returned, that Scarlet would not be left with only memory.

I bent my head slightly, as if willing her to hear me in whatever quiet place she had gone. Please, Sam. Wake up.

DRUISILLA

Dr. Patel's words still lingered in the air—clean, clinical, and suffocating facility.

I folded my arms, careful with my tone when I finally spoke. "It makes sense," I said evenly, almost sympathetic. "She would have round-the-clock care. Specialists. The right environment for recovery."

But what I didn't say pressed heavier than what I did. Outsiders. Nurses with loose tongues. Orderlies who liked to gossip. Reporters who always seemed to circle tragedy like vultures. Samantha in a facility meant questions. Speculation. And the Devereux name could not afford speculation.

Still, I hated the thought. That young woman—lying pale among machines and strangers, stripped of dignity, of protection. Samantha had proven herself over the years. She had obeyed when it was required, yielded when it was demanded, survived when many others would not have. She had been mother, wife, dutiful daughter-in-law. She had been grace itself, even when the bruises showed through. I respected that. Respected her.

My gaze shifted, unbidden, to Marcus. The way he hovered restless in his chair, jaw tight, as though sheer force of will might rouse her. His eyes never left her name on the chart, on the doctor's lips, on the silence that followed. He loved her. There was no mistaking it. And I was certain Jerome would never allow that love to tip the balance.

Jerome sat across from me, his face carved from marble, but I knew him too well. He was already calculating. Facility or estate. Risk or control. Which story would play better, which optics would cost less.

I smoothed the silk of my sleeve, voice quiet, measured. "Perhaps the manor is the better choice. Family close, children close. Outsiders kept at a distance." I let my eyes rest on Jerome's for a beat. "We cannot allow whispers. Not now."

Jerome's nod was the faintest thing—approval, or acknowledgment, or both.

Marcus's jaw clenched, his silence louder than words.

And I thought of Samantha again, her pale face beneath hospital lights, her daughter's curls pressed to Marcus's shoulder. For a flicker of a moment—rare, dangerous—I envied her. Even broken, she was the axis we all revolved around.

CRAIG

"Facilities like that... they can even start therapy," I said, my voice rougher than I wanted. "Muscle work. Stretching. So she's not—" The word stuck, jagged in my throat. Unresponsive. I forced it out more softly. "So when she wakes up, she won't have to fight as hard to walk again."

The room went still. I kept my eyes on the polished table, not on Jerome's calculating stare or Marcus's restless hands.

Inside, my thoughts were louder. Scarlet needed her mother. Not just alive—present. Protecting. Grounding. That girl had a fire in her, but fire without oxygen burned out quick.

I swallowed hard and leaned back, letting silence swallow my words.

JEROME

"A facility." I rolled the word on my tongue, tasting its weakness. "No. That will not do at all."

A facility meant papers, charts, and strangers with loose lips. It meant whispers sliding through town like smoke, speculation about Alexander, about the family name. Outsiders already sniffed around my house—I would not give them reason to sniff deeper.

Samantha was a Devereux now, bound by name and duty, and

she would recover under my roof. My doctors. My staff. My control.

I let the silence lengthen until it bent, everyone waiting. "She comes home," I said finally. My tone was iron, the same tone I used to seal contracts and crush opposition.

Drusilla inclined her head, a small concession. Craig's jaw tightened, though he said nothing. Marcus... Marcus's eyes burned with something he tried to leash. I filed that away.

"The solarium beyond the ballroom will be converted," I continued. "Plenty of light, private enough to keep her recovery contained. The children are never in that wing except for events. It will keep Scarlet from seeing too much, too soon."

Drusilla folded her hands, voice careful. "And the gala?"

"Cancelled." The word landed like stone. "If someone doesn't understand, they don't belong in our ranks. And everyone will understand. You will see to it."

Her nod was sharp. "I'll handle communications. Guests will be encouraged to attend the spring garden party instead."

I turned to Craig. "Begin arrangements. Equipment. Specialists. Spare no expense. I want the best therapist available brought here—quietly."

His answer was a single nod, the sort of obedience I expected.

My gaze shifted back to Drusilla. "Fetch the attending. Now."

When the physician entered, still clutching her chart, I didn't bother with pleasantries. "You will prepare a complete report on what will be required for her recovery before she wakes— and after. Spare me your hedging. I want specifics."

She swallowed, nodded quickly, and retreated with her orders.

I leaned back, steepling my fingers. "We will close ranks. We will control the story. Samantha will return to us, and the family will appear intact. Strong. Untouched."

Privately, I wondered if she'd ever forgive the world she'd been bound into. But forgiveness was not required. Survival was. And under my roof, survival was the only option.

MARCUS

The walk from the conference room to Samantha's room was quiet, each of us wrapped in our own calculations. Craig's shoulders were set like stone, Drusilla's heels crisp against the tile, Jerome's silence heavier than anything he might have said aloud.

At least she would be safe now. Whatever else Jerome was, he would make sure of that. Security would be doubled, staff already loyal would rally around her, and Scarlet could see her mother without layers of red tape and restrictions. It was a cage,

403

yes—but a gilded one. And it was closer to freedom than exile in some sterile facility.

Jerome broke the silence first, his voice cutting through the hum of machines. "Be sure the solarium retains a feeling of home. Not this clinical aspect. Bright. Flowers."

The words landed, wrong, sharp in my ears. Before I could stop myself, I cut in. "No flowers. Sam hates cut flowers."

All three of them turned toward me—Jerome, Drusilla, Craig—like I'd spoken in a foreign tongue.

"Cut flowers remind her of funeral homes," I said more quietly. My hand had settled over hers without my even realizing it. "She likes orchids. Things that are still alive. Don't surround her with death."

No sense pretending anymore. The board Jerome loved so much—the game he thought he controlled—had been overturned, the pieces scattered. We weren't playing the old rules anymore.

And then—movement. The faintest twitch against my palm.

I froze. Did I imagine it? Then Drusilla gasped, sharp enough to snap all of us forward.

Her eyes.

Her eyelids dragged open like heavy curtains, gaze drifting unfocused, catching on nothing at first, lost as though she were wandering back from some distant dream.

Her lips moved, cracked, raw, but the whisper rose. A single word. "Scarl..."

I bent close, heart hammering. "She's safe, Sam. With Genevieve. She's safe."

Her lashes trembled, eyes shifting sluggishly, searching, trying to anchor. Another breath, another word, thinner than air. "...Al...?"

Jerome's voice cut in, calm but too controlled. "Jail. Alexander is in jail."

Finally, her gaze found me. And then—fingers tightening, the barest squeeze, fragile as a bird struggling to take flight.

Her mouth formed one word, faint, almost a sigh. "Y...you."

Relief. Not for Jerome's decree. Not for her husband's absence. For me.

The heat rose behind my eyes before I could stop it. I swallowed hard, forcing myself to stay steady, not to break in front of her.

No one spoke. Not Craig. Not Drusilla. Not Jerome. The room seemed to hold its breath.

Jerome's expression didn't flicker, his posture carved from marble, as if he had expected this outcome all along. He gave no sign of approval, no sign of censure—just quiet observation, absorbing the truth as part of his ledger.

Whatever passed between Samantha and me in that moment, Jerome wouldn't interfere. Not now. Perhaps not ever.

Drusilla's hand darted to the call button, her voice cutting sharp into the silence. "She's awake."

DR. MIRIAM PATEL

The call light was flashing before the words reached me. She's awake. I was already moving, chart forgotten, stethoscope bouncing against my chest.

When I entered, the room was too crowded—family pressing in, emotions suffocating the air. I motioned them back with a sharp hand. "Give her space."

Her eyelids fluttered open, heavy, reluctant. Pupils sluggish, but reactive. The faintest rasp of sound clung to the oxygen around her lips.

"Mrs. Devereux, can you hear me?" I leaned close, voice steady, measured.

Her throat worked. A dry swallow. Then—broken, fragile—
"...y...ye..."

Not much, as expected. "Don't force it. I'm Dr. Patel, my team has you."

I checked her pupils again, swept her vitals, signaling for a nurse. "Let's get neuro on standby, order a swallow screen, and page respiratory to reassess support. Labs too." My voice was brisk, but my pulse quickened. Twenty-one days of silence and now—this.

SAMANTHA

Light pressed against my eyelids—bright, searching. Shapes loomed, blurred at the edges. For days... weeks... I'd floated, half-hearing voices, half-dreaming Scarlet's laugh, Marcus's whisper, Alex's anger. The machines had been my lullaby.

Now the voices were louder. Too loud. Someone—steady, unfamiliar—cut through them.

"Mrs. Devereux, can you hear me?"

I tried to nod, but my body felt heavy, leaden. My lips cracked as I forced them to move. "...yes."

The effort tore me raw. But I was here. I'd been here all along, listening, waiting.

Through the haze, I felt it—warmth against my hand. A grip, trembling but real. Marcus. He'd been talking to me in the dark. And Jerome's voice, too, lower, commanding. Drusilla's clipped tone. Craig's steadiness.

But Scarlet. Always Scarlet. Her chatter, her giggle, her cries. The weight of her little body curled against me in dreams that felt too vivid to be only dreams.

I tried to ask for her. Tried to say her name. My lips shaped the beginning: "Scarl—" but the word withered on the dryness of my tongue.

Hands adjusted my oxygen, voices called for tests. Too many sounds, too much light. But the important part was simple.

I was awake.

And I wasn't letting go.

MARCUS

The doctor's voice cut like a blade: "Out. All of you."

We shuffled back, the hall swallowing us while machines and clipped orders filled the room behind the door. A fury of motion, nurses darting in and out, Patel steady at the center.

But none of that mattered. Not compared to the truth I'd just seen.

She was awake.

After twenty-one days of silence, of wondering if she'd ever come back—she hadn't given up. Not on herself, not on Scarlet.

Not on us.

I leaned against the wall, breath unsteady. My hand still tingled where hers had squeezed, fragile but deliberate. Proof she was still fighting.

Scarlet.

Should I tell her yet? That Mommy's eyes had opened, that she had whispered, that she was here again? Or would it be cruel, too soon, if the doctors tempered hope with caution?

I closed my eyes, pressing my palms into them until the stars burned.

She's awake. That was enough for now.

But the thought that lodged deep in my chest refused to move: Don't let them take this from her. Don't let them take her from Scarlet again.

CHAPTER TWENTY-SEVEN
The Weight of Survival

"He who has a why to live can bear almost any how."

DR. MIRIAM PATEL

The conference room smelled faintly of coffee, though it did not cut through the tension at the table. The Devereux family sat in silence as I set the chart down in front of me, tabs neatly ordered, test results highlighted.

"She is stable," I began. "Yesterday's awakening was the turning point we hoped for. Overnight, we ran a swallow study. Results were excellent for where she is in recovery, but not enough to remove the feeding tube. Neurologically, her responses are strong. No evidence of brain bleed or long-term impairment. Her memory seems intact, her speech will improve in time. These are all excellent signs."

Relief flickered around the table—quiet, but undeniable.

I continued, my tone measured. "That said, her recovery will be long. Multiple rib fractures, an occipital fracture, and surgical complications mean she will require extensive rehabilitation. Physical therapy for mobility, occupational therapy for daily activities, and psychological support given to the trauma she has endured."

The family nodded in understanding. I continued, "You should be prepared for slow progress with eating and speaking. Three weeks of airway support and facial injuries mean her swallowing is weak. She may only tolerate small amounts at first, such as, thickened liquids under supervised trials. It will take time before she can manage regular meals."

"How long before she can speak?" Drusilla inquired.

"Her voice will return gradually, but it will be limited. Soft. Hoarse. Fatigued. Between the cricothyrotomy and the jaw trauma, she won't be speaking in full sentences right away. Weeks, possibly longer, before her strength and coordination come back to her."

I met their eyes one by one. "This is a marathon. She's alive, and she is stable. Everything else will return in small, careful steps."

I let that settle before glancing at Jerome. His gaze was fixed on me, sharp, expectant.

"You asked for a full report on what would be required should she convalesce at your estate," I said evenly. "Here it is: she will need a hospital bed, lift equipment, railings, monitoring equipment, and full-time nursing support. Physical therapy should begin within days, even while she regains strength, and a speech therapist will be necessary for several weeks. She should not climb stairs and will need an accessible environment—somewhere bright, safe, and large enough for her therapy staff to work."

Drusilla's brow arched, already calculating. Craig leaned forward, hands clasped, listening with the intensity of a man memorizing every word. Marcus's eyes never left me.

Jerome folded his hands. "How long until she can come home?"

I paused, checking the final note. "Assuming no setbacks, ten days. That allows us to stabilize her nutrition, transition her to oral medications, and prepare her for discharge with appropriate care coordination. If your staff is ready, she can be transferred directly from here to your compound with medical support in place."

Jerome inclined his head, final as a gavel. "Then ten days it is."

No one argued. The decision, as always, landed like law.

MARCUS

The conference room emptied of doctors, leaving just the four of us and the echo of Patel's prognosis. Recovery was possible. Therapy was necessary. And for the first time in weeks, there was something like hope.

Everyone moved at once, slipping into roles the way only the Devereux clan could.

Drusilla was already making notes on her phone, her voice low but quick: calling caterers and florists would be replaced with contractors and suppliers. The gala could wait; optics would be reshaped around Samantha's recovery.

Craig leaned forward, his tone brisk, controlled. "The solarium can be converted within a week. I've already spoken with a physical therapist—they'll provide a list. I'll take care of the contractors, order the bed, and the monitoring systems. The wing can be closed off for privacy. When she's back, it'll feel like home. We can convert the ballroom parlor into a bedroom, she can see the children play from there."

Even Jerome—stone, immovable Jerome, wasn't arguing. He simply nodded once, giving his approval as if sealing a contract.

And me? I just sat there, watching them all assign themselves tasks with the efficiency of generals in a war room. Part of me burned—because I had no orders, no clear role, no way to fix this with contracts or equipment or signatures.

I swallowed, my voice quieter than I meant. "What do I need to do?"

Jerome dismissed the others with a flick of his hand. Drusilla swept out, already dictating messages into her phone. Craig left next, his stride purposeful.

That left just the two of us. Jerome's gaze fixed on me, steady, unblinking. His voice came stern, as immovable as the man himself.

"Support the woman you love. Protect and love my granddaughter. This is the start of a very long, hard road. It's about them, not you."

The words landed like stone. For once, I didn't argue.

I sat there in the heavy silence, the weight of his command settling deeper than I expected. Maybe it was twisted, maybe it was late—but it was the most fatherly thing he had ever said to me.

And this time, I wouldn't fail.

I would love her, but I wouldn't burden her with it. I would be steady, supportive. A friend she could trust. I wouldn't make the same mistake again—pressing my feelings when all she needed was someone she could lean on.

Later, in the corridor, I pulled out my phone. A promise was a promise. Genevieve picked up on the first ring.

"Well?" she asked, the word tight with worry.

"She's going to recover. The doctors are optimistic. Tests were better than we could have hoped." I breathe deep, "I can tell Scarlet, her mommy is awake."

I could hear her exhale, a rush of relief. "Thank God."

"I promised I'd call you with updates when I knew more," I added softly. "Now you know."

When I hung up, I stood there a long time with the phone still in my hand, the hallway quiet around me.

For the first time in weeks, I let myself believe it: Sam was coming back. And I'd be right where I should have been all along—steady beside her.

JEROME

She had refused all visitors for the last week.

Except Genevieve. And Marcus.

I was certain it was only because they always brought Scarlet with them.

I had stopped by every day. Sat in the waiting room, exchanged words with Patel or Sinclair, and read the reports that landed on my desk. But Samantha would not see me.

I carried the guilt I could not speak. Alexander had done the damage with his hands, but my pushing had set the board. I had played too close to the edge, and she had paid the price.

She was scheduled to transfer to the manor in three days. But today, like it or not, I would see her.

When I entered the room, Marcus sat beside her bed, hand wrapped firmly around hers. Scarlet was curled against her mother's side, fast asleep, her curls spilling across the pillow. One of her stuffed ponies—bigger than she was—lay wedged between them like a sentry.

Outwardly, I was still. Controlled. The mask I had cultivated over decades did not falter. But the set of my jaw betrayed me, and I knew Marcus saw it.

Inside, though, it was something else entirely. Relief first. Anger next. And then the bitter taste of recognition.

Marcus checked his watch, the motion almost apologetic. He leaned close to Samantha, his voice gentle. "I need to get Scarlet back before Mrs. Keene skins me alive. Dinner and bedtime wait for no one."

He squeezed her hand, then turned to the little girl curled at her mother's side. "Scarlet, time to wake up. We're going to see Mrs. Keene."

Scarlet blinked, rubbing her eyes, then grinned. "Mrs. K makes the best rolls."

Samantha's mouth curved into a faint smile—fragile, tired, but it reached her eyes at last. Not laughter. Not yet. But a sign.

Marcus coaxed Scarlet upright, steadying her as she clambered down. "Tell Mommy goodnight. Careful now."

Scarlet tiptoed back, pressing a small kiss to her mother's cheek. "Night-night, Mommy. Don't forget Patches."

Her voice was so light it nearly cracked me. Samantha whispered a response, hoarse and soft, but her gaze lingered on Marcus, following the line of his hand as he guided the child toward the door.

I watched them go—the gentleness, the ease, the devotion—and felt the truth settle in my bones. Marcus would never be a threat to her. But he might destroy himself in the way he loved her, in the way he loved them both.

When the door closed behind them, I lowered myself into the chair Marcus had vacated. Samantha turned her face toward me. The bruises had faded to pale shadows, the swelling around her eye nearly gone. Still, she blinked slowly, deliberate, as though every motion cost effort.

"She's a lovely child," I said into the quiet, my gaze settling back on Samantha.

Her gaze didn't waver, but no words came. Silence was its own answer.

So I sat with it, posture fixed, mask in place. Yet the weight inside me was harder to hold. She had seen it, I was certain my regret, plain enough to register even through her haze.

"I vow to always protect her and by extension you." It was as close to an apology as I could conjure. She blinked, reflex or recognition I could not be sure.

We stayed in that silence until the detective arrived.

THE DETECTIVE

A week had passed. Samantha was awake now—pale, thin, careful in every motion, but awake. She sat propped against the hospital pillows, her hair trimmed shorter where they'd shaved for sutures, one eye still mottled at the edges of healing bruises.

I'd been waiting for this. For her words.

Not just because her testimony could close the case, though it could. But because I'd seen the wreckage—her body, her child's quiet account, the broken glass of her home. I'd carried my own ghosts from childhood, and this was one of the worst cases of domestic violence I had ever stood over. If she chose silence, it would haunt me forever.

Jerome Devereux sat at her bedside when I entered, composed in his chair like a man holding vigil at his own altar. At first, I thought his visits were nothing more than image management, another layer of control. But after a week of watching, I knew better. Power, yes—but also something quieter. Almost paternal. He and Marcus were the constants at her side.

I kept my notepad shut. I wanted her eyes, not her dictation.

418

"Sam," I said gently, "I need you to tell me what you remember about that night. Anything at all."

Her lashes fluttered. A faint nod.

"Do you remember what happened?"

Her gaze slid toward the window, but again, a faint nod. Her throat worked, the threat of tears shimmering in her good eye.

"Do you know who hurt you?"

Her breathing hitched. The machines hummed, steady until her chin dipped once. The blood pressure monitor spiked, green numbers climbing higher with every uneven breath.

Her eyes shifted back to Jerome, raw and pleading.

"Perhaps that's enough for now, Detective. Dr. Patel advised it would be weeks before Samantha would speak in more than broken whispers." Jerome said, calm but final. He didn't rise, didn't shift—just let his words close the door.

Then, softer, to her alone: "Do you need anything, Samantha? Ice chips?"

Her lashes trembled, cracked lips moving with effort. The words came faint but unmistakable, weighted with all the fury her broken body couldn't carry:

"Al...Alex... dead."

The room went still.

Jerome's jaw tightened once, then smoothed. He inclined his head, so slight it was impossible to tell whether it was agreement or not.

I'd heard confessions before, but never one that rang so cleanly of truth. My chest tightened with something I hadn't felt in years—not triumph, not relief. Just a raw ache that this young woman had been beaten to the edge of death by the man who vowed to love her.

Her voice had given me more than evidence. It had given me new purpose.

CHAPTER TWENTY-EIGHT

Epilogue

"He who spares the guilty harms the innocent."

SAMANTHA

Silence isn't silent. It hums, like the monitors beside me, like the ringing in my ears. Too loud to ignore, too steady to escape. I've spent seven days listening, letting it morph me into something harder.

Scarlet's laugh fills the quiet. Her small hand in mine, warm and trusting. She deserves so much more than this—than me. Than Alex. Than the weight of Devereux's blood.

And then Marcus. My first sight when I opened my eyes, his hand closing over mine. No shame, not even with Jerome and Drusilla watching. Relief washed through me like breath after drowning: he's here.

I shouldn't think of him, but I do. My heart has carried him every day since I coldly turned him away. Scarlet's chin, her stubborn tilt—it's his. The way she watches the world—his. Her eyes... stormy, ocean blue. Something all her own. I searched for Alex or Marcus in her for so long, that I barely see myself in her at all.

What if I stole her father from her? What if I denied Marcus the right to tuck her in, kiss her goodnight, watch her grow? He never pressed, never asked, but the truth was always there between us. He loves her as if she were his, and sometimes I believe she really is.

That guilt threads with another—the day of the attack. Did I say something wrong? Did I push too hard? Things had been so good—four years of peace, of laughter, of Alex being the man he promised. I wanted so badly to believe he had changed. Then—snap. His hand in my hair. His fists. Scarlet was crying behind the locked door.

For a breath, I almost let myself believe it was my fault. NO. His violence. His choice. His sickness.

Still, the shame clings. That Scarlet heard. What Marcus might think. That even now, part of me still longs for the steadiness in his hand, when things were good. NO. Don't go there; it gives him access. Alexander Devereux's "Sammie" is dead. He killed her. He beat her. Broke her. I am what is left. Whatever the hell that may be now.

The detective, Ciro something—his steady gaze, his whispered prayer when he thought no one saw. He prayed for me. When was the last time I prayed? My parents would be disappointed. They'd tell me I lost faith, that it could have saved me. But prayer won't save me now. It won't save Alexander. Rage might. Jerome once told me, anger is useful.

Alexander Devereux is not just my nightmare. He is a danger to my daughter. To me. I'll turn my rage into a blade and drive it into him.

Jerome sat beside me, silent, immovable. He said nothing until the detective's questions pushed too far.

"Perhaps that's enough for now, Detective," Jerome said, calm but final. He didn't rise, didn't shift—just let his words close the door.

Then, softer, to me alone: "Do you need anything, Samantha? Ice chips?"

My throat burned. I had been thankful for my imposed silence. The healing process would mute my voice in the weeks to come. I did need something. Jerome needed to hear it. The machines hummed. The pressure monitor slowed. I knew exactly what I wanted, no, needed. The words pressed out, cracked, and raw. Every syllable a burning coal.

"Al...Alex... dead."

THE END

CHAPTER
EPIGRAPHS

Chapter 1 - Deception

"False face must hide what the false heart doth know."

— William Shakespeare, Macbeth, Act 1, Scene 7

Chapter 2 - The House of Devereaux

"I know not how it was—but, with the first glimpse of the building, a sense of insufferable gloom pervaded my spirit."

— Edgar Allan Poe, The Fall of the House of Usher (1839)

Chapter 3 - The Gilded Mask

"The mask, given time, comes to own the face beneath."

— Oscar Wilde (public domain aphorism, 19th c.)

Chapter 4 - Hard Lessons

"Force, and fraud, are the two cardinal virtues."

— Edward Gibbon, The History of the Decline and Fall of the Roman Empire, Vol. I (1776)

Chapter 5 – Whispers & Lies

"When devils will the blackest sins put on, they do suggest at first with heavenly shows."

— William Shakespeare, Othello, Act 2, Scene 3

Chapter 6 – Half in Shadow

"Every truth has two sides; it is as well to look at both, before we commit ourselves to either."

— Aesop (6th century BCE, fable fragment)

Chapter 7 – The Board is Set

"Life is a kind of Chess, in which we often have points to gain, and competitors or adversaries to contend with."

— Benjamin Franklin, "The Morals of Chess" (1779)

Chapter 8 – Knight Takes Pawn

"At the end of the game, the king and pawn go into the same box."

— Italian Proverb

Chapter 9 – Queen's Watch

"Man is tormented not by things, but by the views he takes of them."

— Epictetus, Enchiridion (c. 125 CE)

Chapter 10 – The Price of Love

"The misery of man proceeds not from his wants, but from his desires."

— Jean-Jacques Rousseau, Emile, or On Education (1762)

Chapter 11 – The Offer

"Gold is the spur to do and suffer."

— John Milton, Lycidas (1637)

Chapter 12 – The Fragile Truce

"The chains of habit are too weak to be felt until they are too strong to be broken."

— Samuel Johnson, The Rambler, No. 23 (1750)

Chapter 13 - Shifting Pieces

"In the very cradle of our being, fate plants the seeds of our end."

— Heinrich Heine, Ideas: The Book Le Grand (1827)

Chapter 14 - The Poisoned Picture

"Suspicion is a heavy armor, and with its weight it impedes more than it protects."

— Robert Burns, Poems and Songs (1786)

Chapter 15 - Fractured Lens

"We are always deceiving ourselves in our hopes."

— François de La Rochefoucauld, Maximes (1665)

Chapter 16 - Resort Game

"The most dangerous man is the one who can keep his temper in check."

— Publilius Syrus, Sententiae (1st century BCE)

Chapter 17 - The Bargain of Blood

"Men are not punished for their sins, but by them."

— Elbert Hubbard, A Thousand & One Epigrams (1911)

Chapter 18 - Blood Tithe

"What is bred in the bone will not out of the flesh."

— John Heywood, Proverbs (1546)

Chapter 19 - The Weight of Small Things

"The invisible threads are the strongest ties."

— Friedrich Nietzsche, Human, All Too Human (1878)

Chapter 20 - Legacy

"Trust, once broken, leaves a fracture that never heals."

— Publilius Syrus, Sententiae (1st century BCE)

Chapter 21 - Homecoming

"Every man is the son of his own works."

— Miguel de Cervantes, Don Quixote (1605/1615)

Chapter 22 - The Distance Between

"Absence diminishes little passions and increases great ones, as the wind extinguishes candles and fans a fire."

— François de La Rochefoucauld, Maximes (1665)

Chapter 23 - Unicorns

"The innocent and the beautiful have no enemy but time."

— William Butler Yeats, Death (1914)

Chapter 24 - Family Alignment

"We are never so defenseless against suffering as when we love."

— Sigmund Freud, Beyond the Pleasure Principle (1920)

Chapter 25 - Kill Me Softly

"Hell is truth seen too late."

— Thomas Hobbes, Leviathan (1651)

Chapter 26 – Ashes of the Phoenix

"The boundaries which divide Life from Death are at best shadowy and vague."

— Edgar Allan Poe, The Premature Burial (1844)

Chapter 27 – The Weight of Survival

"He who has a why to live can bear almost any how."

— Friedrich Nietzsche, Twilight of the Idols (1889)

Epilogue

"He who spares the guilty harms the innocent."

— Publilius Syrus, Sententiae (1st century BCE)